CW00433969

Cambridge English

EMPOWER

ELEMENTARY
STUDENT'S BOOK

A2

Adrian Doff, Craig Thaine
Herbert Puchta, Jeff Stranks, Peter Lewis-Jones

Contents

Lesson and objective	Grammar	Vocabulary	Pronunciation	Everyday English
Welcome!	Possessive adjectives; *a* and *an*; Plurals; Question words	Numbers; The alphabet; Colours; Classroom objects and instructions	Noticing word stress	Saying hello and introducing people; Spelling words

Unit 1 People

Getting started Talk about meeting people from other countries

1A Talk about where you're from	*be*: positive and negative	Countries and nationalities	Syllables and word stress	
1B Talk about people you know	*be*: questions and short answers	Adjectives	Sound and spelling: /k/; Sound and spelling: long and short *o*	
1C Ask for and give information			Tones for checking; Consonant groups	Asking for and giving information
1D Write an online profile				
Review and extension More practice		**WORDPOWER** *from*		

Unit 2 Work and study

Getting started Talk about what kind of work you find interesting

2A Talk about jobs	Present simple: positive and negative	Jobs	Word stress; *-s* endings	
2B Talk about study habits	Present simple: questions and short answers	Studying; Time	*do you*	
2C Ask for things and reply			Sound and spelling: *ou*	Asking for things and replying
2D Complete a form				
Review and extension More practice		**WORDPOWER** *work*		

Unit 3 Daily life

Getting started Talk about what you do every day

3A Talk about routines	Position of adverbs of frequency	Time expressions; Common verbs	Sentence stress; Sound and spelling: /aɪ/ and /eɪ/	
3B Talk about technology in your life	*have got*	Technology	Word stress; Main stress and tone	
3C Make arrangements			Main stress; Thinking time: *Mm*	Making arrangements
3D Write an informal invitation				
Review and extension More practice		**WORDPOWER** Prepositions of time		

Unit 4 Food

Getting started Talk about eating with your family

4A Talk about the food you want	Countable and uncountable nouns; *a / an*, *some*, *any*	Food	Sound and spelling: *ea* Sound and spelling: /k/ and /g/	
4B Talk about the food you eat every day	Quantifiers: *much*, *many*, *a lot of*	Talking about food	Sentence stress	
4C Arrive and order a meal at a restaurant			Word groups	Arriving at a restaurant; Ordering a meal in a restaurant
4D Write a blog about something you know how to do				
Review and extension More practice		**WORDPOWER** *like*		

Unit 5 Places

Getting started Talk about what a good home is

5A Talk about towns	*there is / there are*	Places in a city	*there's*; Sound and spelling: /b/ and /p/	
5B Describe rooms and furniture in your house	Possessive pronouns and possessive *'s*	Furniture	Sound and spelling: vowels before *r*	
5C Ask for and give directions			Sentence stress	Asking for and giving directions
5D Write a description of your neighbourhood				
Review and extension More practice		**WORDPOWER** Prepositions of place		

Unit 6 Family

Getting started Talk about a family you know

6A Talk about your family and your family history	Past simple: *be*	Family; Years and dates	Sound and spelling: /ʌ/; Sentence stress	
6B Talk about past activities and hobbies	Past simple: positive	Past simple irregular verbs	*-ed* endings; Sound and spelling: *ea*	
6C Leave a voicemail message and ask for someone on the phone			Sound and spelling: *a*	Leaving a voicemail message
6D Write a life story				
Review and extension More practice		**WORDPOWER** *go*		

Listening and Video	Reading	Speaking	Writing
Five conversations		Saying hello and introducing people	Names and addresses
A conversation about where you're from		Where you're from	Sentences about you
A conversation about people you know	Facebook entries about people you know	People you know	Notes about people you know
At the gym reception		Asking for and giving information; Checking understanding	Unit Progress Test
First day of an English course	Online profiles	Using social networking sites	An online profile; Capital letters and punctuation
A conversation about a TV programme	An article about Ice Road Truckers	Jobs	Sentences about jobs
A survey about study habits	An online forum about study habits	Studying; Study habits	Questions about study habits
Ordering in a café; Asking for help		Asking for things and replying; Reacting to news	Unit Progress Test
Three monologues about studying English; A teacher addressing her class	A competition entry form	Studying English	A form; Spelling
A conversation about family routines	An article about an Indian family	Daily routines; Spending time with your family; Routines you share with others	A dialogue; Notes about routines you share with other people
Three conversations about gadgets	An interview about using the Internet	Using the Internet; Technology in your life	Sentences about gadgets you've got; Questions about gadgets you've got
Making arrangements to go out		Making arrangements; Thinking about what you want to say	Unit Progress Test
A monologue about someone's family	Two informal emails	Your family	An informal email invitation; Inviting and replying
A conversation about buying food	An article about World markets	Buying food; The food you like and don't like	
A conversation about cooking	A factfile about Heston Blumenthal; Two personal emails	Cooking programmes; Cooking; The food you eat	Questions about food
At a restaurant		Arriving at a restaurant; Ordering a meal in a restaurant; Changing what you say	Unit Progress Test
Four monologues about cooking	A cooking blog	Cooking; A good cook you know; Cooking for others	A blog about something you know how to do; Making the order clear
	An article about an unusual town	Places you like; Describing a picture of a town; What there is in a town	Questions and sentences about what there is in a town
A conversation about a new home	A newspaper advertisement	Your home and furniture	Sentences about your home
On the street		Giving and following directions; Checking what other people say	Unit Progress Test
Three monologues about neighbourhoods	A website about neighbourhoods around the world	What makes a good neighbourhood; Your neighbourhood	A description of your neighbourhood; Linking ideas with and, but and so
A conversation about a family tree		Your family	Notes about your family
A conversation about childhood hobbies	An article about Steve Jobs	Steve Jobs; What you did at different times; A childhood hobby	Notes about a childhood hobby
On the phone		Leaving a voicemail message; Asking for someone on the phone; Asking someone to wait	Unit Progress Test
A monologue about someone's life story	A life story	Important years in your life	A life story about someone in your family; Linking ideas in the past

Lesson and objective	Grammar	Vocabulary	Pronunciation	Everyday English
Unit 7 Journeys				
Getting started Talk about where you'd like to travel to				
7A Talk about past journeys	Past simple: negative and questions	Transport	*did you*; Sound and spelling: /ɔː/	
7B Talk about what you like and dislike about transport	*love / like / don't mind / hate* + verb + *-ing*	Transport adjectives	Word stress	
7C Say excuse me and sorry			Tones for saying *excuse me*; Emphasising what we say	Saying excuse me and sorry
7D Write an email about yourself				
Review and extension More practice		WORDPOWER *get*		
Unit 8 Fit and healthy				
Getting started Talk about sport and exercise for other people				
8A Talk about past and present abilities; Talk about sport and exercise	*can / can't*; *could / couldn't* for ability	Sport and exercise	*Can, can't, could* and *couldn't*; Sound and spelling: /uː/ and /ʊ/	
8B Talk about the body and getting fit	*have to / don't have to*	Parts of the body; Appearance	*have to*; Word stress	
8C Talk about health and how you feel			Joining words	Talking about health and how you feel
8D Write an article				
Review and extension More practice		WORDPOWER *tell / say*		
Unit 9 Clothes and shopping				
Getting started Talk about shopping in your town or city				
9A Say where you are and what you're doing	Present continuous	Shopping; Money and prices	Word stress in compound nouns; Sentence stress	
9B Talk about the clothes you wear at different times	Present simple or present continuous	Clothes	Sound and spelling: *o*; Syllables	
9C Shop for clothes			Joining words	Choosing clothes; Paying for clothes
9D Write a thank-you email				
Review and extension More practice		WORDPOWER *time*		
Unit 10 Communication				
Getting started Talk about how you use your mobile phone				
10A Compare and talk about the things you have	Comparative adjectives	IT collocations	Sentence stress	
10B Talk about languages	Superlative adjectives	High numbers	Word stress; Main stress	
10C Ask for help			Main stress and tone	Asking for help
10D Write a post expressing an opinion				
Review and extension More practice		WORDPOWER *most*		
Unit 11 Entertainment				
Getting started Talk about what you enjoyed when you were a child				
11A Ask and answer about entertainment experiences	Present perfect	Irregular past participles	Sound and spelling: /ɜː/	
11B Talk about events you've been to	Present perfect or past simple	Music	Syllables	
11C Ask for and express opinions about things you've seen			Main stress and tone	Asking for and expressing opinions
11D Write a review				
Review and extension More practice		WORDPOWER Multi-word verbs		
Unit 12 Travel				
Getting started Talk about photographs				
12A Talk about holiday plans	*going to*	Geography	Syllables and word stress Sentence stress	
12B Give advice about travelling	*should / shouldn't*	Travel collocations	*Should / Shouldn't*	
12C Use language for travel and tourism			Tones for showing surprise; Consonant groups	Checking in at a hotel; Asking for tourist information
12D Write an email with travel advice				
Review and extension More practice		WORDPOWER *take*		

| **Communication Plus**   p.129 | **Grammar Focus**   p.136 | | **Vocabulary Focus**   p.160 | |

4

Listening and Video	Reading	Speaking	Writing
A conversation about travelling on the Silk Road	An article about the Silk Road; Two blogs about travelling on the Silk Road	Transport people use; Past journeys	
A conversation about transport in Moscow	A webpage about metros around the world; Four reviews of metros	Metros you know; Disagreeing about transport; Transport you use	
On the train		Saying excuse me and sorry; Showing interest	Unit Progress Test
A conversation about choosing a homestay family	Two online profiles; An email about Ahmed	Homestay families; English-speaking countries you'd like to visit	An email about yourself; Linking ideas with *after*, *when*, and *while*
A podcast about how the Olympics can change a city	An article about Paralympian Jonnie Peacock	Famous sport events and people; The Olympics; Present and past abilities	
Two monologues about exercise	An article about High Intensity Training	Getting fit; The things people have to do; Yoga; Parts of the body	Sentences and notes about what people have to do
At the gym		Health and how you feel; Expressing sympathy	Unit Progress Test
A conversation about a free-time activity	An email about a company blog; A blog article about a free-time activity	Free-time activities in your country; Your free-time activities	An article; Linking ideas with *however*; Adverbs of manner
Four phone conversations about meeting		Meeting friends in town; Saying where you are and what you're doing	Sentences about what you are doing
Two phone conversations about what people are wearing	Two blogs about living abroad; Text messages about what people are doing	Shopping; Festivals in your country; The clothes you wear	Notes about what someone you know is wearing
Shopping for clothes		Choosing clothes; Paying for clothes; Saying something nice	Unit Progress Test
Four monologues about giving presents	Two thank-you emails	The presents you'd like; Giving presents and thanking people for them	A thank-you email; Writing formal and informal emails
A podcast about smartphones and tablets	A webpage about smartphones and tablets	Smartphones and tablets; Using the Web; Comparing two similar things	Notes about two similar things
A radio programme about languages	A blog about languages	Languages; Blogs and language websites	
Asking for help		Asking for help; Checking instructions	Unit Progress Test
Three monologues about text messages	Four text messages; Six posts on an online discussion board	Sending messages	A post expressing an opinion; Linking ideas with *also*, *too* and *as well*
A conversation about a magazine quiz	Three fact files about actresses; A magazine quiz about actresses; An article about actresses	Famous Australians	
A conversation about music in Buenos Aires	An article about Buenos Aires	Buenos Aires; Kinds of music; Entertainment events in your town or city	Notes about entertainment events in your town or city
A night out		Going out in the evening; Asking for and expressing opinions; Responding to an opinion	Unit Progress Test
A conversation about a film	Two online film reviews	Films	A film review; Cohesion in paragraphs
Two conversations about holidays	A webpage about holidays	Natural places; Important things when on holiday; Holiday plans	
Two monologues about things people like when travelling	An article about living in a different country	Living in a different country; Travelling and holidays; Giving advice about travelling	Unit Progress Test
A prize holiday		Checking in at a hotel; Asking for tourist information; Showing surprise	Notes about surprising things
A conversation about a planned holiday	An email with travel advice; An email asking for travel advice	Planning holidays; Sweden	An email with travel advice; Paragraph writing

Welcome!

G Possessive adjectives; question words; *a/an*; regular plural forms
V Numbers; the alphabet; colours; classroom objects and instructions

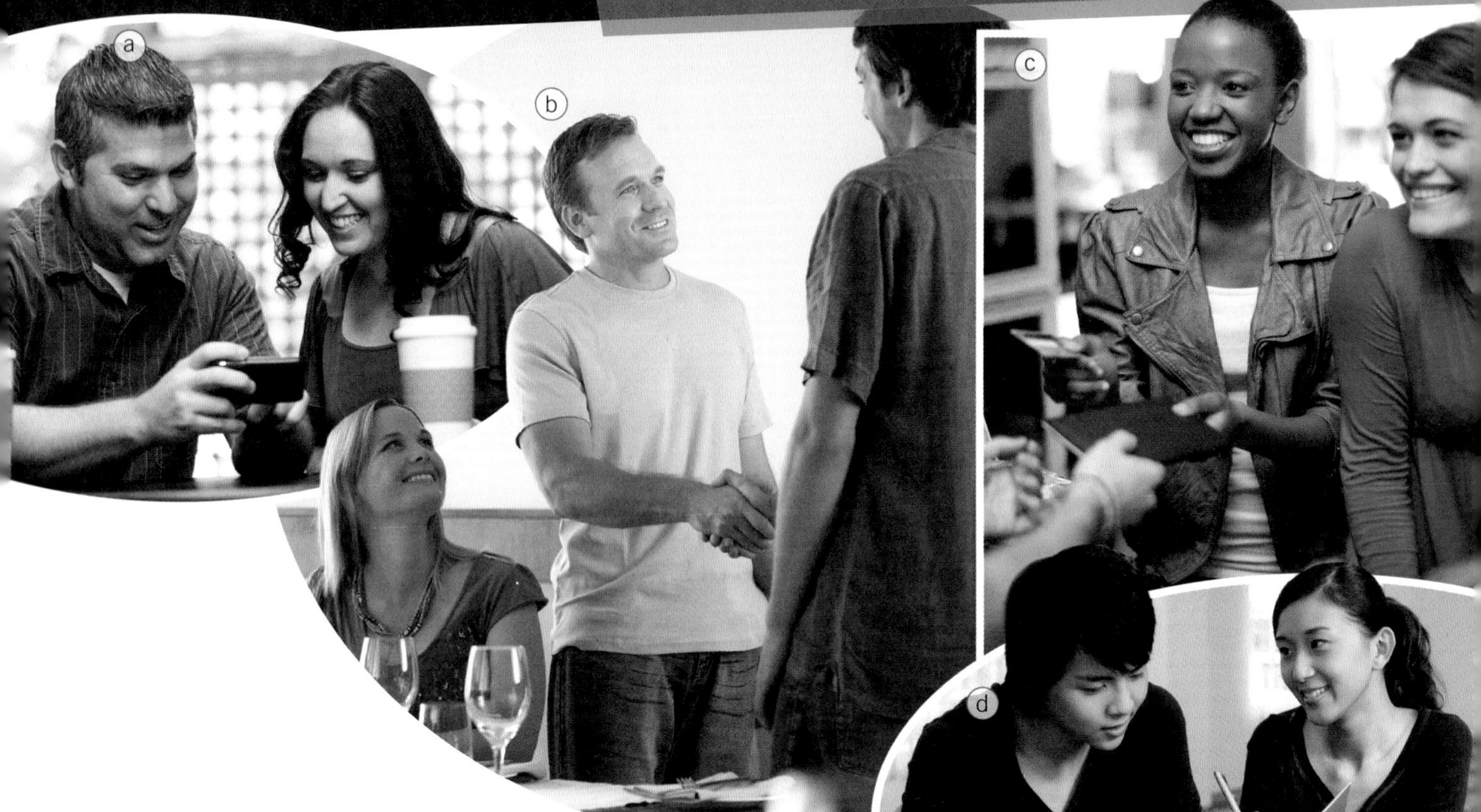

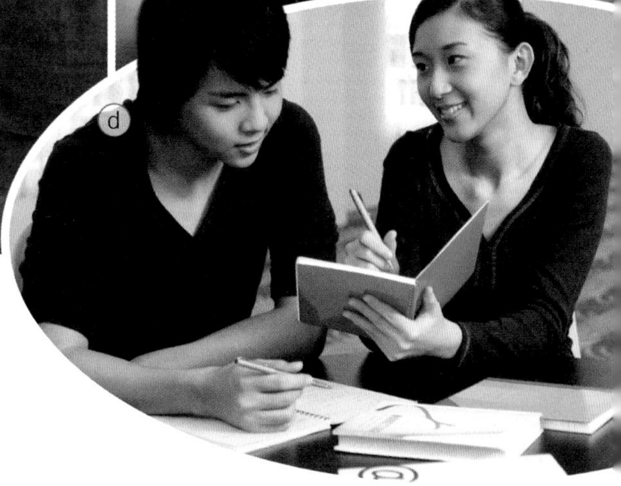

1 FIRST CONVERSATIONS

a 1.2–1.6 Listen to five short conversations. Match them with pictures a–e.

b 1.2–1.6 Listen again. Who says these sentences? Match them with pictures a–e.

1 [b] Nice to meet you.
2 [ ] How are you?
3 [ ] What's your name and address?
4 [ ] How do you spell that?
5 [ ] Can we pay, please?
6 [ ] Is that your flat?

2 SAYING HELLO

a Read Conversation 1. Put the sentences in the correct order.

[ ] Hello. Nice to meet you. I'm Pierre.
[ ] Hello, Pierre. Nice to meet you.
[ ] Hello. I'm Tony, and this is my wife, Joanna.

1.2 Listen and check your answer.

b In pairs, say hello and say your name.

c In groups of four, say hello. Say your name and introduce your partner.

d 1.3 Read Conversation 2 and complete the sentences. Listen and check your answers.

fine thanks how

A Hi, Nick. 1____________ are you?
B I'm 2____________, thanks. And you?
A I'm OK, 3____________.

e Meet other students. Have a conversation with two or three people in the class.

3 NUMBERS

a 1.4 Listen to Conversation 3. Complete the bill.

2 coffees	€ _____
2 ice creams	€ _____
TOTAL	€ _____
Thank you	

How much do they pay? € _____

b 1.7 Listen and circle the numbers you hear. Then say all the numbers.

13 15 16 17 12
30 50 60 70 20

c Choose the correct answer.

25 = twenty and five / twenty-five
61 = sixty-one / one and sixty
110 = a hundred ten / a hundred and ten

d Read the numbers aloud. Then say the next three numbers.

1, 2, 3, 4, …
10, 20, 30, …
15, 25, 35, …
31, 33, 35, …
50, 100, 150, …

d Say these colours and spell the words.

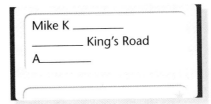

e 💬 Write two words you know in English. Say the word and ask your partner to spell it.

f ▶️**1.5** Listen to Conversation 4 and complete the name and address.

> Mike K _____
> _____ King's Road
> A_____

g 💬 Work in pairs. Student A, tell Student B:

– your first and last name   – your address.

Student B, ask Student A to spell their name and address. Write the information down. Then swap roles.

> How do you spell your … ?

5 POSSESSIVE ADJECTIVES

a ▶️**1.6** Read and listen to Conversation 5. <u>Underline</u> the correct answer.

A This is a nice photo. This is *my / your* wife and *his / her* brother.

B Oh yes. Is that *our / your* flat?

A Yes, that's *our / their* flat in London.

B Mm, it's very nice.

b Complete the table.

our   their   her   his

I live here.	This is _my_ flat.
Do you live here?	Is this _your_ flat?
He lives here.	This is _____ flat.
She lives here.	This is _____ flat.
We live here.	This is _____ flat.
They live here.	This is _____ flat.

c Complete the sentences with a word from the table in 5b.

1 This is my brother. _____ name is George.
2 Jenny and Phil are old friends and that's _____ old car.
3 That's a good photo of you. And is that _____ daughter?
4 In this photo, we're on holiday with _____ friends Sue and Bill.
5 I know that girl in the photo. What's _____ name?

4 THE ALPHABET

a ▶️**1.8** Listen to the letters of the alphabet and say them.

A B C D E F G
H I J K L M N
O P Q R S T U
V W X Y Z

b **Pronunciation** Which letters have:

1 the same long sound as s**ee** /iː/
2 the same long sound as d**ay** /eɪ/
3 the same short sound as **e**gg /e/

c 💬 Test a partner. Student A, point to a letter. Student B, say the letter.

6 CLASSROOM OBJECTS

a Match objects 1–10 with a–j in the picture.

1 a <u>note</u>book	6 a <u>cup</u>board
2 a <u>dic</u>tionary	7 a desk
3 a pro<u>jec</u>tor	8 a <u>white</u>board
4 a <u>ques</u>tion	9 an <u>an</u>swer
5 a pen	10 a <u>course</u>book

b ▶1.9 **Pronunciation** Notice the stressed syllable in the words in 6a. Listen, then practise saying the words.

c When do we use *an*? Choose the correct answer.
a before *a, e, i, o, u*   b before other letters

d Write *a* or *an* next to each word.

① _____ book   ② _____ apple   ③ _____ camera

④ _____ glass   ⑤ _____ egg   ⑥ _____ baby

⑦ _____ ice cream   ⑧ _____ box

e Choose one of the words from 6a or 6d. Other students ask questions to guess the word.

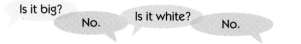

Is it big?   No.   Is it white?   No.

f Look at how words change in the plural. Complete the rules.

Singular → Plural	Rule
a pen → pens	Most words add _____ in the plural.
a baby → babies	Change a final *-y* to _____ and add _____.
a glass → glasses	If a word ends in *-s*, *-x*, *-sh* or *-ch*, we add _____.

7 CLASSROOM INSTRUCTIONS

a ▶1.10 Listen and do what the teacher says. Then listen again. Which verbs do you hear each time?

open   close   look at   read   turn to   write   ask   work

b ▶1.11 <u>Underline</u> the correct words. Listen and check.
1 *What's / Who's* this? An apple or an orange?
2 *When's / Where's* Tokyo?
3 *How / What* do you say this word?
4 *Who's / When's* the president?
5 *When's / What's* your English lesson?

c Match questions 1–4 with answers a–d.

1 What's 'amigo' in English?	a It's a boat for cars and people.
2 How do you spell 'night'?	b 'Pee-pl'.
3 What's a 'ferry'?	c Friend.
4 How do you say this word?	d N-I-G-H-T.

d Write a question like questions 1–4 in 7c. Then ask other students your question.

CAN DO OBJECTIVES

- Talk about where you're from
- Talk about people you know
- Ask for and give information
- Write an online profile

UNIT 1
People

GETTING STARTED

a ⬭ Look at the picture and answer the questions.

1 What different countries are the people from?
2 Why are they together?
   - for a sports game   • for a party   • for a music concert
3 How do they feel? Here are some ideas:
   - bored   • excited   • good   • happy
   - sad   • tired

b ⬭ When do you meet people from other countries?
Here are some more ideas:
   - on holiday   • at work
   - on a language course   • at parties
   - never

1A I'm from France

Learn to talk about where you're from
- **G** *be*: positive and negative
- **V** Countries and nationalities

1 LISTENING AND READING

a 💬 Look at pictures a–f and answer the questions.

1 What sport do all the people like?
2 Match countries 1–6 with pictures a–f.

1 ☐ Brazil	4 ☐ Japan
2 ☐ Spain	5 ☐ Russia
3 ☐ Germany	6 ☐ France

b ▶1.12 Listen and check. Practise saying the countries.

c ▶1.13 Thomas and Lena are at the World Cup. Listen and tick (✓) the three things they talk about.

1 ☐ football	4 ☐ a city
2 ☐ countries	5 ☐ TV
3 ☐ food	

d ▶1.13 Listen again. Complete the conversation.

THOMAS Hi there! My name's Thomas. What's your ^{1}_____?
LENA I'm Lena.
THOMAS Hi, Lena! Where are you ^{2}_____? Russia?
LENA Yeah, you're right! I'm Russian. I'm from St Petersburg.
THOMAS Oh yes! It's a really beautiful city.
LENA Yes, I think so too. So, ^{3}_____ are you from, Thomas?
THOMAS Me? I'm from ^{4}_____. I'm French.
LENA Oh, the French team's really good!
THOMAS Of course, we're ^{5}_____!

e Are sentences 1–4 true or false?

1 Thomas and Lena are friends.
2 Lena is from Russia.
3 Thomas likes St Petersburg.
4 Lena says the football team from France is very bad.

f <u>Underline</u> the two nationalities in the conversation in 1d.

2 VOCABULARY
Countries and nationalities

a Thomas says:

I'm from **France**. I'm **French**.

▶1.14 Find other pairs of countries and nationalities in the box below. Listen and check.

Ru|ssia	Bra|zil|i|an	Spa|nish	Ja|pan	Ru|ssian
Ger|many	Jap|an|ese	Ger|man	Bra|zil	Spain

b ▶1.14 **Pronunciation** Notice how many syllables each word has. Underline the stressed syllable in each word in the box in 2a.

c ▶1.14 Listen again and repeat.

d Make sentences about the people below with the words in 2a.

1 Lena: She's _Russian_. She's from _____.
2 The people in pictures a–f: They're _____.
They're from _____.

e 💬 Look at the conversation in 1d again. Complete the question. Then ask your partner.

_____ are you from?

I'm from _____.
I'm _____.

f ▶ Now go to Vocabulary Focus 1A on p.160 for more Countries and nationalities

3 GRAMMAR
be: positive and negative

a ▶1.17 Listen to the next part of the conversation between Thomas and Lena. What do they talk about?

a their football teams
b the town where Thomas is from

b ▶1.17 Underline the correct answers. Listen again and check.

1 Thomas *is / isn't* from Paris.
2 Lena's friends *are / aren't* Russian.
3 Her friends *are / aren't* at the match.
4 *It's / It isn't* 8:00.

c Look at the sentences and complete the rules.

It's a town near Paris. It **isn't** very big.
They're all in the hotel. They **aren't** here.
I'm from France. I'm **not** from Paris.

1 To make *is* and *are* negative, we add _____.
2 To make *I'm* negative, we add _____.

d Complete the table with the correct forms of the verb *be*.

Positive (+)	Negative (–)
I'**m** from St Petersburg.	I'm ___ French.
He ___ a really good player.	She ___ from Moscow.
They say they ___ tired.	They ___ at the match.

e ▶ Now go to Grammar Focus 1A on p.136

f Thomas and Lena talk more in the café. Add the verb *be* to make correct sentences.

Thomas says: 1 My brother at university in Madrid.
2 My mother and father not here.

Lena says: 3 Russia not very hot in April.
4 My friends really interesting and fun.

g Write two positive and two negative sentences about you with the verb *be*. Make two of the sentences false.

h 💬 Read your sentences to a partner and say if your partner's sentences are true or false.

4 SPEAKING

a ▶ **Communication 1A** Student A go to p.129. Student B go to p.132.

b 💬 Work in small groups. Tell other students:

• your name
• your country and nationality
• your home town.

1 READING

a Look at pictures a–d. Where do you think the people are?

b Read the texts and match them with pictures a–d. Are your ideas in 1a correct?

c Who do you think says sentences 1–4?

1 'I have four classes every day.'
2 'It's fun to travel with friends.'
3 'My family live in different places.'
4 'She speaks two languages – Spanish and Portuguese.'

d Who would you like to meet: Suzi, Andrey, Altan or Saddah? Why?

 Suzi

This is me in Rio de Janeiro with my friend Claudia. She lives in Brazil, but she's from Spain. She's a lovely person – very warm and kind.

view Suzi's photos   leave Suzi a message

 Andrey

In this photo I'm in St Petersburg with my cousin Oleg. He's Russian, but I'm from England – his father and my mother are brother and sister. He's a really pleasant guy and he's a brilliant doctor. He's well-known in his part of St Petersburg.

view Andrey's photos   leave Andrey a message

 Altan

In this photo, I'm on holiday with my friend Takor. He's a fantastic friend and he's very cool. He's a great person to be on holiday with.

view Atlan's photos   leave Atlan a message

 Saddah

This is my colleague Maram. We're teachers and we work together in a school. She's quiet, but she's really friendly. She's also very popular with her students.

view Saddah's photos   leave Saddah a message

2 VOCABULARY
Personality adjectives

a Look at the sentence. The <u>underlined</u> words are adjectives. Are they about Rio de Janeiro or Claudia?

She's a <u>lovely</u> person – very <u>warm</u> and <u>kind</u>!

b <u>Underline</u> nine more adjectives in the texts. Then put them in the correct gaps.

1 very good: _____, _____,

    _____, _____

2 nice: *lovely, warm, kind,* _____,

    _____

3 famous: _____

4 he/she doesn't talk much: _____

5 people like him/her: _____

c **Pronunciation** Three words in the texts have the /k/ sound:

<u>k</u>ind   <u>c</u>ool   <u>qu</u>iet

<u>Underline</u> the /k/ sound in these words. Which two words do not have /k/?

cold	car	cheap	kitchen	like
coffee	quick	back	key	know
come	make	school	cat	

d 💬 Talk about people you know. Use adjectives from 2b.

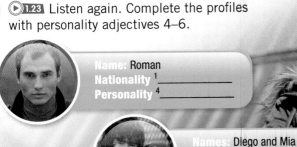

My friend Emma's very friendly and very popular.

My best friend Joe's a cool guy.

My aunt Sophia's fantastic – she's a very warm and friendly woman.

e ▶ Now go to Vocabulary Focus 1B on p.161 for more Adjectives

3 LISTENING

a ▶1.23 Listen to the conversation. Complete the nationalities (1–3) on the profiles below.

b ▶1.23 Listen again. Complete the profiles with personality adjectives 4–6.

Name: Roman
Nationality [1] _____
Personality [4] _____

Names: Diego and Mia
Nationality [2] _____
Personality [5] _____

Name: Laura
Nationality [3] _____
Personality [6] _____

4 GRAMMAR *be*: questions and short answers

a ▶1.24 Complete the answers with the verbs in the box. Listen and check.

aren't	isn't	is	are

1 Is she Italian?   No, she _____. She's from Spain.
2 Is he from Poland?   Yes, he _____.
3 Are they married?   Yes, they _____.
4 Are they Spanish?   No, they _____. They're from Mexico.

b Complete the table with the correct forms of the verb *be*.

Questions (?)	Short answers	
<u>Are</u> you Australian?	Yes, I <u>am</u>.	No, I'm not.
_____ you Spanish?	Yes, we are.	No, we aren't.
_____ he/she Turkish?	Yes, he/she _____.	No, he/she _____.
_____ they Russian?	Yes, they _____.	No, they _____.

c ▶ Now go to Grammar Focus 1B on p.136

d ▶1.26 Complete the conversations. Use contractions *'s, 're* and *isn't* if possible. Listen and check.

A My friend Tony [1] <u>'s</u> English. He [2] _____ very kind.
B [3] _____ he from London?
A Yes, he [4] _____.

A My friends, Joe and Mel, [5] _____ American.
    They [6] _____ very warm and friendly.
B [7] _____ they married?
A No, they [8] _____. They [9] _____ just good friends.

5 SPEAKING

a Write down words about friends, family and famous people you know from other countries.

Camilla – British, cool, popular   Gabriel – Mexican, quiet, kind

b 💬 Talk about the people you know. Look at the conversations in 4d to help you.

1 LISTENING

a 💬 Look at the pictures of Dan and Leo. Use personality adjectives from page 12 to describe them.

b ▶1.27 Watch or listen to Part 1. Choose the correct answer.

1	Dan wants to:	a finish something	b do some exercise
2	Leo wants to:	a do an exercise class	b go for a run.
3	Martina is:	a in the office	b at the gym.

c ▶1.28 Leo talks to the gym receptionist. Watch or listen to Part 2. What does Leo want to do? Choose the correct answer.

a join the gym   b book a fitness class
c pay for a fitness class.

d ▶1.28 Watch or listen to Part 2 again. Are the sentences true or false? Correct the false sentences.

1 The class starts at 7.20.
2 Ten people can go to the fitness class.
3 The class is in Studio 2.

Leo   Dan

2 USEFUL LANGUAGE
Asking for and giving information

a Who says sentences 1–7 at a gym: the receptionist (*R*) or a visitor (*V*)?

1	What time's the next class?	a	Seymour.
2	And what's your address?	b	You're welcome.
3	How can I help?	c	S–E–Y–M–O–U–R
4	Thanks for your help.	d	It's at twenty past seven.
5	Can you spell that, please?	e	It's in Studio 1.
6	And where's the class?	f	I'd like to do a fitness class.
7	What's your surname?	g	18 New Street.

b ▶1.29 Match 1–7 with a–g. Listen and check.

c <u>Underline</u> the correct answers.

1 It's **in** *ten past four* / *Room 6*.
2 It's **at** *eight o'clock* / *Studio 4*.

d ▶1.30 A is a receptionist and B wants information. Complete the conversation. Look at 2a and 2b to help you. Listen and check.

A Hello. How can I [1]_____ you?
B I'd [2]_____ to do a computer course.
A No problem.
B When's the first lesson?
A It's tomorrow at eight o'clock.
B And [3]_____ the lesson?
A It's here in Room 5.
B Great. Can I book a place?
A Certainly. [4]_____ your surname?
B Moore.
A Can you [5]_____ that, please?
B M–O–O–R–F
A Thank you. Enjoy the class.

e 💬 In pairs, practise the conversation in 2d. Use your own surname. Take turns being A and B.

3 LISTENING

a ⏵1.31 Watch or listen to Part 3. Leo talks to Martina at the gym. Answer the questions.

1 Who is Martina?
2 What does she say about Dan?
a He's very busy.   b He's a bit lazy.

b 💬 What is a good time to go to the gym?

- before work / school
- after work / school
- at lunchtime
- never

4 CONVERSATION SKILLS
Checking understanding

a Complete the mini-conversations with the words in the box.

so that's	sorry

SONIA   It's at twenty past seven.
LEO   ¹_____?
SONIA   7:20.

SONIA   It's in Studio 1.
LEO   ²_____ 7:20 in Studio 1.

b Which expression in 4a means:

1 I'm not sure and I want to check.
2 I don't understand. Can you say that again?

c ⏵1.32 **Pronunciation** Listen to what Leo says in 4a. Does the tone go up ↗ or down ↘ on 1 and 2?

d 💬 Work in pairs. Use the dialogue map to practise checking understanding. Take turns being A and B.

A   B

Tell each other your surname and spell it →

Answer with *sorry*.

Repeat the information. ←

5 PRONUNCIATION
Consonant groups

a ⏵1.33 Listen to the time. Notice how the marked consonant groups are pronounced.

ei**ght** o'**cl**o**ck**
 /t/   /kl/ /k/

b ⏵1.34 Listen to the words below. How many consonant sounds do the marked letters have?

three   si**x**   ei**ght**y

c ⏵1.35 Practise saying these times. Listen and repeat.

1 seven o'clock (7:00)
2 six ten (6:10)
3 eight twenty (8:20)
4 three forty (3:40)
5 six thirty (6:30)
6 twelve twenty (12:20)

6 SPEAKING

a ▶ **Communication 1C** Student A go to p.129. Student B go to p.132.

♻ Unit Progress Test

CHECK YOUR PROGRESS

You can now do the Unit Progress Test.

1 SPEAKING AND LISTENING

a ◯ Ask and answer the questions.

1 Do you use a social networking site?
2 Do you have a profile?
3 Which of the following information is on it?

- your name
- your age
- your nationality
- where you live
- your job
- things you like

b Look at Kate and Carla's profiles and complete the table with yes (✓), no (✗) or don't know (DK).

She's ...	20 years old	from London	Italian	a teacher	a student
Kate	DK				
Carla	✓				

c ▶1.36 The people in the picture are on an English course. Listen and answer the questions.

1 Is this the first or the last day of the course?
2 What city are they in?

d ▶1.36 Listen again. Complete the table.

Name	Country	One other thing we know
Kate and Mike	UK	They're _____.
Carla	Italy	She's a _____.
Masato		English is _____ for his work.
Carmen		She's a _____ of IT.
Orhan		His _____ is in London.
Marisa		Her _____ is in London.

Kate Marks

- Teacher, International College
- Age: –
- Lives in London, UK

Friends: 132 **view**
Photos **view**

about Kate >

Carla Dimambro

- Student, University of Milan
- Age: 20
- Lives in Milan
- From Genoa, Italy

Friends: 29 **view**
Photos **view**

about Carla >

e ◯ Work in groups of five or six. It's your first day at International College.

Student A: You're the teacher.
The others: You're one of the students in the picture.

Say who you are and say one more thing.

I'm Masato.

My home town is Kyoto.

2 READING

a Read Kate and Carla's profiles for the new course.
<u>Underline</u> any new information.

I'm Kate Marks. I'm from Wigan. It's a small town near Manchester in England. I live in London and I'm a teacher at International College. I'm married and I have two small children, a boy and a girl.

I like languages, music and films.

back >

I'm Carla Dimambro. I'm Italian. I'm from Genoa, but I study marketing at the University of Milan. It's my first time in London and I'm very happy to be here. Are other people new to London?

I like running, swimming and yoga.

back >

3 WRITING SKILLS
Capital letters and punctuation

a Look at the profiles in 2a. Tick (✓) the words that have capital letters.

1 ☐ first names of people
2 ☐ last names of people
3 ☐ names of companies, schools, universities
4 ☐ names of countries and nationalities
5 ☐ names of sports
6 ☐ names of towns or cities
7 ☐ all nouns
8 ☐ all words at the start of a sentence
9 ☐ the word *I*

b *I'm = I am.* What are the full forms of these words?

1 it's   4 isn't
2 she's   5 aren't
3 you're

c Correct the words. Add an apostrophe (') to each word.

1 Im   4 hes
2 arent   5 were
3 isnt   6 theyre

d Look at the commas (,) and full stops (.) in the online profiles. Which do we use:

a at the end of a sentence?
b after words in a list?

e Correct the sentences. Add capital letters and punctuation (. , ' ?).

i live in paris its amazing → I live in Paris. It's amazing.

1 im from shanghai its a big city in china
2 i like basketball old cars and jazz
3 im a french teacher in australia
4 this isnt my first time in london
5 are the teachers all from britain

4 WRITING

a Write a profile about you. Use the profiles in 2a to help you. Give this information:

- your name
- your nationality
- your home town
- your job
- what you like

b Swap profiles with another student and check the capital letters and punctuation.

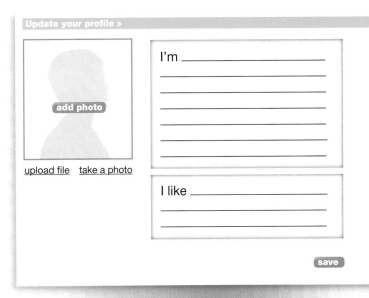

UNIT 1
Review and extension

1 VOCABULARY

a Complete the sentences with the correct nationality word.

1 Vera's from Rio de Janeiro. She's _____.
2 Pedro's from Madrid. He's _____.
3 Kurt and Erika are from Berlin. They're _____.
4 Masha's from Moscow. She's _____.
5 Claude and Sabine are from Paris. They're _____.
6 Takashi's from Tokyo. He's _____.

b Complete the text about Vera with the correct adjective.

Vera's family are all very [1]n___e. Her mother's [2]w___m and
[3]k___d and her father is very [4]p_____t. He's a [5]b_____t
doctor. Her sister Pia is [6]q___t, but she's very [7]f_____y.

2 GRAMMAR

a Complete the text with the correct form of the verb *be*.
Use contractions where possible.

Hi I [1]_____ Paolo and I [2]_____ from Melbourne in Australia.
I [3]_____ a university student. I [4]_____ really lucky because
I live near my sister Barbara. She [5]_____ an English teacher
and she [6]_____ very popular with her students. She [7]_____
very kind and friendly. We [8]_____ Australian, but our parents
[9]_____ from Italy. They [10]_____ doctors.

b Write questions for the answers. Use the word in italics
to start your question.

1 *Are ...?*   No, I'm not. I'm Brazilian.
2 *Is ...?*   Yes, she's very kind.
3 *Are ...?*   No, they aren't. They're from Germany.
4 *What's ...?*   My name's Abdul Aziz.
5 *Where ...?*   I'm from Poland.

c Write questions and short answers.

1 you Russian?   Yes
2 she your sister?   No
3 they friendly?   Yes
4 you both from the USA? No
5 he well-known?   No

d Complete the conversation with one word in each gap.
A contraction (*I'm, you're, he's*) is one word.

A Hello. What's [1]_____ name?
B I'm Juan.
A [2]_____ you from Spain?
B No, [3]_____ from Mexico.
A And that woman over there. Is [4]_____ your sister?
B No, she [5]_____. She's a student at my school.
A OK. And [6]_____ she from?
B She's Italian. [7]_____ from Venice.

e 💬 Practise the conversation in 2d with a partner and
use your own personal information.

3 WORDPOWER *from*

a Match sentences 1–4 with pictures a–d.

1 Is the flight **from** Hong Kong here?
2 I'm not American, I'm **from** Canada.
3 The shops are open **from** 9:00 am to 6:00 pm.
4 My house's about five kilometres **from** the centre of town.

b Match examples 1–4 in 3a with rules a–d.

We use *from* to talk about:
a times
b a starting place
c our country or city
d how far away something is

c Match sentences 1–4 with rules a–d in 3b.

1 Our lunch break is from 12:30 to 1:30.
2 Our hotel's about five kilometres from the airport.
3 The train from Paris is now at platform two.
4 I'm from Argentina.

d Add *from* in the correct place in these sentences.

1 This postcard's New Zealand.
2 Breakfast is seven o'clock every morning.
3 The bank's only 200 metres here.

e Put the phrases in the correct order to make
sentences.

1 from / Denmark / I'm
2 open from / the supermarket's / 7:30 am
3 my place's / from school / two kilometres

f Are the sentences in 3e true for you? Change them
to make them true.

I'm not from Denmark, I'm from Australia.

🔄 REVIEW YOUR PROGRESS

How well did you do in this unit? Write 3, 2, or 1
for each objective.
3 = very well   2 = well   1 = not so well

I CAN ...

talk about where I'm from	☐
talk about people I know	☐
ask for and give information	☐
write an online profile.	☐

CAN DO OBJECTIVES

- Talk about jobs
- Talk about study habits
- Ask for things and reply
- Complete a form

UNIT 2
Work and study

GETTING STARTED

a ⬤ Look at the picture and answer the questions.

1 Where do you think the woman is?
2 What's in her hand?
3 Is the water warm or cold?
4 What's one good thing about her job and one bad thing?

b ⬤ What kind of work do you think is interesting? Here are some ideas:

- working with people
- working with animals
- working with machines
- working on your own

1 READING AND LISTENING

a Look at the pictures. Answer the questions.

1 Is the woman a truck driver or a passenger?
2 Where do you think she's from, the USA or Canada?
3 Do you think her job is easy or difficult?

b Read *Ice Road Truckers* and check your answers.

c Find words in the text to complete the sentences.

1 Water _____ at 0°C.
2 The opposite of *safe* is _____.
3 Bad _____ sometimes happen on roads.

d Read the text again. Find three reasons why Lisa's job is difficult.

e ▶**1.37** Listen to Karen and Peter talking about the TV programme *Ice Road Truckers*. Do they like it?

f ▶**1.37** Listen again. Who thinks these things, Karen (*K*) or Peter (*P*)?

1 It's unusual to see a woman truck driver.
2 The truckers are only interested in the money.
3 The programme is popular because people want to see something bad happen.
4 Lisa Kelly is a really good driver.

g Talk about the questions.

1 Would you like to do Lisa Kelly's job? Why / Why not?
2 What other dangerous jobs do you know?

ICE ROAD TRUCKERS

We see truckers driving on the roads every day, but ice road truckers are different. They drive trucks in the north of Canada. But they don't drive on roads because there are no roads in the north, just lakes and rivers. In winter, the water freezes and the trucks go on the ice. Then the truckers take food to the towns in the north.

❄ LISA KELLY

Lisa Kelly drives a big truck on the ice. It's a long journey of 600 kilometres and she doesn't stop for hours. It's not easy, but the good thing is Lisa doesn't drive in the summer because there's no ice. She makes all her money in the winter so she doesn't work at all in the summer – she has a long holiday.

❄ A DANGEROUS JOB

The weather is bad and ice road truckers have a lot of accidents. Kyle Gulkowski, also an ice road trucker, talks about how he does this dangerous job. 'I drive with one hand on the door handle. Sometimes the ice breaks, you see. Then I get out quickly before my truck goes into the water!
I lose the truck, but not my life!'

Lisa and the other drivers are in *Ice Road Truckers* on Wednesday at 7:30.

2 VOCABULARY Jobs

a Match words 1–9 with pictures a–i.

1 ☐ nurse 2 ☐ shop assistant 3 ☐ police officer 4 ☐ dentist
5 ☐ pilot 6 ☐ engineer 7 ☐ cleaner 8 ☐ photographer
9 ☐ taxi driver

b ▶1.38 **Pronunciation** Listen to the words and <u>underline</u> the stressed syllable.

po<u>lice</u> officer engineer photographer dentist

c 💬 Complete the sentences with jobs from 2a. Talk about your answers.

1 A _____ has a dangerous job.
2 A _____ has an easy job.
3 A _____ has an exciting job.
4 The pay for a _____ isn't very good.

d ▶ Now go to Vocabulary Focus 2A on p.161 for more Jobs

3 GRAMMAR
Present simple: positive and negative

a ▶1.40 Look at the sentences from 1b and 1e and complete them with the verbs from the box. Listen and check.

drive (x3) don't (x2) doesn't like (x2) drives

	I / we / you / they	he / she / it
+	I really _____ *Ice Road Truckers*. They _____ trucks in the north of Canada.	Lisa Kelly _____ a big truck.
–	I _____ _____ *Ice Road Truckers* at all. They _____ _____ on roads because there are no roads in the north.	Lisa _____ _____ in summer.

b <u>Underline</u> more present simple verbs in the text in 1b. Make two lists: positive and negative forms.

c ▶ Now go to Grammar Focus 2A on p.138

d <u>Underline</u> the verbs in sentences 1–2.

1 She makes all her money in the winter.
2 In the winter the water freezes.

e ▶1.42 **Pronunciation** Which verb in 3d has an extra syllable when we add the letter -*s*? Listen and check.

f <u>Underline</u> the correct answers.

1 After the sounds /z/, /s/, /ʃ/ (spelled *sh*) and /tʃ/ (spelled *ch*), we *don't add / add* an extra syllable.
2 We *don't add / add* an extra syllable after other sounds.

g ▶1.43 Listen to these verbs. Tick (✓) the verbs that have an extra syllable.

☐ works   ☐ eats   ☐ teaches
☐ finishes   ☐ listens   ☐ stops
☐ drives   ☐ uses   ☐ watches

h ▶ **Communication 2A** Student A go to p.129. Student B go to p.132.

4 SPEAKING

a Think about your job or the job of someone you know. Write four sentences about the job: two positive (+) and two negative (–). Use the verbs in the box.

work drive have like study
speak go start finish know

+ I start work at 7:00 in the morning.
– I don't drive to work.

b 💬 Tell your partner your sentences. Can they guess the job?

c Tell other students about your partner's job. Can they guess it?

> She starts work at …

2B Do you worry about exams?

1 READING

a 💬 Ask and answer the questions.

1 Are you good at exams?
2 Do you worry about exams and tests?
3 Do you study a lot for an exam or test?

b Read comments 1–3 on the *Unichat* forum and match them with pictures a–c.

c 💬 Read the comments again and answer the questions with a partner.

1 Which study habits are:
 • useful • funny?
2 Put the study habits in the order you want to try them from 1 (really want to try) to 3 (don't want to try).

2 VOCABULARY Studying

a Look at the underlined words in questions 1–7. Match them with pictures a–g below.

1 Do you have a break in the middle of your English lesson?
2 Do you have a timetable for your study routine?
3 Do you make notes when you read something in English?
4 Do you get good marks in English tests?
5 How many weeks is a term at your school?
6 Do you have an exam at the end of the year?
7 Do you enjoy your English studies?

b Match the words in the box with 1–4. You can use some of the words more than once.

get good pass bad make fail

1 an exam
2 marks
3 notes
4 a test

c 💬 Ask and answer the questions in 2a.

UNICHAT

Home Forums Articles Revision

Exam stress!

Hi guys! I have a big exam on Friday. It's really hard to study. I read my study notes for an hour and then I watch really bad TV programmes! What about you? Do you worry about exams? What are your study habits? MIMI23

① Yeah I hate tests. They're really difficult and I can't always remember everything. I need to study every day and make lots of notes. It's not easy but it helps to listen to R&B music – really loud! It helps me think. SOUL BOY2
REPLY ✉

② I agree – exams and tests are really, really hard. In my study breaks I play with my pet rabbit. Some people say that animals stop stress and relax people. I think it's true, well, for me it is! Everybody needs a rabbit (or maybe a cat!) to help them study! BUNNY LOVER5
REPLY ✉

③ I think it helps to have a good study routine. I make a study timetable and that helps me to pass my exams. I always plan lots of breaks and have a cup of tea and something small to eat. I don't want to get tired when I study! But the breaks are only short – about five or ten minutes. Then I go back to studying hard for one or two hours. Good marks come from lots of hard work! SWOTTIE8
REPLY ✉

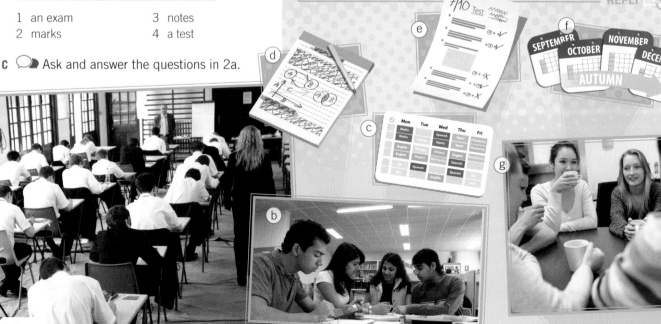

Tania and Jack

3 LISTENING

a ▶ 1.44 Jack (SWOTTIE 8's real name) talks to Tania about her study habits. Listen and tick (✓) the things they talk about.

1 ☐ places to study   3 ☐ exams
2 ☐ hours of study   4 ☐ free time

b ▶ 1.44 Listen again. Complete the information about Tania's studies.

- Part-time or full-time studies?
- Hours a week?
- When?
- Where?

4 VOCABULARY   Time

a Match the times that Tania talks about with the clocks.

1 Usually at **half past eight** …
2 … last night at **quarter past eleven**.

b Complete the sentences with the words in the box.

to	past	o'clock	half

1 four _____   3 (a) quarter _____ four

2 _____ past four   4 (a) quarter _____ five

c ▶ Now go to Vocabulary Focus 2B on p.162 for more practice with Time

5 GRAMMAR   Present simple: questions

a ▶ 1.46 Look at the questions. Which is correct? Listen and check.

1 You study full-time or part-time?
2 Do you study full-time or part-time?
3 Study you full-time or part-time?

b Complete the questions with one word.

_____ … you study part-time?
      … they like tests?

c ▶ 1.47 Jack asks Tania about her daughter, Ellie. Listen and complete the information about Ellie's studies.

- Hours a week?
- When?
- Where?

d Read the question Jack asks Tania.

Does she study more before an exam?

Look at the questions in 5b. How are they different? Why?

e ▶ Now go to Grammar Focus 2B on p.138

f ▶ 1.49 Put the questions in the correct order. Listen and check.

1 a week / do you study / hours / how many?
2 study grammar / or vocabulary / do you?
3 you / when / study / do?
4 study / do / where / you?

g ▶ 1.49 **Pronunciation** Notice the pronunciation of *do you* in each question. Can you hear both words clearly?

6 SPEAKING

a Look at the questions in 5f. Write another question about study.

b 💬 Ask and answer your questions in 6a.

c 💬 Do you have any new ideas about studying now?

> Natalia studies very early in the morning because she isn't very tired. I think it's a good idea, but I prefer to sleep!

1 LISTENING

a 💬 Look at picture a. Dan and Leo are in a cafeteria. Do you think they're:

1 at the airport   2 at work   3 in a shopping centre?

b ▶1.50 Watch or listen to Part 1 and check your answer in 1a.

c 💬 Work in pairs. Choose the correct answers.

1 Dan orders a *small / large* tea, a *small / large* latte and *one croissant / two croissants*.
2 It costs *£3.60 / £4.60*.
3 Dan asks Leo to pass the *milk / sugar*.

d ▶1.50 Watch or listen to Part 1 again and check your answers in 1c.

e ▶1.51 Watch or listen to Part 2. Annie wants to do an online course. What's her problem? Choose one answer.

She can't decide:
a which course to do   b how much to pay   c when to start.

f ▶1.51 Watch or listen to Part 2 again. Are the sentences true or false? Correct the false sentences.

1 Annie asks Dan for help.   3 Annie isn't free on Friday.
2 Dan's free tonight.   4 Annie's happy about dinner.

g 💬 Where do you usually meet friends and family?

- in your home
- in their home
- in a café
- in a different place

2 USEFUL LANGUAGE
Asking for things and replying

a Look at these ways to ask for things. Who says them: Dan (*D*) or Annie (*A*)?

1 Can I have a tea and a latte, please?
2 Could I come to your place tonight?
3 Could we chat about it now?
4 I'd like some help.

b ▶1.50–1.51 Watch or listen to Parts 1 and 2 again and check. Match a–d with 1–4 in 2a.

a Certainly. Small or large?
b Sorry, I have another meeting in five minutes.
c Sure, no problem.
d Sorry, we're not at home tonight.

c 💬 In pairs, take turns asking for things and replying. Use the phrases from 2a and 2b.

3 CONVERSATION SKILLS
Reacting to news

a ▶1.53 Complete the mini-conversations with words in the box. Listen and check your answers.

problem   pity

LEO   Sorry, I have another meeting in five minutes.
DAN   OK, no ¹_____. We can do it later.

DAN   Sorry, we're not at home tonight.
ANNIE Oh, that's a ²_____.

b Read the mini-conversations in 3a again. Which phrase means:

1 'It's not important.'
2 'I'm not happy about it.'

c Match a–d with 1 or 2 in 3b.

a Never mind.
b I'm sorry about that.
c It doesn't matter.
d What a shame.

4 PRONUNCIATION
Sound and spelling: *ou*

a ▶1.54 Listen to the sound of the letters *ou* below.

1 col**ou**r
2 an online c**ou**rse
3 h**ou**se

Do the letters in 1–3 have different sounds?

b ▶1.55 Do these words sound like 1, 2 or 3 in 4a? Listen and check. Listen again and repeat.

out __3__   four _____   neighbour _____
about _____   sound _____

5 SPEAKING

a ▶ **Communication 2C** Student A go to p.129. Student B go to p.132.

d ▶1.52 Listen to three short conversations. Where are they? Match them with pictures a–c.

e ▶1.52 Complete the sentences from the conversations in 2d. Listen again and check your answers.

1 _____ some water, please?
2 _____ a chicken sandwich, please.
3 _____ you this afternoon?

f Look at the situations. What can A and B say? Use expressions from 2a and 2b.

A

① You're in B's home. Ask for some water.

② You're in a café. Ask for a small espresso.

③ You have a problem at work. Ask for some help.

④ You want to meet A on Saturday.

B

Say yes.

You're the waiter. Say yes.

Say no. (You're busy.)

Say no. (You aren't free then.)

g 💬 Work in pairs. Use the dialogue maps to ask for things and reply. Take turns being A and B.

⟳ **Unit Progress Test**

CHECK YOUR PROGRESS

You can now do the Unit Progress Test.

1 SPEAKING AND LISTENING

a 💬 Why do you want to study English?

- to get a good job
- to study something in English
- to meet new friends
- a different reason
- for travel and tourism

b ▶ **1.56** Three International College students talk about where they're from and their reasons for studying English. <u>Underline</u> the correct answers.

I come from *Acapulco / Mexico City* and I need English for my *job / studies*.

I come from *Riyadh / Jeddah* and I need English for my *job / studies*.

I come from *Krakow / Warsaw* and I need English for my *job / studies*.

c ▶ **1.56** Listen again and complete the table with the words in the box.

grammar   the lessons   the teacher
reading and writing   listening   the timetable

	Likes at the college	Needs to improve
Daniela		
Said		
Justyna		

d 💬 Talk about the questions with other students.

1 What do you need to improve in English?
2 Why is this important for you?

e ▶ **1.57** Listen to Kate talk about a competition at International College. What can you win?

f ▶ **1.57** Listen again. Answer the questions.

1 Can students who aren't at International College enter the competition?
2 Is it OK to use a computer for the entry form?
3 Where can students get entry forms?

2 READING

a Look at the information about Daniela. Complete Part 1 of the form. Can you remember her nationality?

> ‹ Inbox   ↺ ↻   ⚑ 🔍 ✉ ✕
> **From:** IC Student Care
> **To:** danielar@supermexmail.com
>
> Dear Daniela
> We're looking forward to welcoming you to
> International College on 6th July.
> You will be in class P1 and your teacher will be
> Kate Marks.
> We hope......

Daniela Romero
074822 294576

🌐 INTERNATIONAL *College*   COMPETITION *entry form*

Part 1

First name: _____

Family name: _____

Gender: ☐ female ☐ male

Nationality: _____

Mobile (UK): _____

Email address: _____

Your class now: _____

Course start date: _____

Part 2

Why is English important for you?

> I work as a [1]_____ in Mexico City. I love my job except for the [2]_____! Every day they speak to me and ask me for information. I can't understand them and it is difficult for me to answer. English is important for me because it helps me do my [3]_____ well.

What do you want to improve in your English?

> I think my speaking in English is OK for my level. But [4]_____ and understanding is still very difficult for me. I really want to stay an extra month at your school and improve my listening.

b Read Part 2 of Daniela's form. Complete it.

c ▶ **1.58** Listen to Daniela again and check your answers.

3 WRITING SKILLS Spelling

a Read Daniela's first copy of her entry form. Cover page 26. Look at the example spelling problem. Find eight more spelling problems.

b Tick (✓) when it's important to have correct spelling.

1 ☐ a first copy of a text
2 ☐ a final copy of a text
3 ☐ a text other people read
4 ☐ a text only you read

c Find and correct a spelling mistake in each sentence.

1 I really love swimming in the see.
2 Can you please right your name on the form?
3 I don't no the answer to this question.
4 Can you speak more loudly? I can't here you.
5 Where can I bye bread?

d In what way are the incorrect and correct words in 3c the same?

4 WRITING

a Complete the form with your information.

b Use your ideas in 1d to write answers to the questions in Part 2.

c Swap forms with another student. Are your ideas in Part 2 the same?

Part 2

Why is English important for you?

I work as a ~~trafic~~ <u>traffic</u> police offiser in Mexico City. I love my job except for the toorists! Every day they speak to me and ask me for informashion. I can't understand them and it is dificult for me to anser. English is important for me becos it helps me do my job well.

What do you want to improve in your English?

I think my speaking in English is OK for my level. I also find reading and writing quite easy. But listning and understanding is still very hard for me. I really want to stay an extra month at your scool and improve my listening.

Competition entry form

Part 1

First name:

Family name:

Gender: ☐ female ☐ male

Nationality:

Mobile (UK):

Email address:

Your class now:

Course start date:

Part 2

Why is English important for you?

What do you want to improve in your English?

UNIT 2
Review and extension

1 GRAMMAR

a Complete the text with the correct form of the verb in brackets.

I'm a university student, but I [1]_____ (work) in a clothes shop every weekend. On Saturday I [2]_____ (start) work at 9:00 am, but on Sunday I [3]_____ (not start) until 11:00 am. My sister's a nurse so she [4]_____ (not have) a normal timetable. She sometimes [5]_____ (work) all night, but she [6]_____ (not like) it. My parents are both teachers so they [7]_____ (work) from Monday to Friday.

b Write possible questions for the answers.

1 **A** What _____? **B** I'm a receptionist.
2 **A** Do _____? **B** No, I don't. I work in hospital.
3 **A** Do _____? **B** Yes, I do. It's great.
4 **A** When _____? **B** I start at 9 o'clock in the morning.
5 **A** Does _____? **B** Yes, he does. My husband is a teacher.
6 **A** Where _____? **B** He works in a local school.
7 **A** Does _____? **B** Yes, he does. He loves it.

c 💬 Practise the conversation in 1b with a partner. Answer about your life.

2 VOCABULARY

a Put the letters in brackets in the correct order to complete the job.

1 n_____e (s r u)
2 d_____t (t e i s n)
3 p_____t (l o i)
4 e_____r (n n i e g e)
5 c_____r (e e n a l)
6 p_____r (o o h e h p r a t g)

b Write the times in words.

10:15 – (a) quarter past ten or ten fifteen
1 11:30   3 6:00   5 2:40
2 12:45   4 8:15   6 5:20

c Match 1–5 with a–e to complete the sentences.

1 Read the text and make
2 I'm not worried because I usually get good
3 I hope we have
4 He worries because he often fails
5 I need to study for the end of

a a break soon because I'm tired.
b exams at the end of courses.
c notes on a piece of paper.
d term test next week.
e marks in tests.

3 WORDPOWER *work*

a Match sentences 1–3 with pictures a–c.

1 I **work in** a hospital.
2 I **work for** Larkin Computers
3 I **work as** a receptionist.

b Look at the marked phrases in 3a. Match them with 1–3.

1 the job we do
2 the place of work
3 the company

c Is *work* a verb or a noun in sentences 1–5?

1 I start **work** at 8:00 am each day.
2 She leaves **work** at about 6:00 pm.
3 I can't talk to you now – I'm at **work**.
4 I'm an actor, but I'm out of **work** at the moment.
5 They go to **work** very early in the morning.

d Which *work* phrase in 3c do we use when … ?

a we don't have a job
b we are at the place we work

e Put the word in brackets in the correct place in the sentence.

1 He works a nurse at night. (as)
2 We all work at 6:00 pm. (start)
3 She'd like a job because now she's of work. (out)
4 She's a photographer and works *The Times*. (for)
5 When I'm work, I have no free time. (at)
6 We both work a large office in the centre of town. (in)

f Write four sentences about people you know. Use *work* in different ways.

My brother works for a shoe shop in the centre of town.

🔄 REVIEW YOUR PROGRESS

How well did you do in this unit? Write 3, 2, or 1 for each objective.
3 = very well   2 = well   1 = not so well

I CAN …

talk about jobs	☐
talk about study habits	☐
ask for things and reply	☐
complete a form.	☐

CAN DO OBJECTIVES

- Talk about routines
- Talk about technology in your life
- Make arrangements
- Write an informal invitation

UNIT 3
Daily life

GETTING STARTED

a 💬 Look at the picture and answer the questions.

1 What country do you think this is? Why?
2 What time is it: morning or evening? Why?
3 Where do these three men go when they get off the train?
4 What are their jobs?

b 💬 In pairs, ask and answer the questions.

1 What things do you do every day?
- take a bus or train
- buy a newspaper
- read your emails
- go for a walk

2 What do you do on a train or bus?
- read
- talk to other passengers
- listen to music
- use your phone
- sleep

A DAY IN THE LIFE ...

Breakfast, work, home, dinner: we all know the typical daily routine of people all over the world. But it's the little differences in our lives that make those routines interesting.

Today, we continue our series about daily life around the world with the Chopra family in India. One in six people in the world lives in India. Many of them live in big modern cities, but over 263 million of them – including the Chopras – work on farms across the country.

Garjan Chopra is a farmer in a small village near Delhi. He lives with his wife, Anjani, his children and grandchildren. They work in the fields every day. Garjan and Anjani get up every morning at 4:00 am. They work in the fields from 7:00 am to 6:00 pm. At 9:00 am they always stop work for breakfast. They don't have their breakfast together because in their culture men and women don't usually eat together. They stop work for a rest at midday when the sun is very strong. In the afternoon, their grandchildren usually help them. In the evening, the family never eats together. First, the men and children have dinner, then the women of the family eat together in the kitchen. They often go to bed at around 9:00 pm, ready for another busy day on the farm.

Garjan Chopra and his wife Anjani

1 READING

a  Look at the pictures and answer the questions.

1 Where do they work – in the city or the countryside?
2 What job do the people do?
3 Is their work easy or hard?

b Read the text. Are your ideas in 1a correct?

c Read the text again. Are the sentences true or false? Correct the false sentences.

1 Garjan and Anjani get up early and immediately have breakfast.
2 They work for about 11 hours a day.
3 They work without a break all day.
4 Their grandchildren usually help them in the mornings before school.
5 The children in the family don't eat with their mothers.

d 💬 What are the good things about the life of the Chopra family?

2 GRAMMAR Position of adverbs of frequency

a Look at this sentence from the text. The adverb of frequency is underlined.

At 9:00 am they always stop work for breakfast.

Underline more adverbs of frequency in the text.

b Put the adverbs of frequency in the correct place on the time line.

~~sometimes~~ usually never often always

100% |———————|———————|———————| 0%
sometimes

c ▶ Now go to Grammar Focus 3A on p.140

d 💬 Talk about the questions.

1 What do you always do in the morning?
2 What do you usually do in the afternoon?
3 What do you sometimes do in the evening?

> I always get up at 6 o'clock.

> I often play tennis in the afternoon.

3 LISTENING

a 💬 Ask and answer the questions.

1 Do you spend a lot of time with your family? Why / Why not?
2 What do you like doing with your family?

b ▶1.60 Listen to Martin and Katherine. Answer the questions.

1 Do they talk about their jobs or free time?
2 What does Martin want the family to do?

c ▶1.60 Listen again. Complete the timetable with the correct activity from the box.

Spanish lesson   band practice   work late   volleyball training

d 💬 Talk about the questions.

1 The Chopra family and the Lawson family do something that is the same. What is it?
2 Is your family routine more like the Chopras' or the Lawsons'? Or is it different?

The Lawson Family Week

	Martin	Katherine	Liz	Pete
Monday				
Tuesday				
Wednesday				
Thursday				
Friday				

4 VOCABULARY Time expressions

a ▶1.61 Complete the sentences. Listen and check.

twice   a   every   once

1 I go to my Spanish lesson _____ a week.
2 She goes to volleyball training _____ a week on Monday and Thursday.
3 He has band practice three times _____ week.
4 I work late _____ Tuesday.

b Underline the correct answer to complete the rule.

We put time expressions *before the verb* / *at the end of a sentence*.

c ▶1.62 Pronunciation Listen to the question and answer. Notice the stressed words.

MARTIN   How <u>of</u>ten does she <u>go</u>?
KATHERINE   <u>Twice</u> a <u>week</u> on <u>Mon</u>day and <u>Thurs</u>day.

d Which words do we usually stress? Choose the correct answer.

a Important words like time expressions and verbs.
b Less important words.

e ▶1.63 Put the words in each sentence in the correct order to make a dialogue. Listen and check.

A you and your family do / how often do / things together?
B a week / about once.
A you do / what do?
B we usually / to a restaurant / go for a picnic or.
A do that at / do you / the weekend?
B but we sometimes / yes, every Sunday / go to the cinema.
A do anything else / do you?
B away for a weekend / a year we go / well, about twice.
A with your family / a nice time / it sounds like you have.

f ▶ Now go to Vocabulary Focus 3A on p.163 for Common verbs

5 SPEAKING

a Think of a group of people you know well. Think of things you do together every day, week or year. Make notes.

My mum – have a cup of tea every morning
Rob and Andy – usually go on holiday every June
My classmates – study English three times a week

b 💬 Talk about what you do with the people you know well and how often. Look at the conversation in 4e to help you.

3B Imagine you haven't got the Internet

Learn to talk about technology in your life
- Ⓖ *have got*
- Ⓥ Technology

1 READING

a How do you use the Internet? Tick (✓) the things you sometimes do. Tick (✓✓) the things you do every day.

- ☐ find information
- ☐ talk to friends
- ☐ send emails
- ☐ watch films or TV
- ☐ upload pictures
- ☐ play games
- ☐ buy things
- ☐ download music

b 💬 Talk about your answers with other students.

c Read the first part of *Tech Blog*.

1 Is it about … ?
   a using the Internet more
   b using the Internet less
2 What is unusual about the Kim family this month?

d Read *The Interview* and answer the questions.

1 Which of activities a–f does Ha-eun do more without the Internet?
   a reading books   d getting news
   b talking to people   e doing homework
   c contacting friends   f going out
2 Which activities are now more difficult for Ha-eun and her family?

e 💬 Talk about the questions.

1 Would you like to live without the Internet? Why / Why not?
2 What do you think is good and bad about the Internet?

2 VOCABULARY Technology

a Match the words in the box with pictures 1–10.

computer	smartphone	tablet	e-reader	satnav
keyboard	printer	headphones	camera	laptop

b ▶ 1.66 **Pronunciation** Listen and repeat the words in 2a. Underline the stressed syllable in each word.

c What are the people talking about? There is sometimes more than one answer.

1 I talk to my friends on it.
2 I use it to write emails.
3 I use these when I listen to music.
4 I often print out maps, so it's very useful.
5 I use it in the car.

TECHBLOG

HOME   REVIEWS   FORUMS   DOWNLOADS   Login   Search

THIS MONTH ON TECHBLOG

These days, we all use the Internet – for everything. It's on our computers, our smartphones … it's everywhere. But imagine you haven't got the Internet. So you can't send emails, you can't upload photos, and you can't go online to get information.

How long could you live like that? A day? A week maybe, if you're on holiday? Two weeks?

Here at Tech Blog we asked the Kim family in Seoul, South Korea, to live without the Internet for a whole month. Read our Interview with Kim Ha-eun the mother of the family, about what it's like to go offline.

THE INTERVIEW

Ha-eun, is your life different without the Internet?
Ha-eun: Yes, it is different in many ways. Our TV comes over the Internet so now we can't watch it. And I usually read the news online and now I can't do that. But I've got more time to do other things – I read books and I go out more.

Is it easy to live without the Internet?
Ha-eun: No, it certainly isn't easy. I usually do all my shopping online, but now I go to the supermarket and carry my shopping home. And my son uses the Internet for his homework. But now he hasn't got the Internet, so he has to buy books or go to the library.

What about talking to friends?
Ha-eun: Yes, that's a problem too: we've got friends in Japan and in the USA, but if you aren't on Facebook or Skype, it's difficult to contact them. But in some ways life is good without the Internet. Now I often visit my neighbours and we drink tea together!

3 LISTENING

Don

Bella

Chris

a ▶**1.67** Listen to Don. Bella and Chris's answers. Match the people with the questions.

1 Have you got a computer?
2 Have you got a smartphone?
3 Have you got a digital camera?

b ▶**1.68** Listen to the conversations and complete the table.

	What gadgets have they got?	Do they often use them?
Don		
Bella		
Chris		

c ▶**1.68** How do Bella and Chris use each gadget? Listen again and check.

4 GRAMMAR *have got*

a Look at the sentences. Which are from the Reading text (R) and which are from the Listening (L)?

1 I've got my daughter's phone.
2 We've got friends in Japan and in the USA.
3 She's got a new phone.
4 Imagine you haven't got the Internet.
5 Now he hasn't got the Internet.
6 Have you got a digital camera?

---

b Underline the forms of *have got* in 1–6 in 4a. Does *I've got* mean:

a I am   b I have   c I get?

c Complete the table.

	I / We / You / They	He / She
+	I _____ got her old phone.	She _____ got a new phone.
−	I _____ got a PC, but I've got a laptop.	He _____ got his phone with him. It's at home.
?	_____ you got a computer at home? Yes, I have. / No, I haven't.	_____ she got a new camera? Yes, she has. / No, she hasn't.

d ▶**1.69** **Pronunciation** Listen to the sentence. The main stress is on *camera*, the last important word.

I've got a digital <u>camera</u>.

e ▶**1.70** Listen to sentences 1–3. <u>Underline</u> the main stress.

1 They've got a computer.
2 He's got a smartphone.
3 She's got a new laptop.

f ▶**1.70** Listen again. Does the tone go up ↗ or down ↘ on the main stress?

g ▶ Now go to Grammar Focus 3B on p.140

h Write sentences that are true for you. Use *have got* or *haven't got* and the words and phrases in the box.

---
a laptop   a camera   a car   a smartphone   an e-reader
a lot of online friends   friends in another country

I've got a smartphone.

i Write three *have got* questions with words and phrases in 4h.

Have you got a smartphone?

---

5 SPEAKING

a Put the words in the correct order to make questions.

1 use it / how often / you / do?
2 you / do / like it?
3 it / is / what kind?
4 is / it / how old?
5 where / they / do / live?
6 like one / would / you?

b 💬 Ask and answer your questions in 4i with a partner. Then ask questions from 5a to find out more.

Have you got a car?

Yes, I have.

What kind is it?

It's a ...

c 💬 Work in new pairs. Tell a new partner what you know about other students.

Pavel's got a smartphone. It's one year old and he uses it every day.

HA-EUN AND HER HUSBAND

Learn to make arrangements

S Thinking about what you want to say
P Main stress

1 LISTENING

a 💬 Ask and answer the questions.

1 How often do you watch TV?
2 Are there programmes you watch every week?
3 Do you have a favourite TV programme? Who do you watch it with?

b ▶1.72 Watch or listen to Part 1. Do Martina, Annie and Dan all like the same TV programme?

c ▶1.72 Watch or listen to Part 1 again. Are the sentences true or false?

1 The programme Annie wants to watch is *Best Cook*.
2 Martina and Dan don't see this programme very often.
3 Annie loves everything to do with eating.

d ▶1.73 Watch or listen to Part 2. What do they plan to do?

e ▶1.73 Answer the questions. Watch or listen to Part 2 again and check your answers.

1 Which day does Martina work late?
2 Which day do they decide to go out?
3 Who does Dan want to ask to dinner?
4 How does Annie feel about Dan's idea?

2 USEFUL LANGUAGE Making arrangements

a Match beginnings 1–6 with endings a–f.

1	Why	a	be great.
2	How	b	free next Friday?
3	Are you	c	don't we try it?
4	That'd	d	love to.
5	That's a	e	about next Wednesday?
6	I'd	f	good idea.

b Which questions in 2a do we use to make suggestions? Which sentences do we use to say *yes* to suggestions?

c Martina says *no* to an idea. Underline the phrase that means *no*.

MARTINA I'm sorry, I can't. I need to work late next Wednesday.

d ▶1.74 Put the conversation in the correct order. Listen and check.

B ☐ I'm sorry, I can't. I'm away this weekend.
A ☐1 Why don't we go to the cinema?
B ☐ Yes, Monday's fine.
A ☐ How about this Saturday?
A ☐ Are you free on Monday?
B ☐ The cinema? That's a good idea.

e 💬 Practise the conversation in 2d. Then have similar conversations using your own ideas.

Why don't we go for a picnic?

3 PRONUNCIATION Main stress

a ▶1.75 Listen to the sentences. Notice the main stress in each sentence.

1 That'd be <u>great</u>.   2 That's a <u>good</u> idea.   3 I'd <u>love</u> to.

b Choose the correct answer.

The words in 3a that have the main stress are
a short and loud   b long   c long and loud?

c ▶1.76 Listen to the sentences. Underline the main stress.

1 We'd love to.   3 That's a lovely idea.
2 That'd be good.   4 That'd be fantastic.

d 💬 Practise the sentences in 3c.

4 CONVERSATION SKILLS
Thinking about what you want to say

a Look at the <u>underlined</u> phrases in the conversation. Choose the correct answer below.

ANNIE How about next Wednesday?
MARTINA <u>Mm, maybe</u>. <u>Let me see</u>. I'm sorry but I can't. I need to work late next Wednesday.
ANNIE Are you free next Friday?
MARTINA <u>Mm, possibly</u>. Friday's fine. Dan?
DAN Friday? Sure, I'd love to.

Martina uses the <u>underlined</u> phrases because they:
a have an important meaning in the conversation.
b give her time to think.

b   **Pronunciation** Listen and notice how *Mm* is pronounced. Do you have short words or sounds like this in your language?

c   In pairs, ask and answer the questions. Think about your answer before you reply.

1 Are you free this weekend?
2 Do you want to have a coffee after the lesson?
3 Would you like to go to the cinema tomorrow?
4 Why don't we do our homework together?

5 SPEAKING

a   **Communication 3C** Student A look at the information below. Student B go to p.133.

Conversation 1. Read your first card. Think about what you want to say. Then start the conversation with Student B.

> ① You want to have a picnic on Saturday morning with Student B. Decide the following and invite Student B.
> • where to have the picnic
> • what time
> • what you'd like to do/eat

b **Conversation 2.** Now look at your second card. Listen to Student B and reply.

> ② You aren't free next Friday after work/school because you have an exercise class at the gym. You'd like to go out on Saturday night.

c Tell other students about arrangements in each role play.

Unit Progress Test

CHECK YOUR PROGRESS

You can now do the Unit Progress Test.

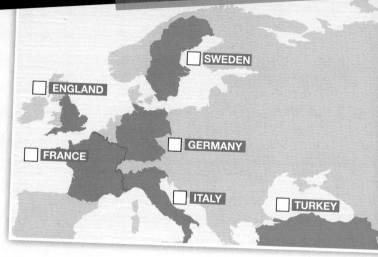

1 SPEAKING AND LISTENING

a 💬 Ask and answer the questions.

1 Have you got family or friends in other countries, or in other places in your country?
2 Where are they?
3 What do they do?
4 How often do you see them?

b ▶1.78 Emrah from Turkey talks about his family. Listen and number the countries where he's got family in the order you hear them.

c ▶1.78 Listen again. Correct the mistakes in the text below.

Emrah comes from a large family and [1]they all live in Izmir in Turkey. [2]He hasn't got any brothers or sisters. His family keep in contact by Skype, and every [3]ten years they all meet in [4]London. They stay [5]in a large hotel and they have a big [6]meal. This [7]is only for people in the family – they [8]don't invite friends.

1 *They live in many different countries.*

2 READING

a Read Emrah's emails to his brother and sister. Why does he email them?

b Complete the information about the family party.
- Place
- Date
- How many days?
- Where to stay?

Hi Mustafa
[1]How are you? Hope the family's well.
[2]In September it's our family party again and we all plan to meet in Izmir as usual. [3]We're there from Friday 14 to Sunday 16 September. [4]Would you like to come? I hope so, as I'd love to see you. [5]Mert (you know, my friend from school) says he's got a bedroom free so you can stay at his house. [6]Please let me know if you would like to join us.
I hope you can come!
Love,
Emrah

Hi Ayda
[1]How are things? Hope you like your new job.
[2]In September it's our family party again and we all plan to meet in Izmir as usual. [3]We're there from Friday 14 to Sunday 16 September.
[4]Can you join us? I hope you can, as it would be great to see you. [5]Melis (you know, my friend from school) says she's got a bedroom free so you can stay at her house. [6]Please let me know if you can come. Hope you can make it!
Love,
Emrah

3 WRITING SKILLS Inviting and replying

a Read Emrah's email to Ayda again. In which of sentences 1–6 does he … ?

a [4] invite Ayda
b [ ] ask how she is
c [ ] ask her to reply
d [ ] give the reason for his message
e [ ] talk about where to stay
f [ ] give details of dates

b Compare sentences 1–6 in Emrah's emails to Mustafa and Ayda on p. 36. <u>Underline</u> phrases that are different.

c Tick (✓) the correct questions to invite people.

1 [ ] Can you come?
2 [ ] Can you join?
3 [ ] Can you join us?
4 [ ] Can you to join us?
5 [ ] Would you like come?
6 [ ] Would you like to come?
7 [ ] Would you like to join us?

d Put the words in the correct order. Add question marks (?) and full stops (.).

1 things / are / how
2 you / see / to / be / it / would / great
3 hope / it / can / you / make
4 to / I'd / you / love / see
5 are / you / how
6 I / can / come / you / hope

e Which sentences and questions in 3d mean the same?

f Read the emails from Mustafa and Ayda. Can they come?

> ✉
>
> Hi Emrah
> It's good to hear from you and many thanks for the invitation. Yes, I'd love to come. I'm really looking forward to it. Please tell Mert I'd love to stay with him if he's got a free room. See you soon.
> Love,
> Mustafa

> ✉
>
> Hi Emrah
> Great to hear from you and thanks for the invitation. I'd love to come but I'm afraid I can't. I've got a business trip to Los Angeles that weekend and I can't change it.
> Hope you all have a great time, and hope to see you soon.
> Keep in touch!
> Love,
> Ayda

g <u>Underline</u> phrases in the emails from Mustafa and Ayda that mean:

1 I want to come.
2 I can't come.
3 Have a good time.

4 WRITING AND SPEAKING

a Plan a party or other event. Make notes.

• Where? • When? • Why? • Who?

b 💬 Talk about your plan with other students.

> My party is at the Grand Hotel.

> It's at 7 pm on Saturday.

> It's for my brother's birthday.

c Write an invitation to your event to another student in your class. Use the emails on page 36 to help you.

d Swap invitations with another student and check the information.
Does it include the information in 4a?

e Write a reply to the invitation. Use the emails in 3f to help you. Give your reply back to the student who invited you.

UNIT 3
Review and extension

1 GRAMMAR

a Put the frequency adverbs in the correct place in the sentences.

1　He gets up often at about 10 or 11.
2　He goes to bed before 2:00 am never.
3　He studies all sometimes night.
4　He has usually black coffee and toast for breakfast.
5　He is away for a week often or more.
6　His windows are closed always, even in summer.

b Complete the text with the correct forms of *have got* or *haven't got*.

My brother and I are very different. He and his wife
[1]_____ good jobs and they [2]_____ a large house near
London. Their house [3]_____ a big garden with a swimming
pool. They both work ten hours a day so they [4]_____ any
free time and they never go on holiday.

I'm a school teacher, so I [5]_____ much money, but I [6]_____
a lot of free time in the holidays. Every summer I travel to a
different country and I [7]_____ friends all over the world.

c Make the notes into questions with *have got* or *has got*. Then write true short answers.

1　you – a car? *Have you got a car? No, I haven't.*
2　your neighbours – children?
3　your flat or house – a garden?
4　you – TV in your bedroom?
5　someone in your family – a laptop?
6　you – a lot of free time?

d 💬 Ask and answer the questions in 1c.

2 VOCABULARY

a Change the words in italics into a time expression.

1　She phones ~~on Tuesday and Sunday~~. *twice a week*
2　There are English courses *in March, May and October*.
3　We go on holiday *in June and in January*.
4　There's a boat *on Monday, Wednesday and Saturday*.
5　I check my emails *before I start work and in the evening*.
6　Her mother phones on *Monday, Tuesday, Wednesday and Thursday*.

b Write the names of the objects.

3 WORDPOWER Prepositions of time

a Match sentences 1–5 with pictures a–e.

1　He only works in the winter.
2　He works all the time – in the evening, at the weekend, sometimes even at night.
3　He gets up at 6 am, but he finishes work at 1 pm.
4　He works on weekdays, but on Sunday he gets up late.
5　In January he works at a ski resort.

b Answer the questions.

1　Do we use *at*, *in* or *on* with a–f?
a　times
b　days
c　months
d　parts of days (morning, afternoon)
e　seasons (summer, winter)
f　the words *the weekend* and *night*

2　How many examples of a–f can you find in 3a?

c Add *at*, *in* or *on* in the correct place in these sentences. Some sentences may need more than one word.

1　I always get up 6:30 the morning weekdays.
2　It's usually cold here the winter and it often snows January.
3　Are you free the weekend? I've got tickets for a concert Saturday. It starts 7:30 pm.

d When do you usually do these things? Write sentences.

1　get up
2　go to bed
3　have lunch
4　go on holiday
5　go shopping
6　drink coffee or tea
7　clean your flat or house
8　cook meals

e 💬 Ask and answer questions about when you usually do the things in 3d.

⟳ REVIEW YOUR PROGRESS

How well did you do in this unit? Write 3, 2, or 1 for each objective.
3 = very well   2 = well   1 = not so well

I CAN ...

talk about routines	☐
talk about technology in my life	☐
make arrangements	☐
write an informal invitation.	☐

CAN DO OBJECTIVES

- Talk about the food you want
- Talk about the food you eat every day
- Arrive at and order a meal in a restaurant
- Write a blog about something you know how to do

UNIT 4
Food

GETTING STARTED

a 💬 Look at the picture and answer the questions.

1 Do you think they're friends or family?
2 What meal is it – breakfast, dinner or lunch?
3 Is it the beginning, middle or end of the meal?

b 💬 In pairs, ask and answer the questions.

1 How often do you eat together as a family?
2 What do you usually have for … ?
   - breakfast
   - lunch
   - dinner
3 What things do you talk about when you eat together?

1 READING

a 💬 Look at the pictures of places to buy food. Which one would you like to visit? Why?

b Read *World markets* and match 1–3 with pictures a–c.

c Read the sentences. Where is each person?

RON I love freshly baked bread – it's still warm.
MAGGIE I really only need a snack, but look at all the food I can buy!
SARAH Now I know a new way to cook these vegetables.

d 💬 Talk about the questions.

1 Are there any markets in your town? What do they sell?
2 Where do you prefer shopping for food, in a market or a supermarket? Why?

2 GRAMMAR
Countable and uncountable nouns

a Look at the four nouns from *World markets*. Which two have plural endings?

fruit   vegetables   tomatoes   cheese

b Complete the rule.

We can't count some nouns (they are uncountable). We *always / never* add *-s* or *-es*.

c Look at the table. Add food nouns from *World markets*.

Countable nouns (You can say *1, 2, 3 vegetables.*)	Uncountable nouns (You can't say *1, 2, 3 fruits.*)
vegetables, tomatoes	fruit, cheese

WORLD MARKETS 🍃

Markets can be the best places to see the daily life of a city and to eat some fantastic local food. Today, read about different markets around the world.

1 COOK AS YOU SHOP

If you want to buy food and learn how to cook it at the same time, go to the Union Square Greenmarket in New York. It's open four days a week and it has about 250,000 customers. Farmers from all of New York State sell food there. You can find different kinds of fruit and vegetables, such as potatoes, carrots, mushrooms and tomatoes. The farmers show the best ways to cook the food and you can even try the dishes they make for free!

2 FRESH ITALIAN FOOD

Italian food is famous all over the world. You can find pasta and a pizza restaurant in almost any city but one of the best places to try it is in Modena, Italy. There you can find the Mercato Albinelli. It's not a big market, but the food's amazing. Many Italians go there to buy some fresh pasta made by hand – you can't get better pasta anywhere else! You can also buy fresh meat, fruit and vegetables and, of course, fantastic cheese and bread.

3 FOOD AND HISTORY

In the centre of Moscow on Tverskaya Street, you can visit a beautiful and historic building. Inside there's Yeliseyevsky's Food Hall, a large market with things to eat and drink. From chocolate to fish, you can find just about anything at Yeliseyevsky's. For Russians, it's a popular place to go for a quick snack. Many tourists also visit because it's fun to go and look at the beautiful building and try some interesting food. It's open 24 hours a day, so you can't ever be hungry!

3 VOCABULARY Food

a Match the food words with pictures 1–10.

> beans lemons chicken
> mushrooms onions
> lamb pears steak
> carrots grapes

b Underline the different word in 1–3. Why is it different?

1 lemon pear carrot grape
2 bean lamb onion mushroom
3 steak chicken grape lamb

c ▶2.2 **Pronunciation** Answer the questions. Then listen and check.

1 What is the same about the spelling of these words?
  • steak   • bean   • pear
2 Which word above has the same sound as these words?
  gr**ee**n /iː/   h**air** /eə/   m**a**ke /eɪ/

d ▶2.3 What sound do the marked letters have in the words in the box? Add the words to the sound groups below. Listen and check.

> **ea**t wh**ere** th**e**se **eigh**t r**ai**n
> gr**ee**n w**ear** d**ay** f**air**

Sound 1 /eɪ/	Sound 2 /iː/	Sound 3 /eə/
steak	bean	pear

e 💬 Talk about the food you like and don't like.

f ▶ Now go to Vocabulary Focus 4A on p.164 for more Food vocabulary

4 LISTENING

a 💬 Ask and answer the questions.

1 Do you like cooking?
2 How often do you (or does someone in your family) buy food to cook?

b ▶2.7 Listen and answer the questions.

1 Does Milly want to cook?
2 Who doesn't want to do anything at the weekend – Tom or Milly?
3 Where do they buy food at the weekend – at the supermarket or farmers' market?
4 Who says they can pay – Tom or Milly?

c ▶2.7 Listen again. Tick (✓) the food on the shopping list that Tom and Milly need.

Meat:
☐ chicken   ☐ steak   ☐ fish
Vegetables:
☐ carrots   ☐ an onion   ☐ potatoes
☐ tomatoes   ☐ mushrooms

5 GRAMMAR a/an, some, any

a ▶2.8 Complete the sentences with the words in the box. Listen and check.

> some a/an any (x2)

1 We've got _____ potatoes.
2 Have we got _____ mushrooms?
3 And I need _____ onion.
4 I haven't got _____ money.

b Complete the table with a, an, some and any.

	Countable	Uncountable
+	_a_ potato ____ potatoes	____ fruit
– / ?	____ onion ____ onions	____ cheese

c ▶ Now go to Grammar Focus 4A on p.142

d ▶2.10 Complete the conversation with a/an, some or any. Listen and check.

SARAH	Hello, I'd like ¹___ lemon and ²___ onion, please.
STALLHOLDER	Just one?
SARAH	Yes, and I'd like ³___ potatoes too.
STALLHOLDER	Is this bag OK?
SARAH	Yes, fine. Have you got ⁴___ small tomatoes?
STALLHOLDER	I'm sorry but I haven't got ⁵___ small tomatoes.
SARAH	OK, the big ones there are fine. Also I'd like ⁶___ cheese.
STALLHOLDER	I'm sorry, I don't sell cheese. Try that guy over there.

6 SPEAKING

a ▶ **Communication 4A** Student A go to p.129. Student B go to p.132.

1 READING

a 💬 Answer the questions with other students.

1 Do you have any famous cooking TV programmes in your country?
2 Do you like the food they make on those programmes? Why / Why not?
3 Do you know the chef in the picture?
4 Read the information about Heston Blumenthal. Would you like to try one of his restaurants? Why / Why not?

b Read Josh's email to his father. Answer the questions.

1 Who lives in London – Josh or his dad?
2 Which restaurant does Josh want to go to?
3 Why does Josh want to go to this restaurant?

c Read his dad's reply. Does he want to go to *Dinner*?

d Read his dad's email again. What does he think about these things? <u>Underline</u> the correct answers.

1 Heston Blumenthal's food: *boring* / *different*
2 His wife's food: *normal* / *strange*
3 The restaurant: *expensive for him* / *expensive for Josh*

e 💬 Talk about the questions.

1 Do you like going to restaurants with your family? Or do you prefer to eat at home? Why / Why not?
2 Do you like trying unusual or strange food? Why / Why not?

Introducing ...
Heston

Who is Heston Blumenthal?
A famous chef and TV star, Heston has two well-known restaurants, *Dinner* and *The Fat Duck*.

What's he famous for?
Heston makes strange and unusual food. On his menu you can find dishes such as brown bread ice cream. Or try his duck with orange dish – the duck is inside the orange!

---

visit

Hi Dad,

When you come to London next week, I want to take you for dinner. Would you like to go to Heston Blumenthal's restaurant *Dinner*? It looks fun and I can pay! Do you remember my friend, Pete? Well, he goes to *Dinner* every time his parents are in town. He always has the fish dish and he says it's amazing! And his mum says the brown bread ice cream is great, too. I really want to take you there!

Josh

5 ▶ 132

Re: visit

Hi Josh,

Thanks for the invitation to *Dinner*. I know about that guy Blumenthal from TV. His food is interesting and it's certainly a bit unusual. But really I'm happy to go to a normal restaurant and have some roast chicken and boiled potatoes, like your mum makes at home. Or I'm also fine with a can of soup at your place. It's a nice idea to go to the restaurant, but you don't need to do anything special for me.

Dad

2 VOCABULARY Cooking

a Read the cooking instructions 1–5 and match them with the pictures a–e.

1 **Fry** the onions in a little oil.
2 Put water and rice in a pan and **boil** for 12 minutes.
3 **Grill** the chicken for 10 minutes until it's brown.
4 Put some oil on the lamb and **roast** it in the oven.
5 **Bake** the bread in a hot oven for 30 minutes.

b ▶2.11 Complete the table. Use verbs from 2a and adjectives from Josh's dad's email. Listen and check.

Verb	Adjective
boil	
	fried
	grilled
	baked
roast	

c Complete the examples with adjectives in 2b.

- add -ed   boiled
- add -d   _____
- changes -y to -ied   _____
- the same as the verb   _____
- ends with the sound /t/   _____

d 💬 Talk about the questions.

1 Which kinds of cooking do you think are healthy? Which do you think are unhealthy?
2 Choose two kinds of food. What is your favourite way to cook that food?

e ▶ Now go to Vocabulary Focus 4B on p.164 for Containers.

3 LISTENING

a ▶2.13 Listen to Olivia and Harry talk about Heston Blumenthal recipes. Tick (✓) which two recipes they choose.

☐ Ultimate mashed potato   ☐ Three times cooked chips
☐ Cheese-on-toast ice cream   ☐ Coffee and chocolate sauce

b ▶2.13 Listen again. <u>Underline</u> the correct food words in the instructions for Olivia and Harry.

1 Olivia needs *potatoes / chips* and *cream / butter*.
2 She needs to *boil / roast* the ingredients.
3 Harry needs *honey / sugar, coffee beans / black coffee,* and *milk chocolate / dark chocolate*.
4 He needs to *grill / boil* the ingredients.

c 💬 Which recipe would you like to make?

4 GRAMMAR Quantifiers: *much, many, a lot (of)*

a ▶2.14 Complete the sentences with the correct words in the box. Listen and check.

| much   a lot   many   a little |

1 That's _____ _____ of butter.
2 How _____ chocolate? Only _____ _____ – 60 grams.
3 How _____ grams of butter?

b Look at the phrases in italics in 1–3. Can you use them with countable (C) or uncountable (U) nouns, or both (B)?

1 **A** *How much* butter does Olivia need?
 B *A lot / Quite a lot / A little / Not much.*
2 **A** *How many* beans does Harry need?
 B *A lot / Quite a lot / A few / Not many.*
3 I need *a lot of / quite a lot of* potatoes and chocolate.

c ▶ Now go to Grammar Focus 4B on p.142

d ▶2.17 Complete the conversation. Then put the conversation in order. Listen and check.

B ☐ A ¹_____ – about five or six pieces.
A ☐ Really? That's ²_____ a lot.
B ☐ About four or five.
A ☐ And what about drinks? How ³_____ cups of coffee do you have a day?
A ☐1 How ⁴_____ fruit do you eat a day?

e 💬 Do you think that Speaker B in 4d is healthy or unhealthy? Why?

5 SPEAKING

a Write questions to ask your partner about the food they eat.

Do you eat much fish?

What fruit do you like?

How many pieces of bread do you eat a day?

How much rice do you eat a week?

b 💬 Ask your questions and write down your partner's answers.

c 💬 Go to page 135 and read about food that is healthy to eat every day. Look at your partner's answers and decide if your partner eats in a healthy way.

4C Everyday English
Do we need a reservation?

Learn to arrive at and order a meal in a restaurant
- **S** Changing what you say
- **P** Word groups

1 LISTENING

a Ask and answer the questions.

1 How often do you go to a restaurant?
2 What kind of restaurant do you like?
3 Do people eat out a lot in your country?

b Work in pairs. Look at picture a. Why do you think the restaurant is empty? Choose an answer.

1 The restaurant isn't open.
2 People think the waiter isn't very nice.
3 It's very early.

Annie　Leo　Martina　Dan

c 2.18 Watch or listen to Part 1 and check your answers in 1b.

d 2.18 Watch or listen to Part 1 again. Are the sentences true or false? Correct the false sentences.

1 They have a reservation for four people.
2 They want a table by the door.
3 Annie finds it difficult to choose a table.

2 USEFUL LANGUAGE
Arriving at a restaurant

a Read the sentences. Who is the waiter – A or B?

A No problem.
B Can we have a table by the window?
A Good evening. Do you have a reservation?
A Yes, of course. This way, please.
B No, we don't. We'd like a table for four.

b 2.19 Put the sentences in 2a in the correct order. Listen and check your answers.

c Practise the conversation with a partner.

d Change what B says in 2a. Use the sentences below.

1 We'd like a table outside.
2 Yes, we have a reservation for two people. The name's Morton. But we're twenty minutes late.

3 LISTENING

a Read the restaurant menu. Read what the friends say about food in picture b. What do you think they choose for their main course?

Martina _____　Dan _____
Annie _____　Leo _____

b 2.20 Watch or listen to Part 2.

1 Which of your answers in 3a are correct? Change the wrong answers.
2 Who can't decide what they want to have?

c Do you sometimes find it difficult to choose at a restaurant? Why / Why not?

Starters

Smoked chicken salad

Mixed bean salad

Fried fish in lemon sauce

Fresh mushroom soup

Main course

Spaghetti with tomato sauce

Egg and vegetable pie

Lamb with roast potatoes

Thai chicken curry

I think I want to eat meat tonight.

I really like Asian food.

4 USEFUL LANGUAGE
Ordering a meal in a restaurant

a Complete the conversations from Part 2 with the words in the box.

| have   then   with   I'll   like |

WAITER	What would you like for your starter?
MARTINA	I'd [1]_____ the mushroom soup, please.
WAITER	And for your main course?
MARTINA	[2]_____ have the lamb with roast potatoes.
WAITER	And for your starter, sir?
DAN	I'll [3]_____ chicken salad.
WAITER	Chicken salad.
DAN	[4]_____ lamb with roast potatoes.
WAITER	Would you like rice [5]_____ that?
LEO	Yes, please.

b Tick (✓) the two phrases we use when we want to order food in a restaurant.

1 ☐ I have   3 ☐ I'd want
2 ☐ I'd like   4 ☐ I'll have

c ▶ 2.21 Put the words in the correct order to make sentences. Listen and check.

1 salad / my / bean / I'd / starter / for / like
2 course / I'll / my / spaghetti / for / have / main
3 I'd / rice / chicken / like / with / curry

The only meat I eat is fish or chicken.

I love Italian food, but everything on the menu looks good!

5 PRONUNCIATION Word groups

a ▶ 2.22 Listen to the sentences. In each sentence there are two or more word groups. Write ‖ where you hear the start of a new word group.

1 For my <u>starter</u> ‖ I'd like raw <u>fish</u>.
2 And I'll have <u>vegetable</u> pie for my <u>main</u> course.
3 I'd like <u>chicken</u> salad for my <u>starter</u>.

b ▶ 2.22 Listen again. Notice the main stress in each word group.

c ▶ 2.23 Write ‖ where you hear the start of a new word group. Listen and check.

For my <u>starter</u> ‖ I'll have <u>mushroom</u> soup. And then I'd like <u>chicken</u> <u>curry</u> for my <u>main</u> course. And I'll have some <u>rice</u> with my <u>curry</u>.

d 💬 In pairs, practise saying the order in 5c.

6 CONVERSATION SKILLS
Changing what you say

a Look at the two sentences from the conversation. <u>Underline</u> the phrases Annie uses when she wants to change what she wants to say.

1 **ANNIE** What about the one on the right?
  DAN If you prefer …
  ANNIE Maybe not. The one on the left is fine …

2 **ANNIE** OK, for a starter I'll have the fish. No, wait. I'll have chicken salad.

b ▶ 2.24 Complete the sentences. Listen and check.

1 I'll have mushroom soup. Maybe _____. I'd like the chicken salad.
2 I'd like spaghetti, I think. No, _____. I'll have the vegetable pie.

7 SPEAKING

a 💬 Work in groups of three or four. Use the menu on page 44. Write one more starter and one more main course.

b You are at a restaurant. Take turns to be the waiter and the customer. Order a meal from the menu. Use phrases from 4a to help you. Practise changing what you say when you order.

🔄 **Unit Progress Test**

CHECK YOUR PROGRESS

You can now do the Unit Progress Test.

1 SPEAKING AND LISTENING

a 💬 Ask and answer the questions.

1 Which of the dishes in pictures a–d would you like to eat?
2 Can you make any dishes like these?
3 Who does most of the cooking in your house: you or another person? Why?

b ▶️ **2.25** Four people talk about cooking. Listen and <u>underline</u> the correct answers.

Name	Talks about		
Jake	*himself / his wife*	a *good / bad* cook	picture *a / b / c / d*
Rosie	*herself / her husband*	a *good / bad* cook	picture *a / b / c / d*
Johanna	*herself / her father*	a *good / bad* cook	picture *a / b / c / d*
Toby	*himself / his mother*	a *good / bad* cook	picture *a / b / c / d*

c ▶️ **2.25** Listen again. Answer the questions.

1 Who always wants to eat more?
2 Who can only make one thing?
3 Who doesn't understand how you can make a really good dish from only a few things?
4 Who enjoys their own food?

d Think of someone you know who is a good cook. Make notes.

• Who?   • Why?   • What dishes?

e 💬 Ask and answer about the good cook you know.

Who do you know who is a good cook?

My father – he's a great cook.

Why is your father a good cook?

He can cook lots of different things.

What does he make?

He makes fantastic chicken salad.

2 READING

a Read *Jake cooks!* Who is it for?

a People who know how to cook very well.
b People who want to learn how to cook.

HOME   **POSTS**   **LINKS**   **CONTACT**

Jake cooks!

Hi everyone and welcome to my cooking blog.

I'm not a good cook, but I want to become better. I just want to learn how to cook simple dishes and eat well. I don't want to cook difficult things and I don't want to be a famous chef. In this blog, I want to tell you about the help I get from my family and friends and the things I try out. So if you want to be a better cook, but not a chef, then maybe I can help you!

b Read *My food – shared!*. What does Jake talk about?

  a the food he eats

  b planning a dinner

c Read *My food – shared!* again. Are the sentences true or false? Correct the false sentences.

  1 Jake hopes the blog can help other people plan dinner for friends.

  2 It's not a good idea to invite a lot of people for dinner.

  3 It's always fun to try a new dish because friends can tell you if it's good or not.

  4 Decide the night of the dinner and then tell your friends.

  5 It helps to do all the cooking before your friends come.

d 💬 Do you prefer making meals for other people or going to someone's home for a meal? Why?

3 WRITING SKILLS Making the order clear

a In Jake's blog, the words *first* and *next* help make the order clear. <u>Underline</u> two more phrases in the blog that also make the order clear.

b Answer the questions.

Which two phrases can we change with *then*?
What punctuation do we use after these phrases?

c Read the recipe for a bean salad. Only sentences 1 and 5 are in the correct order. Put the other sentences in the correct order.

  ☐1 Cook the beans in hot water with a little salt.

  ☐ Add salt and pepper and mix everything together.

  ☐ Put lemon and oil on the warm beans – not too much.

  ☐ Leave the beans until they are warm.

  ☐5 Place the bean salad in a nice bowl and serve to your guests.

d Add the words in the box to the sentences in 3c.

first	after that	next	then	finally

First, cook the beans in hot water …

4 WRITING

a Plan a blog about something you know how to do.

  • What are good ideas to become better?

  • What's a good order to do things?

b Write your blog. Use *My food – shared!* to help you.

c Swap blogs with another student and check the order is clear.

HOME   POSTS   LINKS   CONTACT

My food – shared!

Added at 12.47 today

Do you like the idea of cooking dinner for friends? Here are my ideas for planning a dinner for friends – I hope you find them useful …

First, think about how many people you want to invite. Don't invite too many – I think four people is a good number.

Next, ring or email to invite your friends and all agree on a night that's good for everyone.

After that, decide on your menu. Only choose food that you know how to prepare. Don't choose new and difficult dishes – it's just too hard. Your friends know that you are not a chef and your house is not a restaurant!

Finally, on the day of the dinner, you need a lot of time to prepare everything – the food and the table. (The weekend is good because you have all day to prepare.) If everything is ready before your guests arrive, you can enjoy the dinner much more.

Cooking for friends can be easy and fun. I hope it is for you!

UNIT 4
Review and extension

1 GRAMMAR

a Correct the words (1–10) that are wrong.

There's a very good market near my home. I always go there to buy [1]*food*. Some stalls sell [2]*vegetable* and [3]*fruits*. I usually buy [4]*potato* and [5]*onions* there because they're very cheap. At my favourite stall an old lady sells [6]*butters*, [7]*cream* and [8]*egg* from her own farm. There is also a building where they sell [9]*fishes* and [10]*meat*.

b Underline the correct answers.

1 Have we got *an / any* onions?
2 How *much / many* coffee do you drink?
3 How *much / many* bananas would you like?
4 Can you buy *a / some* spaghetti?
5 Is there *any / many* milk in the fridge?
6 How *a lot of / much* money have you got?

c Choose the correct answer.

1 I haven't got _____ money, but I can buy a cup of coffee.
   a some   b many   c much
2 There aren't _____ bananas. Let's buy some more.
   a much   b many   c some
3 The party's going to be great – _____ people want to come.
   a much   b a lot of   c any
4 He's got _____ good books about food and cooking.
   a some   b much   c any

2 VOCABULARY

a Match the words in the box with 1–5. Then add one more word to each group.

| pear | chicken | grape | cheese | grilled |
| lamb | potato | boiled | carrot | yoghurt |

1 kinds of meat
2 vegetables
3 kinds of fruit
4 things which come from milk
5 ways of cooking food

b Look at 1–9. Which are normal (✓) and which are unusual (or impossible) (✗)?

1 grilled chicken ✓
2 roast butter ✗
3 boiled egg
4 grilled rice
5 fried fish

6 fried grapes
7 roast lamb
8 fried mushrooms
9 boiled potatoes

3 WORDPOWER *like*

a Read the three conversations. Which one matches the picture?

1 **A** What fruit **do you like**?
   B I like most kinds of fruit, but not bananas.
2 **A** What vegetables **would you like**?
   B I'd like potatoes and carrots, please.
3 **A** We want to have a party. **Would you like** to join us?
   B Yes, thanks. I'd love to.

b Look at the questions in 3a. Which question … ?

1 is about what B wants now
2 invites B to go somewhere
3 is about what B likes in general (not just now)

c Match a–c with similar meaning 1–3 in 3b.

a I don't like *Big Brother*. I think it's a terrible programme.
b Would you like to come to my birthday party?
c I'd like two lemons, please.

d Match the marked words in 1–4 with meanings a–d.

1 **What's it like** to live without the Internet?
2 They haven't got a computer. I couldn't live **like that**.
3 I eat a lot of fruit, **like** apples, pears, melons and bananas.
4 She's 20 and she studies Russian, just **like** me.

a the same as
b for example
c how is it
d in that way

e Write a question with *like* for each situation.

1 Invite a friend to the cinema on Friday.
2 You're in a shop. Ask for some apples.
3 You're a waiter in a café. A customer says 'A coffee, please.'
4 Someone is a guest in your home. You want to know what to cook for him/her.
5 At a party, someone says he/she lives in New York. Ask him/her about the city.

f 💬 Ask and answer the questions in 3e with a partner.

CAN DO OBJECTIVES

- Talk about towns
- Describe rooms and furniture in your home
- Ask for and give directions
- Write a description of your neighbourhood

UNIT 5
Places

GETTING STARTED

a 💬 Talk about the picture. Which ideas do you think are true?

1 A family lives here.
2 People go here for a quiet weekend.
3 Wild animals live inside.
4 You can stay here on holiday.
5 People use it when it rains a lot and the river is high.

b 💬 Imagine you go into the house. Answer the questions.

1 How many rooms are there?
2 What three things can you see?

c 💬 In pairs, ask and answer the questions.

1 Why is this a good place for a home?
2 Why is it a bad place?
3 What is a 'good home'?

Here are some ideas:

- It's in a quiet place.
- It's expensive.
- It's in the centre of town.
- It's got lots of of rooms.
- It's got a garden.
- It's modern.

1 READING

a 💬 Where do you think pictures a–c are from? Choose from the countries in the box.

> England   China   Spain
> Germany   the USA   France

b Read *Strange towns* and check your answers.

c Read the text again and answer the questions.

1 How is Thames Town unusual?
2 Can you see other towns like this near Shanghai?
3 Why do people visit Thames Town?
4 What's the best way to get there from Shanghai?

d 💬 Talk about the questions.

1 Would you like to visit Thames Town? Why / Why not?
2 Would you like to live there?

Strange towns ·Thames Town·

Why is it strange?

Thames Town is an unusual English town. There's a town square with beautiful buildings and there are some nice restaurants. There are streets with cafés and big, green parks where you can sit and relax. You can walk by the river in the centre of the town. So, what's unusual? Well, there aren't any English people apart from some tourists. Thames Town isn't in England, it's in China. And the buildings aren't actually old. Thames Town is new – they finished it in 2006.

Thames Town is in Songjiang 30 km west of Shanghai, a big city in the east of China. It was part of the building project 'One city, nine towns'. There's also a German town with modern apartments and a river with bridges and a Spanish town with squares and windmills.

Who lives there?

A lot of the buildings are still empty because it's very expensive to live there. But young Chinese people often go there and take photos when they get married. And, of course, lots of tourists visit because they can see so many different places in one day!

How can I get there?

It's easy to get there. There isn't a metro station in the town, but Songjiang New City metro station is only 4 km away – take Shanghai Metro Line 9 from the centre of Shanghai and then take a taxi or a bus. You can travel from China to 'England' in less than an hour!

2 VOCABULARY Places in a city

a <u>Underline</u> twelve words in *Strange Towns* for places in a town or city. Which ones can you see in pictures a–c?

b ▶ Now go to Vocabulary Focus 5A on p.165

c 💬 Work with other students. Write words for more places in a city. Think of:
- places to go in the evening
- things to see
- places to relax in the daytime

d 💬 Talk about three places you like in your town or city.

3 GRAMMAR *there is / there are*

a Complete the sentences from *Strange Towns* with *there's*, *there are*, *there isn't* or *there aren't*.

1 _____ a metro station in the town.
2 _____ some nice restaurants.
3 _____ any English people.
4 _____ a town square with beautiful buildings.

b Complete the table with forms of *there is* or *there are*.

+	–
There_'s_ a good hotel in the town centre.	There ___ a cinema in the town.
___ ___ some nice cafés.	There ___ any parks.

c Match questions 1–4 about Thames Town with answers a–d.

1 Is there a river?
2 Is there a metro station?
3 Are there any cafés?
4 Are there any old buildings?

a No, there aren't. They're all new.
b Yes, there is. It's in the town centre.
c Yes, there are. There are lots.
d No, there isn't. There's one in Songjiang.

d Complete the table with forms of *there is* or *there are*.

Yes/No questions	Short answers	
___ ___ a good hotel in the town?	Yes, there ___.	No, there ___.
___ ___ any good restaurants?	Yes, ___ ___.	No, ___ ___.

e ▶ Go to Grammar Focus 5A on p.144

f ⏵**2.29** **Pronunciation** Listen to the sentences from 3a and 3c.

1 When do the speakers use *there's*?
   a in sentences   b in questions
   c in short answers
2 Does the word *there* have:
   a a long vowel sound
   b a short vowel sound?

g ▶ **Communication 5A** Student A go to p.130. Student B go to p.134.

4 SPEAKING

a ⏵**2.30** Tom asks his Italian friend, Paola, about visiting Venice, her home town. Complete the conversation with the correct form of *there is* or *there are*. Listen and check your answers.

TOM Is Venice a good place to visit?
PAOLA Oh, it's a fantastic city to visit. [1]_____ lots of interesting old buildings, and [2]_____ some beautiful squares.
TOM [3]_____ any good restaurants?
PAOLA Yes, [4]_____, but they're quite expensive.
TOM What about cafés? [5]_____ any good cafés?
PAOLA Oh yes, [6]_____ lots of good cafés. The coffee's very good in Italy.
TOM And how can I get to places? [7]_____ a metro?
PAOLA No, [8]_____ a metro, but we don't need one. [9]_____ lots of canals, so you can go everywhere by boat.

b 💬 Work in groups of four: Pair A and Pair B.

shops and markets   things to see   buses and trains
restaurants and cafés   parks   famous buildings

Pair A: You are visitors to a town or city. Write questions to ask about the things in the box.

Is there a …? Are there any …?
Can I …? Where can I …?

Pair B: Think about a town or city that you know well. Make notes about the things in the box.

The city is great to visit because … and …
There's a famous … It's called …
There are lots of …

c 💬 Use the conversation in 4a and your notes in 4b to have a conversation.

Pair A: Ask about the town.
Pair B: Answer the questions about the town.

5B Whose wardrobe is that?

Learn to describe rooms and furniture in your home
- **G** Possessive pronouns and possessive 's
- **V** Furniture

1 VOCABULARY Furniture

a 💬 Ask and answer the questions.

1 Do you live in a house or an apartment?
2 How old is your home?
3 In your country where can you buy furniture?

> My apartment is very old.

> I always buy furniture online.

b Read the advertisement for a furniture shop. Who is the store for?

a People who like expensive furniture.
b People who don't want to spend too much money on furniture.

c Match the words in the box with pictures a–l.

mirror   washing machine   bookcase   curtains
sink   cupboard   armchair   wardrobe   lamp
chest of drawers   cooker   sofa

d ▶2.31 **Pronunciation** Listen to the pronunciation of the marked letters. Are the sounds long or short?

1 **a**m	3 w**a**rdrobe	5 c**u**t
2 c**u**rtains	4 **ar**mchair	6 b**a**d

e Answer the questions.

1 What letter is in the spelling of all the long sounds in 1d?
2 Can you hear this letter in the examples?
3 Match *far*, *her* and *door* with three words with the same long sound in 1d.

f Look at the room you are in now. Write a list of the furniture in it.

g 💬 Compare your list with a partner.

> What have you got?

> I've got …

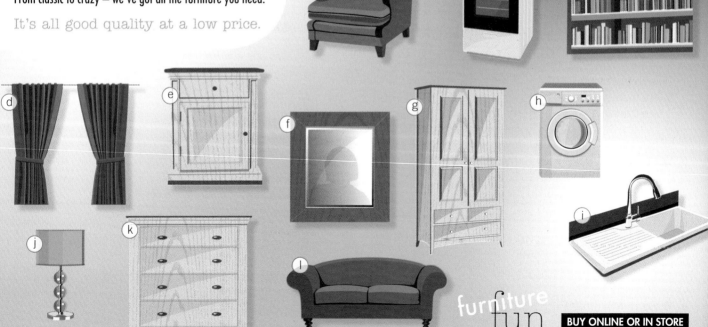

NEW APARTMENT?
Have you got all the furniture you need?

furniture fun

We sell new and second-hand furniture:
- beds • chairs • sofas • wardrobes
- bookcases • chests of drawers …

From classic to crazy — we've got all the furniture you need.

It's all good quality at a low price.

furniture fun   **BUY ONLINE OR IN STORE**

2 LISTENING

a 💬 Ask and answer the questions.

1 Which is your favourite room in your home?
2 Do you have a favourite piece of furniture?

b ▶ 2.32 Jim's sister, Ruth, comes to visit him in his new flat. Listen to their conversation. Which rooms does Jim show Ruth?

a the kitchen   c the bathroom
b the living room   d the bedroom

c ▶ 2.32 Listen again and write down the furniture they talk about in each room.

Room 1 _____
Room 2 _____

d What does Ruth think about the furniture in Jim's flat?

3 GRAMMAR
Possessive pronouns and possessive 's

a ▶ 2.33 Complete the conversation with words from the box. Listen and check your answers.

your	Mum and Dad	David's	mine
yours	of	David	Mum and Dad's

RUTH I love that armchair.
JIM Yes, it's quite … interesting.
RUTH Is it ¹_____?
JIM No, it's ²_____. He's my flatmate.
RUTH I love it. That mirror over there. Is that ³_____?
JIM Well, yes, but really it's ⁴_____ now.

b Tick (✓) the correct sentences.

1 ☐ It's the flat of Jim.
2 ☐ It's Jims flat.
3 ☐ It's Jim's flat.
4 ☐ It's my parent's flat.
5 ☐ It's the flat of my parents.
6 ☐ It's my parents' flat.

Jim's flatmate, David

Jim and Ruth

c Look at the sentences and answer the questions.

Whose mirror is that?   a *It's my mirror.*
                           b *It's mine.*

1 Do we need to repeat *mirror* in the answer?
2 Which answer is better?

d Complete the sentences with the words in the box.

yours	hers	mine	his	theirs

1 It's my bed.   → It's _____.
2 It's your lamp.   → It's _____.
3 It's her sofa.   → It's _____.
4 It's their mirror. → It's _____.
5 It's his chair.   → It's _____.

e ▶ Now go to Grammar Focus 5B on p.144

f ▶ 2.37 Read about Jean Paul's flat. Complete the text with the words in the box. Listen and check your answers.

sister's	parents'	mine (x3)
mother's	hers	yours

I live in a flat with seven rooms. It's not ¹_____ – it's my ²_____. In my bedroom, there's a really big bookcase that I love. It's my ³_____, but she doesn't live at home now so I don't think it's ⁴_____ any more – it's ⁵_____ now. My father's got a study with a beautiful old desk. It's really my ⁶_____, but Dad always says to Mum, 'It's not ⁷_____ now, it's ⁸_____.'

4 SPEAKING

a Write four sentences about your home, the furniture in it and whose furniture it is. Look at Jean Paul's words in 3f to help you.

b 💬 Read your sentences to a partner. Listen to your partner's sentences and try to remember the information.

c 💬 Tell your partner what you remember about their home. Who can remember the most?

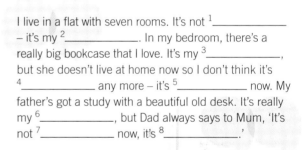

In the living room there's a very large sofa.

No, there are two large sofas.

The lamp in your bedroom is your brother's.

Yes, that's right.

5C Everyday English
Is there a bank near here?

Learn how to ask for and give directions
- **S** Checking what other people say
- **P** Sentence stress

1 LISTENING

a 💬 Answer the questions about pictures a and b.

1 Where do you think Dan and Leo want to go? Say why.
  a shopping   b the gym
  c a meeting   d lunch
2 There's a problem. What do you think it is?

b ▶2.38 Watch or listen to Part 1 and check your answers in 1a.

2 CONVERSATION SKILLS
Checking what other people say

▶2.39 Look at the sentences from Part 1 and answer the questions.

DAN   Are you **sure** it's here?
LEO   I think so.

DAN   Are you **certain**?
LEO   Yes.

a Are the questions still correct if we swap the two marked words?
b Why does Dan ask the questions? Choose the correct answer.
  a He agrees with Leo.
  b He wants to check something with Leo.

3 LISTENING

a 💬 When you're lost, what do you usually do? Choose one idea.

1 Look again for the correct street on your phone.
2 Continue along the street and look for the correct street.
3 Ask someone for help to find the correct street.

b ▶2.40 Watch or listen to Part 2. Do Dan and Leo have the same idea as you in 3a?

c ▶2.40 Watch or listen to Part 2 again. Are the sentences true or false? Correct the false sentences.

1 Dan and Leo want to find a bank that is on the corner of Park Road and South Street.
2 The man on the street says there's a bank 150 metres away.

d 💬 Work in pairs. Look at picture c. Dan and Leo find a bank, but there's another problem. What do you think it is?

e ▶2.41 Watch or listen to Part 3. Answer the questions.

1 Do they find the correct bank?
2 Does the woman they talk to know where South Street is?

c ▶2.38 Watch or listen to Part 1 again. Choose the correct answer.

1 The street name on Leo's phone is:
  a Bedford Street   b Park Road.
2 Leo says South Street is:
  a off Park Road   b off North Street.
3 Dan doesn't want to be:
  a too early   b late.

f ▶2.41 Watch or listen to Part 3 again. Follow the woman's directions. Write *South Street* on the map.

 Park

 Café

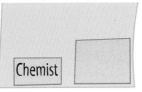 Chemist

Park Road

 Bus station

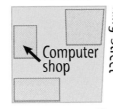 Computer shop

King Street

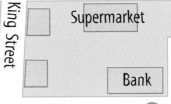 Supermarket   Hotel

Bank

Hudson Lane ←

Henrietta Street

Dan + Leo

---

4 USEFUL LANGUAGE
Asking for and giving directions

a Complete the questions with the words in the box.

tell   where   there   how

1 Is _____ a bank near here?
2 Can you _____ us how to get to South Street?
3 _____ do I get to Park Road?
4 _____ can I find a supermarket?

b Look at the phrases for giving directions. Change the marked words with the words in the box.

a supermarket   on   left

1 Go straight **along the road**.
2 The bank is on your **right**.
3 Go straight on until you come to **Park Road**.

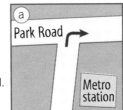
ⓐ Park Road

Metro station

ⓑ Metro station

Park Road

c Match the directions with maps a–b.

1 Turn right **at** the metro station.
2 Turn right **into** Park Road.

d ▶2.42 Complete the conversation with the words in the box. Listen and check.

go (x3)   turn (x2)   get   can   come

A Excuse me, ¹_____ you tell me how to ²_____ to the park?
B Yes, ³_____ straight on and ⁴_____ right at the corner.
A Is that right into King Street?
B Yes and ⁵_____ along King Street until you ⁶_____ to Park Road, then ⁷_____ left.
A Left into Park Road?
B Yes and ⁸_____ straight on for about 50 metres. The park is on your right.
A Thank you very much.

e 💬 In pairs, practise the conversation in 4d. Take turns being A and B.

---

5 PRONUNCIATION
Sentence stress

a ▶2.43 Read and listen to B's directions in 4d. Notice the stressed words.

Go straight on and turn right at the corner. Go along King Street until you come to Park Road, then turn left. Go straight on for about fifty metres. The park is on your right.

b Choose the correct answer.

When we give directions, we stress:
1 only the verbs and nouns
2 the words for direction and place
3 the little words that join ideas.

c 💬 In pairs, take turns asking for and giving directions like the conversation in 4d. Use phrases from 4, the map in 3f and give directions to different places.

---

6 SPEAKING

a ▶ **Communication 5C** Student A go to p.131. Student B go to p.133.

🔄 Unit Progress Test

CHECK YOUR PROGRESS

You can now do the Unit Progress Test.

1 SPEAKING AND LISTENING

a What makes a good neighbourhood? Tick (✓) four ideas.

- [ ] lots of shops
- [ ] a football stadium
- [ ] no shops or cafés
- [ ] a supermarket
- [ ] lots of cafés and restaurants
- [ ] a cinema
- [ ] a sports centre
- [ ] a museum

b 💬 Talk about your ideas in 1a.

c ▶2.44 Antonella, Keith and Jia talk about what they think makes a good neighbourhood. Listen and answer the questions.

1 Who likes a neighbourhood that is:
   a new   b busy   c quiet?
2 Who do you agree with?

Antonella

Jia

Keith

d ▶2.44 Listen again. Write the places in the box next to the people who talk about them.

houses restaurants shopping mall clubs
shops cafés museum cinema park

a Antonella _____
b Keith _____
c Jia _____

Who likes their neighbourhood? Who doesn't?

e 💬 Ask and answer questions about your neighbourhoods.

> Are there any shops in your neighbourhood?

> Yes, there are lots.

> There's a really good café near my house.

2 READING

a Read *Around the world online* and answer the questions.

1 What can you read about on this website?
2 What does the website want you to do?

b Read *In my neighbourhood*. Do Anita and Irena live in the same kind of neighbourhoods?

c Underline the correct answers.

1 *Anita / Irena* lives close to the centre of the city.
2 *Anita / Irena* likes a neighbourhood that isn't noisy.
3 *Anita / Irena* can often go shopping.
4 It's easy for *Anita / Irena* to eat in a restaurant.
5 There's a place where *Anita / Irena* can get some exercise near her home.

ARTICLE EDIT DISCUSS

AROUND *the world* ONLINE
Travel the world without leaving home!

READ about different neighbourhoods from around the world. You can learn about real life in lots of different countries by looking at photos and reading about where people live – these are places tourists never go to!

And we want you to write about your neighbourhood. Tell us all about it and what you think of it.

CLICK HERE TO ENTER A DIFFERENT WORLD.

3 WRITING SKILLS
Linking ideas with *and*, *but* and *so*

a Underline one word in each sentence below that links two ideas.

1 There are lots of good restaurants in my neighbourhood and my apartment's opposite a really good Thai restaurant, Siam Café.
2 My neighbourhood isn't very exciting, but it's a nice place to live.
3 There aren't any restaurants or bars in the area so it's nice and quiet.

IN *my* **NEIGHBOURHOOD**

MY neighbourhood's about two kilometres from the centre of town. It's easy for me to get into the centre of the city, but everything I need is in my neighbourhood so I don't go into the centre very often. It's near the City Museum and there are some beautiful old buildings here so it's an interesting part of the city. There are lots of good restaurants in my neighbourhood and my apartment's opposite a really good Thai restaurant, Siam Café. I love their food and it's cheap so I eat there often.

Anita

MY neighbourhood's about eight kilometres from the city centre, but there's a metro train station near my house so it's easy to get there. There aren't any restaurants or bars in the area so it's nice and quiet. About a kilometre away there's a big shopping mall with a lot of shops. Opposite it, there's a park and a sports centre. I go there three times a week to use the gym. My neighbourhood isn't very exciting, but it's a nice place to live.

Irena

b Look at the sentences in 3a and complete the rules with the words in the box.

so   and   but

1 We use _____ when we want to add an extra idea.
2 We use _____ when we want to add a different idea.
3 We use _____ when we want to add an idea that is the result of the first idea.

c Read *In my neighbourhood* again. Underline sentences that contain linking words.

d Put the linking words in the correct place in the sentences.

1 My neighbourhood's in the centre of town there are lots of different shops near my house. (and)
2 I live near the university there are lots of interesting shops in my neighbourhood. (so)
3 My neighbourhood's quite busy during the day it's nice and quiet at night. (but)
4 My house is near a park there's a small river with a bridge in the park. (and)
5 My neighbourhood is very friendly it's a nice place to live sometimes it's noisy in the evening. (so, but)
6 There's a popular café in my neighbourhood I don't like coffee I never go there. (but, so)

4 WRITING

a Plan a description of your neighbourhood. Make notes.

- where
- near
- what
- adjectives

b Write about your neighbourhood. Use Irena and Anita's texts and your notes in 4a to help you. Use *and*, *but* and *so*.

c Swap descriptions with another student and check the linking words.

d Read about other students' neighbourhoods. Which one is most different from yours?

UNIT 5
Review and extension

1 GRAMMAR

a Complete the conversation with the correct form of *there is* or *there are*.

MARCEL   Can you tell me about your free room?
LANDLADY   ¹_____ a bed, two armchairs and a big window.
MARCEL   ²_____ a desk?
LANDLADY   No, ³_____, but ⁴_____ a small table.
MARCEL   And ⁵_____ a shower?
LANDLADY   No, but ⁶_____ a bathroom on the same floor.
MARCEL   I see. And ⁷_____ other students in the house?
LANDLADY   Yes. ⁸_____ four other students.

b Change the marked words to make them shorter. Use *mine*, *yours*, *his*, etc.

A   Is this bag ¹*your bag*?   yours
B   No, it isn't ²*my bag*.

A   Look, I think this is Theresa's phone.
B   I know it isn't ³*our phone*, so maybe it's ⁴*her phone*. Let's call and ask her.

A   Whose car is that?
B   It's ⁵*my brother's car*. And the motorbike's ⁶*his motorbike*, too.

A   I think that's my book.
B   No, this book's ⁷*my book*. I don't know where ⁸*your book* is.

2 VOCABULARY

a Underline the correct words.

1   They live in a big *flat / river* near the centre.
2   It costs a lot to stay in this *bridge / hotel*.
3   There are lots of good *restaurants / parks* in the main *river / square*.
4   Let's go to the *flat / park*. We can play football.
5   There's only one *square / bridge* over the river.
6   The train gets in to the *park / station* at 6:30.

b Complete the sentences with things you find in a room.

1   Look in the m_____. Your face is dirty.
2   I just want to wash my hands in the s_____.
3   You can put your clean clothes in the w_____.
4   I'm tired. I'll lie on the s_____ for a bit.
5   Put your dirty clothes in the w_____ m_____.
6   Don't touch the c_____. It's hot!
7   There are some plates in the c_____.

3 WORDPOWER Prepositions of place

a Match cafés 1–6 with a–f on the map.

①   **Alpha Café** A busy student café <u>on</u> Newton Street, <u>next to</u> the Rex Cinema. Cheap, but usually full.

②   **Café Uno** On the corner of Newton Street and Green Street. Good coffee and great cakes, but expensive.

③   **Café Express.** A small café just in front of the station.

④   **La Roma.** A small café on Green Street, between the market and the library. They have good pasta dishes.

⑤   **Shane's.** At the end of Newton Street, opposite the station. Popular with mothers and young children.

⑥   **Café Casablanca.** A Moroccan café with a nice garden. It's in a small street behind the Rex Cinema.

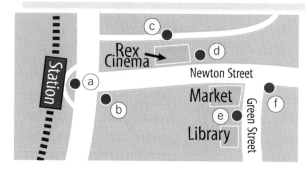

b Look at the <u>underlined</u> examples in 3a. Words like **on** and **next to** are prepositions of place that tell us where something is. <u>Underline</u> more prepositions of place in 3a.

c Add one more word to make the sentences correct.

1   The cinema is on King Street, next the supermarket.
2   There's a cash machine the end of Green Street.
3   I'll meet you in front the bank on Newton Street.
4   There's a new bookshop the corner of New Street.

d 💬 Work in pairs. Choose four numbers on the map. Take turns describing and guessing where they are. Use prepositions of place.

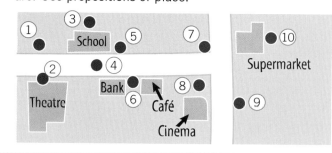

CAN DO OBJECTIVES

- Talk about your family and your family history
- Talk about past activities and hobbies
- Leave a voicemail message and ask for someone on the phone
- Write a life story

GETTING STARTED

a Look at the picture and answer the questions.

1 Who do you think the people in this family are? Use family words you know, like 'mother', 'sister'.
2 Do you think they all live together in one house?
3 Choose someone in the photo. Write two questions to ask them.

b Talk about a family you know well – not your own family.

1 How many people are there in the family? Who are they?
2 Who do you know best in the family? Why?

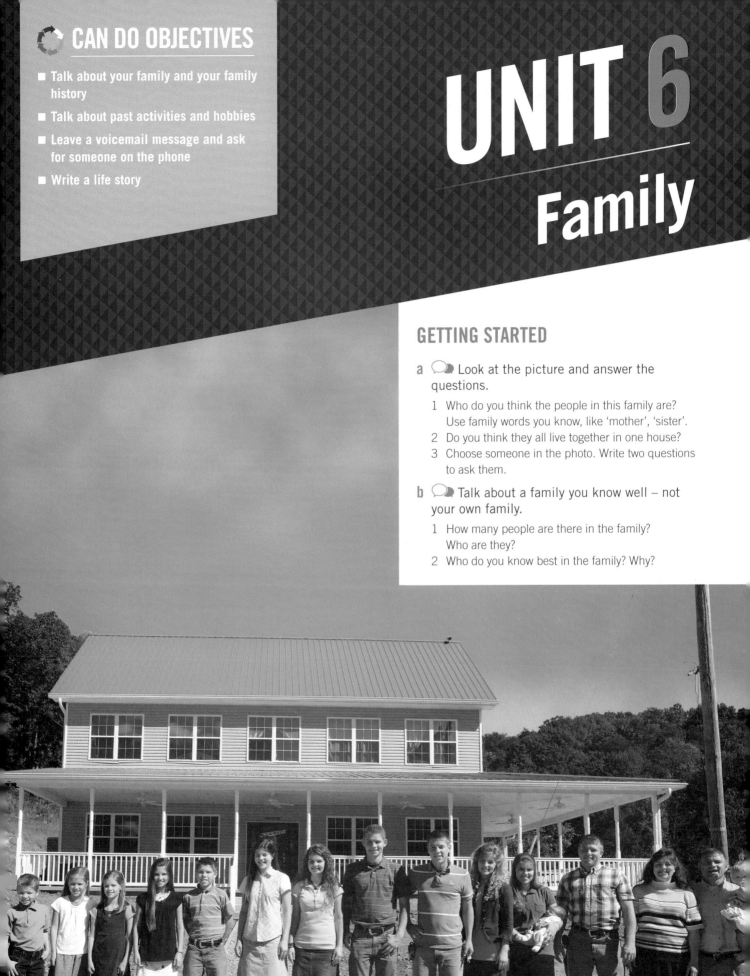

1 VOCABULARY Family

a 💬 Talk about your parents, brothers or sisters. Think about:
- their names • what they do • adjectives about them

b ▶2.45 Listen to Part 1. Greg talks about his family. Tick (✓) the people he talks about.

☐ aunt ☐ sister ☐ grandmother
☐ grandparents ☐ granddaughter ☐ cousin
☐ uncle ☐ brother ☐ grandfather
☐ grandchildren ☐ grandson ☐ parents

c Choose words in 1b to complete Greg's family tree.

d ▶2.45 Listen again and check your answers in 1c. Whose parents were born in India?

e ▶2.46 **Pronunciation** Listen to the sound of the marked letters. Tick (✓) the words that have the same sound as *but* /ʌ/.

c**ou**sin **u**ncle **au**nt grandm**o**ther grands**o**n

f Look at the family tree again. Who can say these sentences? Write the names.
1 'Alice is my aunt.' _Greg, Ella, Rick_
2 'Ravi's our uncle.' _____
3 'Ella's our granddaughter.' _____
4 'Rick, Ella and Greg are our cousins.' _____
5 'Sally and Nathan are our grandparents.' _____
6 'We've got three grandchildren.' _____

g 💬 Draw your own family tree. Show it to your partner and talk about how many people there are.

2 LISTENING

a ▶2.47 Listen to Part 2. Greg talks more about his family. Tick (✓) the people he talks about.

☐ his mother ☐ his grandmother
☐ his grandfather ☐ his uncle
☐ his grandparents in India

b ▶2.47 Put the life events in the correct order on the timeline. Listen again and check your answers.

1 got married
2 grandfather was born
3 grandmother finished work
4 photographer took the picture
5 went to university
6 grandmother was born

☐ 1937 ☐ 1958 ☐ 1963
☐ 1939 ☐ 1962 ☐ 2004

NATHAN   SALLY

ALICE   RAVI   SANJIT   MARY   MICHAEL
_____ _____ Father _____ Mother _____

KARL   KAVITA   GREG   ELLA   RICK
_____ _____ _____ Me! _____ _____

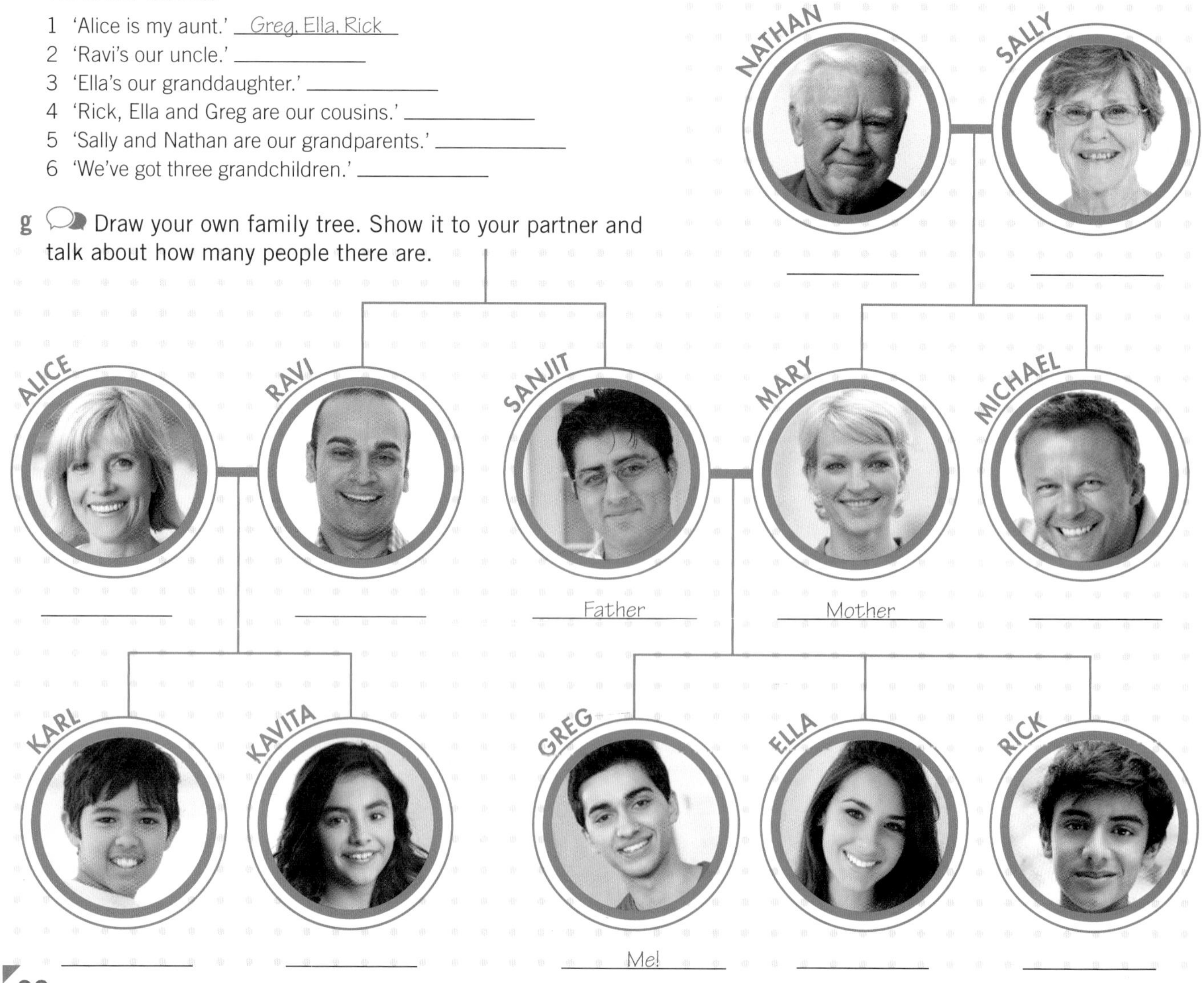

Nathan and Sally

3 GRAMMAR Past simple: *be*

a Underline the correct words.

1 Greg's grandparents *are / aren't* still alive.
2 His grandmother *is / isn't* a doctor now.
3 His grandmother *was / wasn't* a doctor.
4 His grandparents *were / weren't* at the same school.
5 They *were / weren't* friends at school.

b Choose the correct answers to complete the rules.

1 We use *was / were* to talk about: a now   b the past
2 To make a negative sentence, we add: a *'nt*   b *n't*

c Complete the table with *was, were, wasn't* or *weren't*.

+	–
I __was__ ill. She _____ a beautiful woman.	I __wasn't__ ill. He _____ a teacher. He was a doctor.
We __were__ at school together. They _____ friends at university.	No, we _____ in the same class. In 1960 they _____ married.

d ▶ 2.48 Listen again and complete the conversation. Which words are repeated in the question and answer?

A What about your grandfather? [1]___ he a doctor too?
B Yes, he [2]___.
A [3]___ they in the same class?
B No, they [4]___.
A When [5]___ she born?
B She [6]___ born in 1939 I think.

e ▶ Now go to Grammar Focus 6A on p.146

f ▶ 2.50 **Pronunciation** Listen to the sentences. If *was* or *were* are stressed, underline them.

1 She was a doctor.
2 They were at school together.
3 When was she born?
4 Was she a doctor? Yes, she was.

g Complete the rules with *are* or *aren't*.

In positive sentences and questions, *was* and *were* _____ stressed.
In short answers, *was* and *were* _____ stressed.

h Complete the questions with the correct past forms of the verb *be*.

1 Where ___ you born?
2 Who ___ your first teacher?
3 What ___ your first school called?
4 ___ yesterday a good day for you?

i 💬 Ask and answer the questions in 3h.

4 VOCABULARY Years and dates

a ▶ 2.51 In Part 2, Greg talks about years and dates. Listen and answer the questions.

1 How do we say 1939?
   a one thousand, nine hundred and thirty-nine
   b nineteen thirty-nine
2 How do we say 2004?
   a two thousand and four
   b twenty oh four
3 What extra words do we use when we say *16 July*? What do we add to *16*?

b ▶ 2.52 Listen and tick (✓) the years you hear. Then practise saying them.

☐ 2002 ☐ 1930 ☐ 1918 ☐ 2011
☐ 2012 ☐ 1913 ☐ 1989 ☐ 2001

c ▶ Go to Vocabulary Focus 6A on p.162

5 SPEAKING

a Make notes about the people in your family tree in 1g.
   • When were they born?   • How old are they?
   • Where do they live?   • What do they do?

b 💬 Ask and answer questions about your family trees.

1 READING

a 🗩 Ask and answer the questions.

1 Who's the man in the pictures?
2 What do you know about his company?
3 What do you know about his family life?

b 🗩 The text is called *His family secret*. What do you think the secret is? Talk about the ideas and choose one.

1 His grandfather married four times.
2 He had a secret sister.
3 His father was a famous actor.
4 He never met his brother.

c Read *His family secret* and check your answer in 1b.

d Put the events from Steve Jobs' life in the correct order.

a ☐ Steve started a new hobby: electronics.
b ☐ His sister Mona was born.
c ☐ Steve became friends with Steve Wozniak.
d ☐ Steve's real parents couldn't keep him.
e ☐ Steve met his sister.
f ☐ Clara and Paul Jobs became Steve's parents.
g ☐ The two Steves became very rich.
h ☐ Apple Computers began.

HIS FAMILY *Secret*

His name is famous around the world and every day millions of people use the products he made – our phones, computers, laptops, tablets and MP3 players. We all think we know his story from magazines, newspapers and the Internet, but how much do we really know about him?

Steve Jobs was born in San Francisco in 1955. His real parents were university students. They decided not to keep their son and Steve was adopted by Clara and Paul Jobs.

The Jobs family lived in Mountain View in California. This is now in Silicon Valley, where there are a lot of big technology companies. Steve's hobby as a child was electronics. He made simple computers with his father at the family home. At high school he met Steve Wozniak. They both loved electronics and became good friends. In 1976, they started Apple Computers in Steve's parents' garage. They worked hard and four years later, the company was worth $1.2 billion.

Two years after that, Steve found out about his sister for the first time. After he was adopted, his real parents had another child, Mona, who became a famous writer. This amazing brother and sister were close friends until he died in 2011. People will continue to remember Steve when they see or use an Apple product.

2 GRAMMAR Past simple: positive

a **Underline** the past simple form of verbs 1–5 in the text.

1 work
2 start
3 live
4 decide
5 love

b Complete the rule.

To form the past simple of regular verbs add _____ or _____.

c (▶) **2.55** **Pronunciation** Listen to the infinitive and the past simple form of the verbs in 1a. Which two verbs have an extra syllable in the past?

d Complete the rule with two sounds.

-ed endings have an extra syllable /ɪd/ only after _____ and _____.

e (▶) **2.56** (🗨) Practise saying these past simple forms. Which have an extra syllable? Listen and check your answers.

- looked
- waited
- arrived
- finished
- hated
- wanted
- remembered
- needed

f **Underline** the past simple form of verbs 1–4 in *His family secret*. Are these verbs regular or irregular?

1 have   2 find   3 make   4 become

g ▶ Now go to Grammar Focus 6B on p.146

3 LISTENING

a Steve Jobs' hobby when he was a child was electronics. Tick (✓) the hobbies you did when you were a child.

☐ reading   ☐ taking photos
☐ drawing pictures ☐ playing the guitar

Can you think of other hobbies?

b (▶) **2.58** Listen to Hannah and Charlie. What were their childhood hobbies?

c (▶) **2.58** Listen again and complete the notes about Hannah and Charlie.

	Hannah	Charlie
hobby details	basketball	cakes
parents' problem		
now		

4 VOCABULARY
Past simple irregular verbs

a Hannah and Charlie use the past simple irregular verbs in the box in their conversation. Match them with 1–9.

went spent got made told
came bought cost ate

1 buy   4 go   7 make
2 eat   5 cost   8 get
3 tell   6 spend   9 come

b ▶ Now go to Vocabulary Focus 6B on p.163

c (🗨) Use the verbs *go, eat, buy, make* and *get* to talk about things you did:

- last night
- yesterday
- last week
- last year

5 SPEAKING

a (▶) **2.62** Read about Becky's hobby. Complete the text with the past simple form of the verbs in the box. Listen and check your answers.

play buy like listen have start

When I was young my hobby was playing the piano. I only
1_____ jazz not modern or classical music. My parents
2_____ me a piano when I was eight years old and I
3_____ lessons then. They 4_____ a lot of jazz CDs and I always 5_____ to them. So they were happy for me to play jazz. I 6_____ jazz piano all the time. I still play the piano now and jazz is still my favourite music.

b Think of a hobby you had when you were a child. Make notes. Read Becky's example in 5a to help you. Think about:

- what you did
- how your parents helped you

c (🗨) Talk with a partner about your childhood hobby. Start the conversation with this question.

> What was your hobby when you were a child?

1 LISTENING

a If you phone a friend and there's no answer, what do you usually do? Say why.

- leave a message
- send them a text
- call again later

b ▶2.63 Watch or listen to Part 1. Which two people leave messages?

c ▶2.63 Watch or listen to Part 1 again. Are the sentences true or false?

1 Annie tells Dan to only call her on her mobile.
2 Dan tells Annie where he is.

2 USEFUL LANGUAGE
Leaving a voicemail message

a Which sentences do Dan (*D*) or Annie (*A*) say? Which are on their voicemail (*V*)?

1 Please leave a message after the tone.
2 Can you call me back?
3 Could you call me back?
4 You can call me on my work number or my mobile.
5 I'm not here right now.
6 Hi, Dan – it's Annie.

b ▶2.63 Watch or listen to Part 1 again and check your answers in 2a.

c ▶2.64 Complete the voicemail message and the caller's message with the words in the box. Listen and check.

this   message   it's   call   here   back

Voicemail
Hello, ¹_____ is Alex. Sorry, I'm not ²_____ just now. Please leave a ³_____ and I'll call you later.

Caller
Hi, ⁴_____ Pam. Could you call me ⁵_____? You can ⁶_____ me at work.

d Work in pairs. Use the dialogue map to leave a message. Take turns being A and B.

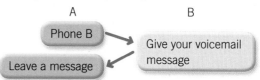

A   B

Phone B → Give your voicemail message

Leave a message ←

3 LISTENING

a ▶2.65 Put events a-e in the order they happened. Watch or listen to Part 2 and check your answers.

a ☐ Annie chats to Leo.
b ☐1 Dan goes to make coffee.
c ☐ Leo answers the phone.
d ☐ Dan brings some coffee.
e ☐ Dan talks to Annie.

b Answer the questions.

1 What do Leo and Annie talk about?
  a how they are   b the weather   c work
2 How does Leo feel?

4 USEFUL LANGUAGE
Asking for someone on the phone

a ▶2.65 Look at Annie's questions and Leo's answers. Underline the correct words. Then watch or listen to Part 2 again and check your answers.

ANNIE Is Dan [1]*here / there*?
LEO He's not [2]*here / there* just now.
ANNIE Can he call me [3]*again / back*?
LEO He'll be [4]*back / there* soon.

b 💬 Work in pairs. Use the dialogue map to ask for someone. Take turns being A and B.

A   B

Phone Student B. You want to speak to another student.

Answer and say that he/she isn't here.

Ask him/her to call you back.

5 CONVERSATION SKILLS
Asking someone to wait

a Complete the conversation with the words in the box.

just wait minute (x2)

LEO Can you [1]_____ a [2]_____? He'll be back soon.
ANNIE Sure.

LEO It's Annie.
DAN Oh, good. [3]_____ a [4]_____.

b What does *a minute* mean in the conversation?
  a 'exactly one minute'   b 'a short time'

c 💬 Practise the conversation in 4b again. Use expressions in 5a.

6 PRONUNCIATION
Sound and spelling: *a*

a ▶2.66 Listen to the sound of the letter *a* in the words below.

Sound 1 /æ/	Sound 2 /ɔː/	Sound 3 /ɪ/	Sound 4 /eɪ/
th**a**nks	c**a**ll	mess**a**ge	l**a**ter

b ▶2.67 What sound do the marked letters have in the words in the box? Add them to the sound groups in 6a. Listen and check. Listen and repeat.

t**a**lk vill**a**ge w**ai**t t**a**ll b**a**ck lugg**a**ge
voicem**ai**l s**a**me sm**a**ll t**a**ble bl**a**ck

c 💬 Work in pairs. Cover the table in 6a. Student A: say a word from 6b. Student B: say a word that has the same sound. Then swap roles.

7 SPEAKING

a ▶2.68 Listen and complete the phone conversation.

SUE Hello, Sue Parker.
NICK Hi, Sue. [1]_____ Nick. Is Melanie there, please?
SUE No, sorry. She's not [2]_____ just now. She's at her English class. Do you want to leave a [3]_____?
NICK No, it's OK. Can she call me [4]_____?
SUE OK, I'll tell her.
NICK Thanks. She can [5]_____ me on my mobile.
SUE OK. ... Just a [6]_____. I need to find a pen to write the number.
NICK It's OK, she knows my number.

MELANIE Hi, Nick. [7]_____ Melanie.
NICK Hi, Melanie!
MELANIE Sue says you [8]_____.
NICK Yes, that's right. Do you want to meet on Friday? We can go for a meal.
MELANIE Yes, I'd love to.

b ▶ Communication 6C Student A go to p.130. Student B go to p.134. Student C go to p.135.

🔄 Unit Progress Test

CHECK YOUR PROGRESS

You can now do the Unit Progress Test.

UNIT 6
Review and extension

1 GRAMMAR

a Complete the conversation with the correct form of the verb *be*. Use contractions if possible.

ANNA Hi, Jenny. How [1]_____ you?
JENNY I [2]_____ fine thanks.
ANNA [3]_____ you at the meeting yesterday?
JENNY Yes, I [4]_____, but it [5]_____ very useful.
ANNA What about Phil? [6]_____ he at the meeting?
JENNY No, he [7]_____. He [8]_____ at home sick.
ANNA Oh dear, the poor guy. [9]_____ he OK today?
JENNY Yes, I think so. He [10]_____ here today.

b Complete the text with the correct past simple form of the verbs in brackets.

When I [1]_____ (be) a child I [2]_____ (want) to be a truck driver. I [3]_____ (love) big trucks and I [4]_____ (have) a lot of toy trucks. But when I [5]_____ (be) about twelve years old I [6]_____ (decide) that trucks were boring. After school I [7]_____ (study) business at university, but I [8]_____ (find) that boring too. Now I'm a chef and I love it.

c Complete the sentences with the present simple or the past simple form of the verbs in brackets.

1 Last night we _____ (stay) at home and my husband _____ (cook) an amazing dinner.
2 I _____ (go) to the countryside with my family last weekend. We _____ (have) a really nice time together.
3 My sister _____ (play) volleyball on Tuesday nights. She usually _____ (get) home at about 7:30 pm, but tonight she _____ (get) back at 8:15 pm.
4 My brother and I _____ (spend) a lot of time together when we _____ (be) children, but now we almost never _____ (see) each other.

2 VOCABULARY

a Complete the text with the correct family words.

Peter and Barbara are my father's parents, so they are my [1]_____. I'm very close to my [2]_____ Barbara, and to my [3]_____ Peter, too. My father has only one sister, Helen, and she married Jonathan. My mother doesn't have any brothers or sisters so Helen is my only [4]_____ and Jonathan is my only [5]_____. They have three children so I have three [6]_____.

b Write the date in words.

25/12/1982 – *the twenty-fifth of December nineteen eighty-two*
1 19/10/2014   4 22/4/2008
2 12/6/1985   5 31/8/2009
3 3/9/1990   6 9/1/2012

3 WORDPOWER go

a Read the conversation and answer the questions.

SARAH I need to [1]**go home** now. It's hot and I feel tired.
VIV I can drive you.
SARAH No, no. I can [2]**go by** bus.
VIV Are you sure?
SARAH Yes, I need to [3]**go shopping** on the way home. The supermarket is next to the bus stop.
VIV Do you want to [4]**go for** a swim later on?
SARAH Yes, that'd be nice. And after that I'd really like to [5]**go out** to a restaurant.
VIV Sounds like a good idea.

1 Who's got a car?
2 What plans do Sarah and Viv have for later on?

b Match the marked phrases in 3a with meanings a–e.

a travel by
b have
c leave and return to where I live
d buy some things
e leave home and do something fun

c Match 1–4 with a–d to make more phrases with *go*.

1 go to   a train
2 go by   b to the cinema
3 go for   c a party
4 go out   d a walk

d Correct the mistakes in the sentences.

1 They want to go to home now.
2 I need to go for shopping in town this afternoon.
3 I'd like to go the cinema this evening.
4 Would you like to go a coffee?
5 He usually goes to work for bus.

e Write sentences about your life using phrases with *go*.

1 every day / usually / go home
   Every day I usually go home at 5:30 pm.
2 each week / go shopping
3 often go / city centre by
4 this evening / would like / go out to
5 sometimes / go for a walk / in

f 💬 Tell a partner your sentences in 3e. How similar are you?

↻ REVIEW YOUR PROGRESS

How well did you do in this unit? Write 3, 2, or 1 for each objective.
3 = very well   2 = well   1 = not so well

I CAN ...

talk about my family and my family history	☐
talk about past activities and hobbies	☐
leave a voicemail message and ask for someone on the phone	☐
write a life story.	☐

⟳ **CAN DO OBJECTIVES**

■ Talk about past journeys
■ Talk about what you like and dislike about transport
■ Say excuse me and sorry
■ Write an email about yourself

UNIT 7
Journeys

GETTING STARTED

a 💬 Look at the picture and answer the questions.

1   This man is on a journey. What country do you think he's in? Why?
2   What do you think the man and women talk about?
- directions
- the weather
- personal information
- shopping
- their families
- something else
3   Think of their questions and answers.

b 💬 In pairs, ask and answer the questions.

1   Where would you like to travel to?
2   Would you like to travel by …?
- car
- boat
- plane
- something else
3   What would you like to see and do there?

Learn to talk about past journeys

G Past simple: negative and questions
V Transport

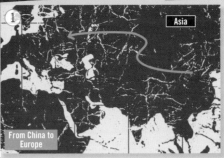
① Asia — From China to Europe
② Africa — From South Africa to Egypt
③ South America — From Ecuador to Chile

THE SILK ROAD

More than 2,000 years ago, China began looking for new places in Europe to sell products such as silk. Different routes opened and these routes were called the 'Silk Road'. It was a difficult journey and could take six months on foot. Today, companies such as Hewlett Packard use the 'New Silk Road' to transport laptops between China and Germany by train – and it only takes 13 days! The Old Silk Road is also very popular now with tourists – more than 50 million tourists visit Xi'an, the city at the start of the Old Silk Road, every year.

1 READING

a 💬 Look at maps 1–3. Which journey would you like to go on? Why?

b Read *The Silk Road* and answer the questions.
  1 Which journey in 1a does it describe?
  2 Was it always a tourist route?

c Read *Travelblog* and match the texts with pictures a and b.

d Read the blogs again. Who do you think said each sentence after their trip, Murat (M) or Ingrid (I)?
  1 I saw some unusual sports on my trip.
  2 We made sure our bags were light.
  3 Sometimes we didn't want to get on our bikes.
  4 The places we stayed in were usually two-star.
  5 I needed to show my passport a lot.
  6 We loved seeing where people lived.

e 💬 Whose trip do you think was better? Why?

TRAVEL BLOG

bike

HOME   FORUMS   PHOTOS   VIDEOS   LINKS

b   motorbike

MY BEST TRIP EVER!! MURAT AKAN

It really was a great trip and I can remember so many amazing things that we did. For example, when we were in Kyrgyzstan, we saw some very exciting competitions with horses. We didn't understand them, but it was a lot of fun! We didn't normally travel much more than 300 kilometres a day – and sometimes less – but one day we travelled 500! I slept well that night! We stayed in hotels, but we didn't use luxury hotels because they were too expensive. There was only one thing we didn't like – going from one country to another. The border police checked everything again and again and it took a long time – six hours one day!

2 VOCABULARY Transport

a Match the words in the box with pictures 1–8.

> aeroplane (plane) scooter tram ship
> helicopter coach ferry train

b 💬 Which kinds of transport:

- do people often use to go on holiday?
- do people normally use to get to work or school?
- are unusual for people to use in your country?
- do you normally use?

c ▶ Now go to Vocabulary Focus 7A on p.166

3 GRAMMAR Past simple: negative

a Complete the sentences from Ingrid's blog.

1 We _____ go very far at all.
2 We didn't _____ to take anything that we didn't _____.

b Look at the sentences in 3a and complete the rule.

> To make the past simple negative, we use:
> _____ + the infinitive

MY DREAM JOURNEY ON THE SILK ROAD INGRID LEIDENROTH

This was my dream holiday!! It wasn't a fast way to travel, but there was a lot to see and a lot of time to think! Before we left, we packed our bags very carefully because we didn't want to take anything that we didn't need (too heavy!). Some days we travelled about 80 kilometres, but other days – when we were tired – we didn't go very far at all. And sometimes, when we were very tired, we didn't want to cycle and we got lifts on trucks. We didn't plan our trip very carefully, and we often changed our plans. We slept in tents next to the road and watched the stars for hours. The best thing about travelling this way is that you can meet the people who live there. They were interested in us and wanted to find out about our trip. We even saw inside a traditional home – a yurt – and had dinner with the family!

4 LISTENING

a 💬 You can also travel along the Silk Road by bus or train. Which would you prefer to do?

b ▶2.73 Klara talks to her friend Hans about the Silk Road. How did Hans travel?

c ▶2.73 Listen again and underline the correct answers.

1 Country started in: *Turkey / Russia / China*
2 Cities visited: *Samarkand / Tashkent / Kabul / Almaty*
3 Change trains: *yes / no*
4 Price: *$2,500 / $25,000*

d ▶2.73 Listen again. Are the sentences true or false?

1 Hans thinks the train is the best way to travel on the Silk Road.
2 He liked visiting the cities in Central Asia.
3 He didn't like the train very much.
4 He didn't think the trip was too expensive.

5 GRAMMAR Past simple: questions

a ▶2.74 Complete these questions from Klara and Hans' conversation. Listen and check.

1 How _____ you travel?
2 Where _____ you catch the train from?
3 _____ you go through Central Asia?

b Look at the questions in 5a and complete the rule.

> To make questions in the past simple, we use:
> _____ + subject + infinitive

c ▶2.74 **Pronunciation** Listen to the questions in 5a again. Notice the pronunciation of *did you* in each question. Can you hear both words clearly?

d ▶ Now go to Grammar Focus 7A on p.148

e ▶2.76 Klara went on the Silk Road and told another friend about her journey. Complete their conversation using the verbs in brackets. Then listen and check.

PAUL How ¹_____ (be) your journey along the Silk Road?
KLARA It ²_____ (be) amazing – incredible!
PAUL How ³_____ you _____ (travel)?
KLARA We ⁴_____ (cycle), but sometimes we ⁵_____ (take) trains or ⁶_____ (travel) by coach.
PAUL How many countries ⁷_____ you _____ (visit)?
KLARA Most countries in Central Asia, but we ⁸_____ _____ (not go) to Tajikistan.
PAUL What ⁹_____ you _____ (enjoy) most?
KLARA Meeting the people – they ¹⁰_____ (be) so friendly.

6 SPEAKING

a ▶ **Communication 7A** Student A go to p.130. Student B go to p.134.

b 💬 Would you still like to go on the journey you chose in 1a? Why / Why not?

1 READING

a 💬 Which cities do you know that have metros?

b Read *Metros around the world*. Match the cities with pictures a–c.

c Which metro … ?

1 is very old
2 is very new
3 has good views
4 looks nice
5 has trains with no drivers
6 do you think is the best

d Underline two things in the text that surprise you. Tell a partner.

e Read *Our reviews* and answer the questions.
- Which metro do you think each review is about?
- Which words tell you the answer?

f 💬 The first reviewer gave five stars (= excellent). In pairs, give stars to the other three reviews.

city tripper.com

METROS AROUND THE WORLD

Dubai

The Dubai Metro opened in 2009. It's 76 kilometres long and there are no drivers. The metro goes above ground in many places, so you can see the city really well. Of course it has air conditioning (it needs it because the temperature in Dubai can sometimes be above 40°C!).

Moscow

If you visit Moscow, go on the Moscow Metro. It opened in 1935 and the stations are very beautiful, with statues and lamps. Eight million people use it every day so it can get very crowded. There are police at the stations so it's very safe, even at night.

London

The London Underground – the 'Tube' – was the first underground (or metro) in the world. It opened in 1863. It now has 270 stations and you can go nearly everywhere in London. It's not cheap and the trains are often full, but it's unusual because it's very deep under the ground (50 metres in some places). One station, Hampstead, has 320 steps!

Our reviews

'Amazing' ⭐⭐⭐⭐⭐

The stations are really fantastic. I went from one station to the next and took lots of photos. And the trains are also good. It's a fast and comfortable way to see the city.

'Loved it!'

It was clean and never late so we didn't wait at all. The air conditioning was great and the seats were comfortable – you can really relax. I preferred it to a taxi and it was a cool way to travel when it was hot outside.

'Good but expensive'

It's a fast way to get around such a big city but it's quite expensive. Also, it's sometimes very crowded and uncomfortable – a few times we couldn't even get on the train. And you have to be careful becausa the platforms aren't very wide so there's not much space!

'Difficult to find your way'

We don't speak Russian and there's nothing in English at the stations, so it's not easy to know where to go. But it's very cheap – you can go across the city for 30 roubles.

2 VOCABULARY
Transport adjectives

a Find the opposite adjectives in the texts. Write them in the table.

fast	slow
	dangerous
empty	/
comfortable	
	expensive
	dirty

b ▶ **2.77** **Pronunciation** Listen and check your answers. Practise saying the words.

c Which of the adjectives are positive? Which are negative?

d ▶ **2.78** Listen to the words and <u>underline</u> the stressed syllable in each word.

comfortable   dangerous   expensive

e 💬 With a partner, take turns being A and B.

A Make a sentence about transport with an adjective from 2a.
B Say you don't agree and use the opposite adjective.

> The buses in this town are very expensive.

> I don't agree. I think they're quite cheap.

3 GRAMMAR AND LISTENING
love / like / don't mind / hate + -ing

a 💬 When you go to meet a friend, do you usually … ?
- go by car
- use public transport
- cycle
- walk

b ▶ **2.79** Svetlana and Alex live in Moscow and meet in the city centre. Listen and complete the table.

	She came by …	The journey took …
Svetlana		
Alex		

c ▶ **2.79** Listen again. Complete the notes.

	Svetlana thinks	Alex thinks
the metro is …		
the stations are …		
driving is …		
Alex's / Her car is …	–	

d ▶ **2.80** Can you remember what Svetlana and Alex said? Complete the sentences with *love*, *like*, *don't mind*, *don't like* or *hate*. Then listen and check.

1 Svetlana I _____ going on the metro.
2 Alex   I _____ using the metro.
3 Svetlana I _____ the stations.
4 Alex   I _____ driving in Moscow.
5 Svetlana I _____ sitting in traffic.
6 Alex   I _____ it, it's not too bad.

e Which verb in 3d means:
1 I like it a lot.
2 I don't like it at all.
3 It's OK.

f ▶ Now go to Grammar Focus 7B on p.148

4 SPEAKING

a Tick (✓) three kinds of transport that you use.

☐ bus ☐ train ☐ metro ☐ tram ☐ boat ☐ taxi ☐ plane

b Make notes about the transport you ticked. Use adjectives from 2a and verbs from 3d.

bus – hate, crowded, slow, dirty

c 💬 Tell your partner about your ideas from 4b. How similar are you?

> I hate going on buses. They're always crowded …

7C Everyday English
Excuse me, please

1 LISTENING

a 💬 Ask and answer the questions.

1 Do you like going away for the weekend?
2 Where do you like going?
3 What do you like doing there?
4 Do you like going alone or with family and friends?

b 💬 Answer the questions about picture a.

1 Where's Annie?
2 What do you think happened with Annie and the woman?
3 What do you think:
   a Annie says?
   b the woman says?

c ▶️**2.82** Watch or listen to Part 1 and check your answers in 1b.

d 💬 Answer the questions about picture b.

1 Where are Annie and Leo?
2 How do you think Annie and Leo feel? Why?
3 What do you think happens next?
   a Leo gets off the train.
   b Leo gives Annie his seat.
   c Leo helps Annie put her bag on the shelf.

e ▶️**2.83** Watch or listen to Part 2 and check your answers in 1d.

f ▶️**2.83** Watch or listen to Part 2 again. Underline the correct answers.

1 *Annie / Leo* booked a seat.
2 *Annie / Leo* didn't check the seat numbers.
3 *Annie / Leo* takes a different seat.

2 USEFUL LANGUAGE
Saying excuse me and sorry

a Match 1–2 with meanings a–b.

1 Excuse me, please.
2 Excuse me, but …

a She wants to say there's a problem.
b She wants to ask someone to move.

b ▶️**2.84** **Pronunciation** Listen to 1 and 2 in 2a. Notice how the tone goes down ↘ in 1 but goes down and then up ↘↗ in 2.

c Look at 1 and 2 in 2a. What do you say when … ?

a you want to tell your teacher you don't understand something
b you want to leave the room but another student is in front of the door

d *Very, really* and *so* can all be added to the expression *I'm sorry*. Do you say the words before or after *sorry*?

> I'm sorry I took your seat.

e ▶️**2.85** Match 1–5 with a–e. Listen and check.

1 I'm so sorry I walked into you.
2 I'm really sorry I'm late.
3 I'm sorry I didn't answer your call.
4 I'm sorry I didn't come.
5 I'm very sorry I broke your cup.

a I didn't feel well.
b I was in a meeting.
c I missed my bus.
d My hands were wet.
e I didn't see you.

f Tick (✓) the correct replies when people say they're sorry.

1 ☐ That's all right.
2 ☐ That's OK.
3 ☐ No problem.
4 ☐ Excuse me, please.
5 ☐ It doesn't matter.
6 ☐ Don't worry.

g ▶️**2.86** Put sentences a–f in order to make two short conversations. Listen and check.

a ☐ **A** No problem. They all look the same.
b ☐1 **A** Excuse me, but I think that's my coat.
c ☐ **B** Is it? I'm so sorry. I took the wrong one.
d ☐ **A** Don't worry. The seat numbers are hard to read.
e ☐ **B** Oh dear. I'm very sorry. I thought this was number 35.
f ☐1 **A** Excuse me, but I think this is my seat.

h 💬 In pairs, practise the two conversations in 2g.

3 PRONUNCIATION
Emphasising what we say

a ▶ 2.87 Listen to the sentences in 2e. Notice the stress on the underlined words.

1 I'm <u>so</u> <u>sorry</u> I <u>walked</u> into you.
2 I'm <u>really</u> <u>sorry</u> I'm <u>late</u>.
3 I'm <u>sorry</u> I didn't <u>answer</u>.
4 I'm <u>sorry</u> I didn't <u>come</u>.
5 I'm <u>very</u> <u>sorry</u> I <u>broke</u> your <u>cup</u>.

b Why are *so*, *very* and *really* stressed? Choose the best answer.

1 We don't want the other person to hear *sorry* clearly.
2 We want to sound more sorry.
3 We want to speak loudly.

c ◯ Practise saying the sentences in 3a.

4 CONVERSATION SKILLS
Showing interest

a ▶ 2.88 Watch or listen to Part 3. Are the sentences true or false?

1 Annie and Leo are both on their way to Bristol.
2 Annie is visiting a friend in Bristol.
3 Leo went to university in Reading.

b Look at these parts of the conversation from Part 3. Two words aren't correct. Replace them with the words in the box.

Great!	Really?

ANNIE Are you on your way to Bristol?
LEO No, Reading. I went to university there.
ANNIE Right.

ANNIE My mum lives there. I go to see her every month.
LEO Oh.

▶ 2.88 Listen again and check your answers.

c Why do they say *Great* and *Really*?

1 to say something is true
2 to show they are interested

d ▶ 2.89 **Pronunciation** Listen to the sound of the marked letters and answer the questions.

Gr**ea**t!   R**ea**lly?

1 Do the letters make the same sound in both words?
2 Are the sounds long or short?

5 SPEAKING

a ◯ Work in pairs. Use the dialogue map to make a conversation in a café. Take turns being A and B.

A

Say hello → Say hello (B)

Say sorry that you're late

Respond (B)

Say you're late because you got a phone call → Show interest (B)

Say the phone call was about a new job. You got the job. → Show interest and offer congratulations (B)

Offer to buy B coffee → Thank A (B)

b ◯ In pairs, practise conversations like the one in 5a but with different reasons for being late. Take turns being A and B.

◯ Unit Progress Test

CHECK YOUR PROGRESS

You can now do the Unit Progress Test.

1 SPEAKING AND LISTENING

a 💬 You want to stay with a homestay family. What kind of family would you like to stay with? Tick (✓) three ideas and tell a partner.

1 ☐ quiet and friendly
2 ☐ friendly and fun
3 ☐ with young children
4 ☐ with no children
5 ☐ lives near a bus/train station
6 ☐ lives in the city centre
7 ☐ has wi-fi
8 ☐ has no TV

b 💬 Read the profiles of two Sydney homestay families. Which family would you like to stay with? Why?

c ▶ 2.90 Ahmed talks to an Australian friend, Finn, about which family to stay with in Sydney. Does Finn tell Ahmed which family to choose?

d ▶ 2.90 Listen again. Tick (✓) the activities that are true for Ahmed.

1 ☐ enjoys gardening
2 ☐ likes watching sport
3 ☐ likes listening to music
4 ☐ wants to play rugby
5 ☐ loves going to the beach
6 ☐ wants to study hard
7 ☐ likes playing football
8 ☐ wants to have fun

e 💬 Which family is good for Ahmed? Why?

> I think the Philips family are good because they like doing sports.

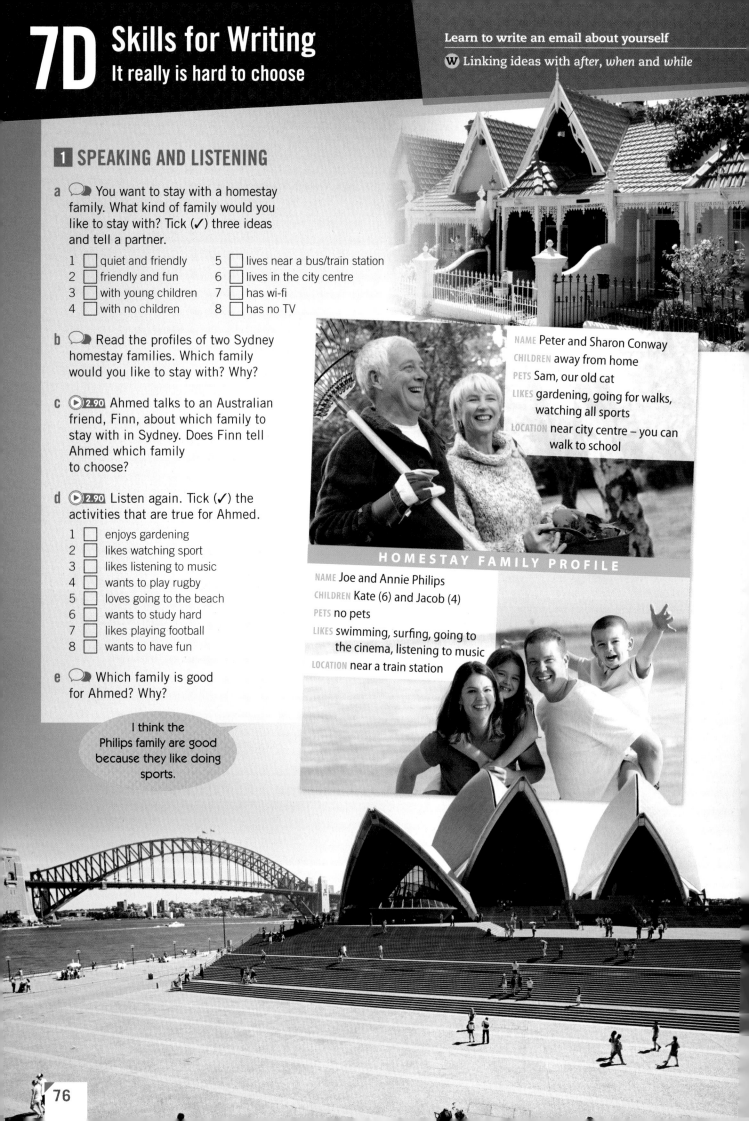

NAME Peter and Sharon Conway
CHILDREN away from home
PETS Sam, our old cat
LIKES gardening, going for walks, watching all sports
LOCATION near city centre – you can walk to school

HOMESTAY FAMILY PROFILE

NAME Joe and Annie Philips
CHILDREN Kate (6) and Jacob (4)
PETS no pets
LIKES swimming, surfing, going to the cinema, listening to music
LOCATION near a train station

2 READING

a Ahmed decided to stay with the Conways. Read his email to them. Tick (✓) the main reason he writes to them.

1 ☐ to ask about their house
2 ☐ to tell them about all the sports he likes
3 ☐ to tell them about himself
4 ☐ to explain how much he wants to study

b Read the email again. Number the information in the order you find it.

☐ his future plans   ☐ his hobbies
☐ his family's jobs   ☐ his hometown

Dubai

Dear Mr and Mrs Conway

My name is Ahmed Al Mansouri and I come from Dubai in the United Arab Emirates. Thank you for offering to be my homestay family when I'm in Sydney.

I am 23 years old and study biology at university. I live with my family in Dubai. My father is a businessman and my mother is a doctor. I've got one brother and one sister. They're university students too.

In my free time, I like playing football (I think you say 'soccer' in Australia!) and meeting my friends. I like watching different kinds of sports with them.

While I'm in Sydney, I really want to study hard and improve my English because I want to become a marine biologist after I finish university. I'd really like to work in a country like Australia.

I'm looking forward to meeting you when I arrive.

Best wishes

Ahmed

Dubai

3 WRITING SKILLS
Linking ideas with *after*, *when* and *while*

a Underline the word in each sentence that's different from Ahmed's email.

1 Thank you for offering to be my homestay family while I'm in Sydney.
2 I want to become a marine biologist when I finish university.
3 I'm looking forward to meeting you after I arrive.
4 When I'm in Sydney, I really want to study hard.

b Look at the sentences in 3a and complete the rules with the words in the box.

after   beginning   while

1 We use *when* and _____ to join two activities that happen at the same time.
2 We use *when* and _____ to join two activities that happen at different times.
3 If the linking word is at the _____ of the sentence, we use a comma (,) between the two parts.

c Underline the correct words. There is more than one possible answer.

1 *After / When / While* I finish my English course, I'd like to go to Canada for a holiday.
2 I'd like to go skiing in the mountains *after / when / while* I'm on holiday.
3 I often play basketball with my colleagues *after / when / while* I finish work.
4 *After / When / While* I watch a game of football, I usually want to play a game myself.
5 My English improved *after / when / while* I was in Sydney.

4 SPEAKING AND WRITING

a Make a list of English-speaking countries you know.

b 💬 Which country in 4a would you like to visit? Why?

> I'd like to go to …

> I like warm places.

> They say the people are friendly.

c Plan an email about yourself to a homestay family in that country. Make notes about:

- your age
- study / job
- what you'd like to do in that country
- free-time interests
- family

d Write your email. Tick (✓) each box.

☐ Start the letter with *Dear*
☐ Say thank you
☐ Say who you are
☐ Talk about study / work / free time
☐ Talk about your family
☐ Say what you want to do in the country
☐ Include *I'm looking forward …*
☐ Finish the letter with *Best wishes*
☐ Use *after, when* and *while* to link your ideas

e 💬 Swap emails with another student and check the ideas in 4d.

1 READING

a 💬 Ask and answer the questions.

1 What famous sport events do you know?
2 Which sportsmen and women do you like? Why?
3 Look at the man on the left in the picture and answer the questions.
   a What sport does he do?
   b Where's he from?
   c Where is he in the picture?
   d What would you like to know about him? Write two questions.

b Read the text and check your answers. Does it answer your questions?

c Read the text again. Answer the questions.

1 What was his life like until he was five?
2 How did his life change when he was five?
3 Why were his doctors, friends and parents surprised?
4 What does the text say about some of the Paralympic athletes?
5 Why is Jonnie famous?

d Underline the parts of the text that surprise you. Tell a partner.

e 💬 Are there any famous Paralympic athletes from your country?

2 GRAMMAR
can / can't, could / couldn't for ability

a Complete the sentences from the text. Check your answers.

1 He ___ run around with the other children any more.
2 Only 18 months after he lost his leg, he ___ run, swim and play football again.
3 Some of the athletes in the Paralympics ___ walk.
4 But in their sports, they ___ do things that most people ___.
5 ___ you run that fast?

b Complete the rules with the words in the box.

past question present

To talk about ability, we use *can / can't* for the _____ and *could / couldn't* for the _____.
To make a _____, we change *You can …* to *Can you …?*

c Look at the question. Which two answers are correct?

Can you run that fast?
a Yes, I do.   b Yes, I can.   c No, I can't.   d No, I don't.

d ▶3.2 **Pronunciation** Listen to the sentences in 2a and answer the questions.

1 One word has a long sound. Which is it?
   a *can*   b *can't*   c *could*   d *couldn't*
2 Can you hear a /l/ sound in *could* and *couldn't*?

e ▶ Now go to Grammar Focus 8A on p.150

JONNIE PEACOCK
CHAMPION RUNNER

When Jonnie Peacock was five, he was like most small boys from his hometown of Cambridge – he loved to play sports. Then suddenly his life changed when he became very sick with meningitis. Jonnie's parents took him to hospital and he nearly died. The doctors saved his life, but they couldn't save his right leg. He couldn't run around with the other children any more and he couldn't play football, his favourite sport. In fact, he couldn't do any sports at all.

But the doctors gave him a new, artificial leg. He could walk again, but he wanted to do more than that, so he started dancing and doing other sports. His doctors, his friends and his parents were all surprised that he could do so much. Only 18 months after he lost his leg, he could run, swim and play football again, but running was his best sport.

In 2010, Jonnie started to practise a lot. He wanted to go to the London 2012 Paralympics, the Olympic Games for disabled athletes. Some of the athletes in the Paralympics can't walk, some can't see at all or can't see very well. But in their sports, they can do things that most people can't.

Jonnie Peacock won gold at the London 2012 Paralympic Games when he was only 19 years old. He ran the 100 metres in a time of 10.90 seconds!

CAN YOU RUN THAT FAST?

3 LISTENING

a 🗨 How do you think the Olympics can help a city and its people? Tick (✓) the sentences you think are true. Say why.

1 ☐ The city has better transport.
2 ☐ People have new places to do sport.
3 ☐ The city gets more money.
4 ☐ People want to do more sport.

b ▶3.4 Read the information and then listen to the podcast.

1 Which ideas in 3a does Liv talk about?
2 Which cities does she talk about?

FOCUS ON SPORT

CAN THE OLYMPICS CHANGE A CITY?

Beijing, London, Rio de Janeiro, Pyeongchang … The Olympics don't only make cities famous. They also help the people who live there.
Sports journalist Liv Oldman tells us why.

🔊 LISTEN

c ▶3.4 Listen again and answer the questions.

1 What is the Water Cube? What can you do there?
2 When is Sochi good for a holiday? Why?
3 Why did children in Britain do more sport after 2012?

d 🗨 Do you think Liv Oldman is right? Can the Olympics also be bad for cities? How?

4 VOCABULARY Sport and exercise

a Match the words in the box with the pictures a–f.

do yoga   play badminton   ride a bike   dance   skate   ski

b ▶ Now go to Vocabulary Focus 8A on p.166 for Sport and exercise collocations

c Read the sentences. Put them in order from good (1) to bad (4).

a ☐ I can play baseball quite well.
b ☐ I can't play baseball very well.
c ☐ I can play baseball really well.
d ☐ I can't play baseball at all.

d 🗨 Ask and answer questions about the activities in 4a.

> Can you ski?
> I can't ski at all.
> Yes, I can ski very well.

5 SPEAKING

a Think about sports or other free-time activities. Write sentences about:

- one thing you can do well
  I can …
- one thing you can't do at all, but you'd like to learn
  I can't …
- one thing you could do well when you were a child
  I could …
- one thing you couldn't do very well as a child
  I couldn't …

b 🗨 Ask other students if they can or could do the same things.

> Can you dance the samba?
> Could you swim well when you were a child?
> No, I can't! Can you?
> Quite well, yes.

c 🗨 Who can or could do the same things? Who would like to do the same things?

> Sachiko and I can do yoga quite well.
> Mia and I would like to learn to snowboard.

1 READING

a Ask and answer the questions.

1 What do you think are good ways of getting fit?
2 What exercise do you do?
3 Would you like to do more or less exercise? Why?

b Read the first paragraph of the text. Answer the questions in the text.

c What do you think the new type of exercise is? Read the rest of the text to find out. Were you correct?

d Complete the HIT Fact sheet.

HIT: GET FIT IN FIVE! THE ROUTINE

warm up ➡ __ seconds of hard exercise ➡ rest

HOW OFTEN?
Time: _____ a day

GOOD FOR:
Getting fit, stopping diabetes and _____ disease

Repeat __ times

e Talk about the questions.

1 Would you like to try HIT? Why / Why not?
2 Do you think it works? Why / Why not?

2 GRAMMAR *have to / don't have to*

a Complete the sentences from the text with the words in the box. Use some words more than once.

have   don't   to

1 You _____ _____ cycle really hard.
2 You _____ _____ _____ spend hours and hours in the gym.
3 What do you _____ _____ do?

b Sentences a–c talk about the sentences in 2a. Underline the correct answers.

a In sentence 1 you *need to / don't need to* cycle hard.
b In sentence 2 you *need to / don't need to* spend hours in the gym.
c Sentence 3 asks what you *need to / don't need to* do.

ONLY 5 MINUTES EXERCISE A WEEK...
... and you can get fit!

HOW EASY IS IT TO GET FIT? Do you think it's difficult to do enough exercise? Is having enough time to exercise a problem? Think you know the answers to these questions? Well, think again because a new type of exercise is here and it could change your life.

WHAT IS IT? This new, popular form of exercise is called High Intensity Training (HIT) and it means you don't have to spend hours and hours in the gym. A few minutes a day doing hard exercise is all you need. You can choose to do floor exercises, run or cycle.

WHAT DO YOU HAVE TO DO? Let's take the example of cycling: you begin with a short warm up then you have to cycle really hard for 20 to 30 seconds and then rest. You repeat the routine twice and that's all you have to do!

SO, HOW DOES HIT WORK? No one is sure of the answer to this question. However, some sports scientists in Canada, Norway and the UK think that when we exercise hard, we use a lot more muscles than we do with normal exercise. This helps us get fit, which could also mean we don't get sick so easily from things like diabetes and heart disease.

c ▶ **3.7 Pronunciation** Listen to sentences 1 and 2 in 2a and answer the questions.

1 How does the speaker say *v* in *have*: /v/ or /f/?
2 How does the speaker say *to* – is it stressed or unstressed?

d ▶ Now go to Grammar Focus 8B on p.150

e Work on your own. Think about things you have to do in your life. Write four sentences. Think about:

- daily routine   • work   • study   • family   • pets

I have to take our family dog for a walk every morning.

f 💬 Tell a partner about things you have to do. Ask more questions.

> I have to clean my flat every weekend.

> Do you have to clean all the rooms?

3 LISTENING

a 💬 Look at pictures a and b and answer the questions with a partner.

1 What kind of exercise is this?
2 Do you think it's easy or difficult?

b ▶ **3.9** Listen to Stella and then Mariana talking about exercise. Match the speakers with pictures a and b.

> So if you think you haven't got time to **get fit**, it's not true. You **only need** a few minutes a day with **HIT**. So why not try it?

c ▶ **3.9** Listen again. Are the sentences true or false? Correct the false sentences.

1 Stella thinks yoga is good for everyone.
2 Her favourite yoga exercise is easy to do.
3 She practised doing this exercise for a long time.
4 Mariana thinks beginner yoga is easy.
5 She has to think carefully when she does yoga.
6 She doesn't like the end of each yoga lesson.

d 💬 Do you do yoga? If yes, do you like it? Why do you do it? If no, would you like to try it? Why / Why not?

4 VOCABULARY Parts of the body

a Match the words in the box with the parts of the body in the picture.

leg   back   foot   head   neck
stomach   arm   hand   finger   toe

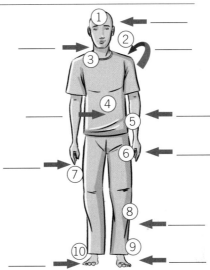

b 💬 Talk about the questions.

1 Which parts of the body can you break?
2 Which parts of the body often give people problems?

c ▶ Now go to Vocabulary Focus 8B on p.167 for Appearance vocabulary

5 SPEAKING

a Look at activities 1–5 and choose one. Think of things people have to do and have to have if they want to do this activity. Make notes.

1 run a marathon
   go running every day   have strong legs
2 climb a mountain
3 swim a long way
4 dance for 24 hours
5 ride a bike along the Silk Road

b 💬 Tell your partner what people have to do to get ready for your activity and what they have to have. Don't tell them what your activity is. Can your partner guess?

> You have to go running every day and you have to have strong legs.

1 LISTENING

a 💬 Answer the questions about the pictures.

1 Where are Dan and Leo?
2 How do you think Dan feels?
3 Which picture do you think is last?
4 Imagine the conversation in picture b.

b ▶️ 3.12 Watch or listen to Part 1. What does Martina tell Dan to do?

c ▶️ 3.13 Watch or listen to Part 2 and answer the questions.

1 What's Dan's problem?
   a He's got a headache.
   b His back hurts.
   c He needs to eat some food.
   d He's got a temperature.
2 What do you think Dan wants to do?
   a go to the aerobics class with Leo
   b go home with Martina
   c go on the running machine again

2 USEFUL LANGUAGE
Talking about health and how you feel

a Complete the mini-conversations. Use the words and phrases in the box.

the matter   feel well   look well   feel a bit tired   all right

MARTINA Are you ¹_____?
DAN I think so.

MARTINA You don't ²_____.
DAN Yes, I ³_____.

MARTINA What's ⁴_____?
DAN I'm not sure. I don't ⁵_____.

b ▶️ 3.12–3.13 Watch or listen to Parts 1 and 2 again and check your answers in 2a.

c Look at some ways to say how you feel.

I feel **tired**.   I've got **a headache**.   My **back** hurts.

Which of the words in the box can you use instead of the marked words?

stomach ache   a cold   sick   hungry   arm
ill   foot   toothache   a temperature

d 💬 In pairs, take turns asking about health and saying how you feel. Use the phrases from 2a and 2c.

3 CONVERSATION SKILLS
Expressing sympathy

a Complete what Martina says with the words in the box.

poor	thing	dear

DAN Actually, I feel awful.
MARTINA Oh [1]_____. Come and sit down.

MARTINA You poor [2]_____. What's the matter?
DAN I'm not sure.

MARTINA So nothing to eat all day?
DAN I ... well ... um ... no. It was a busy day.
MARTINA [3]_____ you. Well, I'm not surprised you don't feel well.

b What do Martina's phrases in 3a mean?

1 I feel sorry for you. 2 I don't feel sorry for you.

c ▶3.14 Listen to the phrases in 3a. Answer the questions.

1 Which word has the main stress in each phrase?
  a the first word   b the last word
2 Does the tone go up ↗ or down ↘ at the end?

d 💬 In pairs, take turns saying these sentences and giving sympathy using phrases from 3a.

1 I've got a cold. 4 I feel really ill.
2 I'm so tired. 5 I lost all my money.
3 My back hurts. 6 No one loves me.

4 PRONUNCIATION Joining words

a ▶3.15 Listen to the sound of the marked letters in these sentences. Then read the sentence below and <u>underline</u> the correct words.

1 Come and si**t** down.   3 You don'**t** look well.
2 I feel a bi**t** tired.   4 Goo**d** to see you.

The sound *joins* / *doesn't join* onto the next word, and there's *a* / *no* pause.

b 💬 In pairs, take turns saying the sentences in 4a and giving a reply.

> Come and sit down.

> OK, thank you.

5 SPEAKING

a ▶ **Communication 8C** Student A look at the information below. Student B go to p.133.

Conversation 1. Read you first card. Think about what you want to say. Then start the conversation with Student B.

> **1** Student B doesn't look well. Ask him/her what's the matter. When he/she tells you, show sympathy using expressions like *Oh dear!* or *Poor you!*
> Then ask if he/she has a temperature. Tell him/her what to do, e.g. *See a doctor. Go to bed.*

b **Conversation 2.** Now look at your second card. Think about what you want to say. Then listen to Student B and reply.

> **2** You're not feeling very well. You've got stomach ache and your eyes hurt. You don't feel hungry. When Student B asks you, tell him/her what's the matter.

♻ Unit Progress Test

CHECK YOUR PROGRESS

You can now do the Unit Progress Test.

8D Skills for Writing
However, I improved quickly

Learn to write an article

W Linking ideas with *however*; adverbs of manner

1 SPEAKING AND LISTENING

a 💬 Ask and answer the questions.

1 Which of these free-time activities are popular in your country? Which aren't popular in your country? Why not?
  - playing chess
  - going dancing
  - cycling
  - playing computer games
  - looking for interesting insects
  - hiking
2 What other activities are popular in your country?

b Read the email Andy and Gina get at work and answer the questions.

1 What's the problem with the company blog at the moment?
  a There's too much information.
  b It's a bit boring.
2 What kind of information can staff put in their article?
  a information about their free time
  b information about their day at work

> **Our staff blog**
>
>
>
> **From:** The management team
> **To:** All staff
> **Subject:** Our staff blog
>
> We want to try to make the company blog more interesting. We would like to find out more about you, the people who work for this company. We'd love to hear about what you do in your free time. Write a short article and send it to us with a photo so we can put it on the blog

c ▶ 3.16 Andy talks to Gina about his free-time activity. Listen and answer the questions.

1 Which activity in 1a does Andy talk about?
2 Does he want to write an article about it?

d ▶ 3.16 Listen again. Match 1–6 with a–f.

1 A year ago, ...
2 Two weeks after his first bike ride, ...
3 A couple of months ago, ...
4 Last weekend, ...
5 Almost every day, ...
6 You always ...

a he bought a bike.
b a car hit him.
c he goes cycling.
d he rode in the hills for two days.
e have to be careful in traffic.
f a friend invited him for a bike ride.

e Think of something you do in your free time. Make notes. Use the questions to help you.

1 When did you start doing this activity?
2 What's something important you did when you started?
3 What do you normally do?
4 What is something interesting you did recently?

f 💬 Ask and answer questions about your activities.

I bought a chess set after two months.

Was it expensive?

I found a very unusual stamp last month.

Where is the stamp from?

2 READING

a Read Dylan's article for the company blog.
Tick (✔) what's the same about Dylan's and Andy's activities.

1 ☐ they do their free-time activities outdoors
2 ☐ they do their free-time activities every day
3 ☐ they get fit doing their free-time activities
4 ☐ they hurt their foot recently

b Read the text again. Are the sentences true or false? Correct the false sentences.

1 Three years ago, Dylan was lonely.
2 He liked the idea of hiking immediately.
3 Hiking was a bit difficult at first.
4 He met his wife on a hike.
5 It's very difficult to learn how to go hiking.

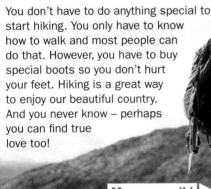

Our staff:
working hard,
playing hard.

Walking my way to love by Dylan Jones

Three years ago, I came to work for this company. I didn't know anyone in the area so I decided to do some exercise to meet new people. However, I felt really unfit. I tried doing different kinds of sports, but I did them all badly. I found an answer to all my problems by going for a walk.

A colleague of mine invited me to go on a walk in the mountains. I didn't say yes immediately because it didn't sound very interesting. However, I decided it could be good exercise for me so I went along. This was the beginning of my love of hiking.

At first, I had to walk slowly because I wasn't very fit. However, I improved quickly and now I can walk quite fast for hours. I began to feel so much better. While I was on a hike with a group of people one weekend, I met Marina. She's now my wife. We go hiking once or twice a month and we love it.

You don't have to do anything special to start hiking. You only have to know how to walk and most people can do that. However, you have to buy special boots so you don't hurt your feet. Hiking is a great way to enjoy our beautiful country. And you never know – perhaps you can find true love too!

Me on a walk! ▶

3 WRITING SKILLS
Linking ideas with *however*; adverbs of manner

a Notice the underlined word that links the ideas in two sentences together.

I didn't say yes immediately because it didn't sound very interesting. However, I decided it could be good exercise for me so I went along.

Is the idea in the second sentence surprising after reading the idea in the first sentence?

b Underline three more sentences in Dylan's article linked by *however*. What punctuation do we use after this word?

c Match the sentences. Link each pair with *however*.

1 I can only do very simple exercises.
2 I started doing yoga about six years ago.
3 I fell off my bike and hurt my leg.

a I didn't stop riding.
b I can't do the difficult positions.
c I feel really fit.

d Notice the underlined adverb of manner in the sentence. Does it tell us what Dylan did or how he did it?

I tried doing different kinds of sports, but I did them all badly.

e Circle the adverbs in Dylan's article that go with these verbs.

1 walk (x2)   2 improve

f We make most adverbs of manner by adding *-ly* to an adjective.

clear   + -ly   = clearly

Which adverb in Dylan's article is different?

4 WRITING

a Plan an article about your free-time activity. Use your ideas in 1e. Think of:

* an interesting way to begin your article
* something you have to or don't have to do with your hobby

b Write your article. Use adverbs of manner.

c Swap articles with another student and check that:

☐ the beginning is interesting
☐ there's useful information about the hobby
☐ the article uses adverbs of manner

UNIT 8
Review and extension

1 VOCABULARY

a Complete the sentences with the words in the box.

> yoga   dance   bike   badminton   baseball   ski

1   When I went to the USA, I learnt to play _____.
    I wasn't very good at it because I could never hit the ball.
2   On my last winter holiday I went to the mountains and
    learnt how to _____. It was great fun.
3   At the weekend, my favourite form of exercise is to get on
    my _____ and go for a ride in the country.
4   I often meet my friend for a game of _____.
    We always play indoors.
5   I'd like to join a _____ class and learn the waltz and
    the tango. It's a fun way to keep fit and make friends.
6   The strange thing about _____ is that you have to
    stay in the same position for a long time.

b Complete the words for parts of the body.

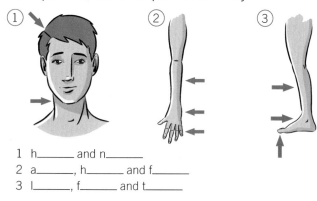

1   h_____ and n_____
2   a_____, h_____ and f_____
3   l_____, f_____ and t_____

2 GRAMMAR

a Complete the text with *can, can't, could* or *couldn't*.

In my family we love playing sport. I ¹_____ play badminton
well and my sister ²_____ ski well. When we were children
we ³_____ both play football very well, but we're both a bit
too slow now. The only sport I ⁴_____ do is swimming. I
didn't learn to swim. My sister did and she ⁵_____ swim very
fast – 50 metres in about 40 seconds. We also tried to learn
musical instruments. I studied the guitar, but I ⁶_____ play
well at all. I was always too busy playing sport.

b Complete the sentences with the correct form of
have to.

1   If you want to go running, you _____ buy
    comfortable running shoes.
2   You _____ go to the gym every day – three
    times a week is enough.
3   _____ I _____ use the same
    machines every time I go to the gym?
4   You _____ take a small towel with you when
    you go to the gym.
5   He _____ be careful on his bike. Last year he
    had a bad accident.

3 WORDPOWER *tell / say*

a Match sentences 1–3 with pictures a–c.

1   My grandmother **told** us **stories** when we were children.
2   What did you **say** to me? I didn't hear you.
3   **Say hello** to your parents when you get there.

b Notice the marked words in the sentences in 3a.
Complete the phrases with *say* or *tell*.

1   _____ hello / goodbye / thank you / sorry
2   _____ a story / the truth / a joke

c Complete the sentences with *to* if it's possible.

1   She told _____ me she doesn't feel well.
2   They said _____ me that they come from Argentina.
3   I'm sure he told _____ the truth.
4   We said thank you _____ them when we left.
5   Can you tell _____ the time?

d Complete the sentences with the words in the box.

> truth   you   sorry   thanks   me   story

1   Could you please tell the children a bedtime _____?
2   My wife told _____ she likes living here.
3   I don't think that's right. He didn't tell us the _____.
4   I just want to say _____ for a lovely dinner last night.
5   Please say _____ to Julia for not going to her party.
6   Yesterday I told _____ to arrive on time, but you're half
    an hour late.

e Complete the sentences with your own ideas.

1   When I was a child, _____ told me stories about …
2   The last person I said sorry to was _____ because …
3   I always say thank you to …
4   … tells really funny / bad jokes.

f   💬 Tell a partner your ideas from 3e.

UNIT 9
Clothes and shopping

GETTING STARTED

a 💬 Look at the picture and answer the questions.

1 Who's the girl talking to?
2 What things does she say? What answers does she get?
3 Do you think this girl enjoys shopping?

b 💬 Where's the best place to go shopping in your town or city for … ?

- food
- clothes
- a present for someone

1 VOCABULARY Shopping

a Match pictures 1–6 with the words in the box.

> a chemist   a department store   a fast food restaurant
> a bookshop   a clothes shop   a café

💬 Which of these shops is your favourite? Why?

b Look at the plan of the shopping mall. Match the words with a–f in the plan.

> stairs   entrance   car park   bus stop   information desk
> cash machine (or ATM)

c ⏵3.17 **Pronunciation** Listen to the words. Which word is stressed: the first word or the second word?

- clothes shop
- department store
- car park
- information desk
- bus stop
- cash machine

d Where can these people go in the shopping mall?

1 'My son needs new jeans.'
2 'Let's get a new sofa.'
3 'I want something to read on the train.'
4 'I've got a headache. I need some aspirin.'
5 'Can you take the shopping to the car?'
6 'Are you hungry? I need to eat!'
7 'I haven't got any money.'

e ▶ Now go to Vocabulary Focus 9A on p.162 for Money and prices

1st Floor

CINEMA

P   f

90

2 LISTENING

a When you meet friends in town, what do you usually do? Here are some ideas:

- go shopping
- go to a café
- go to the cinema
- go for a walk

b A group of friends want to go to the cinema together. Look at the shopping mall. Where is a good place to meet?

c ▶3.19 Listen to Conversation 1. Where does Simon want to meet Susie? What do you think will happen?

d ▶3.20 Listen to the next two phone conversations. Underline the correct answers.

Conversation 2

1 Simon is *in the bookshop* / *in the café*.
2 Susie is *at the bus stop* / *in the car park*.

Conversation 3

3 Amy is *in the clothes shop* / *in the department store*.
4 Sandeep is *at the information desk* / *at the cash machine*.

e Look at the pictures and answer the questions with a partner.

1 Why do you think Simon is running?
2 How do you think Susie feels? Why?

f ▶3.21 Listen to Conversation 4 and check your answers.

Simon

Susie

3 GRAMMAR Present continuous

a ▶3.22 Match the questions and the answers from the conversations. Listen and check your answers.

1 Where are you?
2 Are you having a coffee?
3 Where are you waiting for us?
4 Are you buying furniture?

a I'm standing by the entrance.
b I'm just getting some cash.
c No, we aren't buying anything.
d No, I'm just buying that new book.

b Choose the correct words to complete the rule.

We use *be* + verb + *-ing* to talk about: a now b all the time.

c Complete the tables with the correct form of the verbs in the box.

talk wait read park drink

Positive (+)		Negative (−)	
I'm We're He's / She's	___ a magazine. ___ on the phone.	I'm not We aren't He / She isn't	___ coffee. ___ at the entrance.

Yes/No questions (?)	
Are you Is he / she	___ the car?

d ▶3.23 **Pronunciation** Listen to the sentences and notice the stress.

1 I'm <u>stand</u>ing by the <u>en</u>trance.
2 We're <u>wait</u>ing for you.
3 We <u>aren't buy</u>ing <u>any</u>thing.
4 Are you <u>hav</u>ing a <u>cof</u>fee?
5 <u>Where</u> are you <u>wait</u>ing for us?

When is the word *are* stressed? Choose the correct answer.

a in positive sentences
b in negative sentences
c in *Yes/No* questions
d in *Wh-* questions

e ▶ Now go to Grammar Focus 9A on p.152

f Work on your own.

1 Think of three places in your town or city, but don't tell your partner.
2 Write a sentence to say what you are doing in each place.

g Listen to your partner's sentences. Guess where he/she is.

I'm eating a burger.

Are you in a fast food restaurant?

4 SPEAKING

a ▶ **Communication 9A** Student A go to p.130. Student B go to p.134.

9B Everyone's dancing in the streets

Learn to talk about the clothes you wear at different times

- **G** Present simple or present continuous
- **V** Clothes

1 READING

a 🗨 Talk about when you shop for food, clothes and other things.

- before work/study
- at lunchtime
- at night
- at the weekend

b Lucas is from France and Diana is from the UK. Read *Friends abroad* and answer the questions. Write Lucas (*L*), Diana (*D*) or both (*B*).

Who writes about … ?

a study   c work
b small shops   d shopping malls

c Read *Friends abroad* again. Are the sentences true or false? Correct the false sentences.

1 Lucas only speaks Mandarin at work.
2 The Chinese people he knows like shopping.
3 Lucas would like to go to a party.
4 Diana doesn't like Venice in the winter.
5 She likes the shops in Venice.
6 It's very quiet in Venice at the moment.

d Read the messages below. Which one is Lucas' and which one is Diana's?

e 🗨 Talk about the questions.

1 Which festival would you like to go to? Why?
2 Do you have festivals like these in your country? What do people do?

◁ ▷ ⌂ ⊕   ↻ ⬇

✈ **FRIENDS ABROAD**   **MESSAGES**   INBOX   FIND FRIENDS   SIGN IN

LUCAS   Message posted: 18:36   Send Lucas a message 💬

Hi everyone! I'm really enjoying life here in Shanghai. My new job is quite busy, but my colleagues are very friendly and they all speak English to me. In my free time I sometimes study Mandarin and relax. I often go shopping because this is a popular 'hobby' here. I usually meet friends at a shopping mall. At the moment it's Chinese New Year here. My friends told me there's a great street party this evening – I really want to go.

DIANA   Message posted: 12:23   Send Diana a message 💬

Diana x

Hello to all my friends. I love it here in Venice! It's so beautiful – even in the winter time. I have to spend a lot of time on my art history course, but at the weekends I get some free time. I usually walk around and look at the old buildings, or when it is cold, I go to museums. There are so many interesting little shops here too – it's great. It's very different from going to a mall. This week it's Carnevale and the whole city is like one big party.
Yesterday my friends invited me to a big party in a piazza (that's Italian for a town square). It's tonight and I have to wear a long dress and mask. I need to go shopping!

We're all out in the street. We're watching a big, beautiful dragon go by. And everyone's wearing red – even me!

Everyone's dancing in the streets and having a great time. We're all wearing amazing clothes – I'm even wearing a dress!

2 GRAMMAR
Present simple or present continuous

a Read the sentences from Lucas' online post and message. Match them with meaning a or b.

1 I usually meet friends at a shopping mall.
2 We're watching a big, beautiful dragon.

a Lucas' normal routine   b Happening to Lucas now

b Complete the rule with the correct tense.

present continuous   present simple

We use the _____ to talk about things we usually do.
We use the _____ to talk about things that happen right now.

c Underline more examples of the present simple and present continuous in Diana's online post and message.

d ▶ Now go to Grammar Focus 9B on p.152

e ▶3.25 Complete the conversation with the correct form of the verbs in brackets. Listen and check.

LUCAS   Hello?
JOHANNES   Hi, Lucas! Are you busy?
LUCAS   Hi! Yes, I ¹_____ (get) ready to go out to a street party.
JOHANNES   Oh, sorry. I can call back.
LUCAS   OK, thanks. I usually ²_____ (not go) out much during the week, but it's New Year.
JOHANNES   Of course.
LUCAS   Sorry, Johannes. My friends ³_____ (arrive). I have to go now. We can speak later.

3 LISTENING & VOCABULARY Clothes

a ▶3.26 Tina read Lucas' message and called him. Pete read Diana's message and called her. Listen to the conversations. Why are Tina and Pete surprised?

1 Tina thinks that Lucas doesn't like:
   a parties   b wearing red   c going out at night
2 Pete thinks that Diana doesn't like:
   a going out for dinner
   b being in photos
   c wearing dresses.

b ▶3.26 Listen again and tick (✓) the clothes words you hear. Which words do they not talk about?

Lucas

Diana

c **Pronunciation** The words in the table all have the letter *o* but have a different sound. Write *shoe* in the correct column.

Sound 1 /ɒ/	Sound 2 /uː/	Sound 3 /ʌ/	Sound 4 /əʊ/
sock	boot	glove	coat

d ▶3.27 Write these words in the table in 3c. Listen and check your answers.

come   coffee   know   mother   group   box   phone   two

e ▶ Now go to Vocabulary Focus 9B on p.167

4 SPEAKING

a Think of someone in your family or a friend that you saw earlier today. What's this person wearing today? What colour are their clothes? Make notes.

b 💬 Tell your partner what this person is wearing.

> Today my friend Louise is wearing dark blue jeans with brown boots.

> My brother's at work today. He's wearing black trousers and an orange shirt. He's also wearing black shoes.

9C Everyday English
It looks really good on you

Learn to shop for clothes
- **S** Saying something nice
- **P** Joining words

1 LISTENING

a 💬 Ask and answer the questions.

1 How often do you buy clothes?
2 Which sentence a–c describes you best?
  a I love buying clothes. I buy something new every week.
  b I only buy clothes if I really need them.
  c I don't often buy clothes, but I like looking round clothes shops.

b ▶ **3.31** Watch or listen to Part 1. Who wants to buy clothes: Dan, Annie or both?

c ▶ **3.31** Change three incorrect things in the text below. Watch or listen to Part 1 again to check your answers.

> Dan's meeting Martina to go to a concert. He wants to wear new clothes as a surprise. Annie says she'll meet Dan at 5 pm. She isn't very happy about it.

d ▶ **3.32** Watch or listen to Part 2 and answer the questions.

1 What clothes does Dan want to buy?
2 What size does Dan wear?
3 Do you think Dan enjoys shopping?

e 💬 Do you ever ask friends or family to help you buy clothes? Who do you ask and why?

2 USEFUL LANGUAGE Choosing clothes

a Match 1–4 with a–d.

1 What are you looking for?
2 What size are you?
3 What colour would you like?
4 Why don't you try them on?

a In trousers? 32.
b Oh, I don't know. Something dark?
c A shirt and trousers.
d OK. Excuse me, where are the fitting rooms?

b ▶ **3.32** Watch or listen to Part 2 again and check your answers in 2a.

c 💬 In pairs, practise saying the questions and answers in 2a.

d 💬 Take turns helping your partner choose clothes.

A You want a jacket.   B You want a pair of jeans.

3 LISTENING

a ▶ **3.33** Watch or listen to Part 3 and answer the questions.

1 Does Annie like the clothes Dan tries on?
2 What does Annie think about the last set of clothes Dan comes out in?

b ▶ **3.33** Watch or listen to Part 3 again and complete Dan's receipt.

```
        NORMAN'S
      FOR CLOTHES
=============================
 ITEM      NO.     PRICE
-----------------------------
 SHOES      1    £ _____
 SHIRT      1    £25.99
 TROUSERS   1    £ _____
-----------------------------
        Total    £ _____
=============================
      THANK  YOU
```

4 USEFUL LANGUAGE
Paying for clothes

a ⏵ **3.34** Listen and correct a mistake in each sentence.

1 I take them.
2 How much they are?
3 Can I pay with card?

b Read this conversation in a clothes shop. Add one word in each gap.

A Can I ¹_____ you?
B Yes, how ²_____ are these sunglasses?
A They're £29.99.
B OK, I'll ³_____ them. Can I pay by credit ⁴_____?
A No sorry, only cash. But there's a cash machine just over there.
B OK, thanks. I'll be right back.

c 💬 In pairs, practise the conversation in 4b, but with different clothes. Take turns being A and B.

5 CONVERSATION SKILLS
Saying something nice

a Read what Annie says. Add a verb to both sentences.

1 That _____ great.
2 It _____ really good on you.

b Which sentence could we use … ?
a about anything we see
b only about something someone's wearing

c 💬 Say something nice about what your partner's wearing.

> I like your glasses. They look really good on you.

> Thanks!

6 PRONUNCIATION Joining words

a ⏵ **3.35** Listen to the sentences. Notice the marked words. Is there a pause between them?

1 **Can I** help you?
2 What **size are** you?
3 Can I try **them on**?
4 How **much are** they?
5 The fitting rooms **are over** there.

b Notice how the marked words in 6a are joined.

In 1–4, the consonant sound moves to the start of the next word:

1 Can I → Ca ni
2 size are → si zare
3 them on → the mon
4 much are → mu chare

In 5, we add the sound /r/ to join the words:
5 are over → are **r**over

c 💬 In pairs, take turns saying the sentences in 6a and giving a reply. Try to link the marked words.

> Can I help you?

> Yes, I'm looking for a coat.

7 SPEAKING

a Look at this dialogue map. Make notes about what you want to say.

Shop assistant	Customer
Offer to help.	You want some jeans.
Size? Colour?	Reply.
Show some jeans.	Ask to try them on.
Say they look great!	Ask how much.
Say the price.	Buy them. Credit card?

b 💬 Work in pairs. Use the dialogue map and your notes in 7a to make a conversation in a clothes shop. Take turns being the shop assistant and customer.

c 💬 In pairs, practise conversations like the one in 7a but with different clothes. Take turns being the shop assistant and customer.

🗘 Unit Progress Test

CHECK YOUR PROGRESS

You can now do the Unit Progress Test.

1 LISTENING AND SPEAKING

a 🗩 Look at the picture and answer the questions with a partner.
1 Which presents would you like to get?
2 Which wouldn't you like? Why?

b ▶3.36 Which presents from the picture do you think these people give? Listen and check.

① Axel

I always give my girlfriend an expensive birthday present.

② Bob

We don't buy presents.

③  Fernanda

We buy small presents for the children.

④ Leila

My husband doesn't think clothes or computers are important.

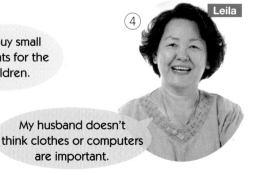

c ▶3.36 Who are these sentences about? Listen again to check.
1 They always buy their own presents.
   Bob's children
2 He doesn't need many things.
   _____
3 They don't get expensive presents.
   _____
4 She loves expensive presents.
   _____
5 They go out for a meal on birthdays.
   _____

d 🗩 Talk about the questions.
1 Who do you give presents to?
   • a child in your family
   • someone you visit
   • grandparents
   • someone who is ill in hospital
   • a colleague
2 How do you thank people for presents?
   • write an email
   • send a text
   • write a letter
   • phone

2 READING

a It was Axel's 30th birthday last week and Molly gave him a present. Complete a–e in his thank-you email with sentences 1–5.

Mail

To: mol@worldwide.net.uk

a Subject: _____

b _____

c _____

d _____

e _____

1 Hi, Molly
2 Love, Axel
3 Thanks very much for the cinema tickets. They're a really great present!
4 Birthday present
5 There's a film I want to see, so I'll use them this weekend.

b Read the email again in 2a. Answer the questions.

1 Who is Molly?
a Axel's sister b a colleague at work
2 How do you know?

c Read Molly's email to Mr Lewis and answer the questions.

1 Who is Mr Lewis?
a someone she worked with b a friend
2 Why did he give her a present?
a It's her birthday. b She's leaving the company.

d Read Molly's email again. Answer the questions.

1 How is her email different from Axel's email in 2a? Think about:
• how she begins
• how she ends
• how she says thank you
2 Why do you think it's different?

Mail

Subject: Thank you

Dear Mr Lewis,

I just want to say thank you very much for the book you gave me on my last day. It's a very nice present.
I really enjoyed working for you and I wish you all the best.
Regards,
Molly

Molly

3 WRITING SKILLS
Writing formal and informal emails

a Sentences 1–4 all say thank you. Add one word to each sentence to make it correct.

⊗
you
✓
¹Thank for the lovely present.

⊗
²I'd just like to say thank you very for the beautiful flowers.

⊗
³Many for the chocolates. They're delicious!

⊗
⁴Thank you the socks. They're a lovely colour.

b Which sentence in 3a is more formal than the others?

c Which of these phrases can you use in an email to someone you know well (1) or to someone you don't know well (2)?

Beginning	Ending
☐ Hello, Mrs Finch	☐ Love
☐ Hi there!	☐ Thanks
☐ Hi, Marie	☐ Best wishes
☐ Dear Mr Parker,	☐ Regards
	☐ See you

4 WRITING

a Think of a present for someone in the class. Write the word on a piece of paper, then give them the 'present'.

chocolates

b Plan a thank-you email for the present.
Think of:
• how to begin the email
• how to end the email
• what to say about the present

c Write your email. Use the email in 2a to help you.

d 💬 Swap emails with another student and check:
☐ the beginning
☐ the sentence saying thank you
☐ the ending

e Write another email to someone you don't know well. What's different about it?

UNIT 9
Review and extension

1 GRAMMAR

a Write questions and answers for the people in the picture.

1 *What's he doing?   He's listening to music.*

b Complete the conversation with the correct form of the present continuous or present simple.

SHARON	Hi, Jason. How are you? What ¹_____ (do)?
JASON	Right now I ²_____ (cook) dinner.
SHARON	Really? But you never ³_____ (cook).
JASON	Well, I'm a bit bored with the meals at the student café. I ⁴_____ (make) spaghetti with tomato sauce.
SHARON	Very good. Usually when I ⁵_____ (make) it I ⁶_____ (put) in lots of pepper.
JASON	Pepper? OK I ⁷_____ (add) it now.
SHARON	But not too much. Jason? Jason? What's that noise? Are you there?
JASON	Sorry, I dropped the phone. I ⁸_____ (try) to cook·and talk to you at the same time.

2 VOCABULARY

a Read the sentences. Which place in a shopping mall is it?

1 Not feeling too well?
2 Want something new to wear?
3 Feeling hungry?
4 Read the best new books!
5 We have 20 kinds of tea!
6 We have everything for your home!

b Write the correct clothes word next to the picture.

3 WORDPOWER *time*

a Look at the marked phrases in sentences 1–5. Match the phrases with meanings a–e.

1 You can **save time** by shopping online.
2 **It takes time** to learn a second language.
3 I'd like to work less so I can **spend time** with my family
4 How do you **find time** to look after four children and work?
5 She always **wastes time** playing computer games when she really needs to study.

a have time together with people
b do things in a short time
c use time badly
d you need a lot of time
e have enough time

b Read the conversations. Underline the adjectives that you can change with *spare* and *good*.

1 **A** See you later. I'm on my way to the cinema.
  B OK. Have a nice time.
2 **A** What do you like doing in your free time?
  B I really love reading.

c Complete the sentences with your own ideas.

1 It takes time to …
2 I save time by …
3 I can never find the time to …
4 I had a good time when I …
5 I sometimes waste time when I …

d 💬 Tell a partner your sentences in 3d. How similar are you?

◯ REVIEW YOUR PROGRESS

How well did you do in this unit? Write 3, 2, or 1 for each objective.
3 = very well   2 = well   1 = not so well

I CAN...

say where I am and what I'm doing	☐
talk about the clothes I wear at different times	☐
shop for clothes	☐
write a thank-you email.	☐

CAN DO OBJECTIVES

- Compare and talk about things you have
- Talk about languages
- Ask for help
- Write a post expressing an opinion

UNIT 10
Communication

GETTING STARTED

a  Look at the picture and answer the questions.

1 Who do you think these people are? Where are they?
2 Who are the men talking to?
3 What is the woman thinking?
4 What happened before this picture? What happens later?

b Which sentences are true for you?

1 I always have my mobile phone with me.
2 If someone calls me on my mobile, I always talk to them.
3 I never phone people during meals.
4 I have my mobile beside me when I sleep.

1 READING

a 💬 Ask and answer the questions.

1 How popular are smartphones and tablets in your country?
2 What do people use them for?

b Read the posts about smartphones and tablets on the *Online Hotline*. What do they talk about?

a different things you can do with them
b differences between them
c different apps you can have on them

c Read the posts again. Find the person who:

1 uses a tablet in their job
2 is happy they bought a tablet
3 takes their smartphone when they go out
4 uses their tablet in their free time.

d 💬 Which is better for Noelle, a smartphone or a tablet?

◁ ▷ ⌂ ⊕   ↻ ⤓

ONLINE HOTLINE
IT ADVICE

HOME | **FORUMS** | NEWS | HELPROOM

Noelle, from Ireland, sent us this message:

Hi everyone. I'd like some advice. I already have a laptop and a phone, but they're both quite old now. I've got some extra money this month, so it's time for something new. I'd like to buy either a smartphone or a tablet. What's the difference? Is a tablet just bigger than a smartphone? Do they do the same things? I work in an office, but sometimes I have to travel around Ireland for my job. Thanks for your help!

We asked our website readers to help her decide!

Size is everything! Which is bigger?

Sabine Easy! A tablet is bigger than a phone.
Hussein Everyone thinks they know the answer here, but these days a lot of new smartphones aren't smaller than some of the mini tablets you see in shops. So maybe there's no difference!

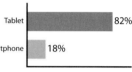
Tablet 82%
Smartphone 18%

How about the price? Which is cheaper?

Susanna A tablet is more expensive than a smartphone. Well, my phone was free, in fact! But I have to pay quite a lot of money every month to the phone company.

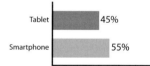
Tablet 45%
Smartphone 55%

Can I carry it around easily? Which is lighter?

Sabine Of course a tablet is heavier than a phone, but that's because it's bigger. The only good thing about a phone is that I can put it in all my small handbags!

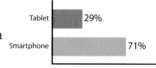
Tablet 29%
Smartphone 71%

Hussein A smartphone is lighter than a tablet, so this means it's easy to take it with me when I go out with my friends.

Tell me about the screen. Which is clearer?

Sabine Smartphone screens are too small. For me, the tablet screen is a lot clearer than the one on my phone. I like to download and watch films, so this is really important for me.

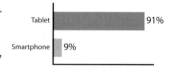
Tablet 91%
Smartphone 9%

Susanna I'm a teacher so I use my tablet to read and work on documents. The screen on the tablet is bigger and better for my work than the phone's small one.

Which is better?

Hussein I think a smartphone is better than a tablet. It's cheaper, it's smaller, so I can take it everywhere without any problems, and, importantly, you can make calls on a phone. I can't easily do that on a tablet.

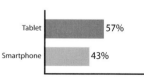
Tablet 57%
Smartphone 43%

Sabine The tablet's the clear winner. Yes, it's expensive, but I think it's worth it. Tablets are the future.
Susanna I can't choose – I like them both.

2 GRAMMAR Comparative adjectives

a Look at the bar charts on the *Online Hotline*. Complete the sentences.

Most people think:

1 a _____ is heavier than a _____.
2 a _____ is better than a _____.
3 a _____ is bigger than a _____.
4 a _____ is more expensive than a _____.
5 a _____ is lighter than a _____.

b <u>Underline</u> the comparative adjectives in the sentences in 2a. Then circle the correct words to complete the rule.

> The adjectives tell us how the smartphone and the tablet are *the same* / *different*.

c Look at the sentences in 2a. Complete the rules and the examples.

1 Short adjectives (e.g. *light*) add _____
 hard ➔ _____
2 Write _____ before long adjectives (e.g. *expensive*)
 interesting ➔ _____ interesting
3 Some adjectives are irregular (e.g. *good*, *bad*)
 good ➔ _____
 bad ➔ <u>worse</u>

d ▶3.37 Complete the sentences. Listen and check your answers.

a My new smartphone is bigger _____ the old one I had.
b Some tablets are more expensive _____ computers.

e ▶3.37 **Pronunciation** Listen again. Is the missing word in 2d stressed or not?

f ▶ Now go to Grammar Focus 10A on p.154

g ▶ **Communication 10A** Student A go to p.131. Student B go to p.135.

3 LISTENING

a ▶3.39 Noelle also listens to a podcast to help her decide. Listen to the podcast. Does it talk about the same ideas as the *Online Hotline* posts?

b ▶3.39 Listen again. Choose the correct answer.

1 Pocketability is about:
 a the size of phones and tablets.
 b how phones and tablets feel when you use them.
2 Eatability is about:
 a using phones and tablets in restaurants.
 b using phones and tablets when you're eating.

c 💬 Talk about the questions.

1 Do you think the ideas in the podcast are useful or not? Why / Why not?
2 Go to page 135 and find out what Noelle decided to buy.

4 VOCABULARY IT collocations

a ▶3.40 Complete the phrases from the podcast with the correct verbs. Listen and check your answers.

1 s _ _ _ the Web   2 c _ _ _ _ emails   3 m _ _ _ calls

b Match verbs 1–5 with nouns a–e. Sometimes more than one answer is possible.

1 download   a a website
2 click on   b a document
3 visit   c a file
4 log on to   d a link
5 save   e a computer

c 💬 Ask and answer questions using the phrases in 4a and 4b.

> How often do you check your emails?

> What kind of websites do you visit?

> Do you surf the Web at work?

5 SPEAKING

a Choose idea 1 or 2.

1 something new you have compared to something old you had (e.g. smartphone / mobile phone)
2 two things that you use and are similar (e.g. desktop computer / laptop computer)

b Make notes about the two things.

- Is one better than the other? How?
 bigger, easier to carry around …
- What can you do with each thing?
 surf the Web, take photos …

c 💬 Talk about the two things. Ask each other questions.

> Are you happy with your new smartphone?

> Which do you think is better, your computer or your laptop?

1 LISTENING

a 💬 Ask and answer the questions.

1 Which languages can you speak?
2 Which languages would you like to learn?
3 Look at the languages in the box. Where do people speak these languages?

Greek Italian English French Arabic Basque
Japanese Mandarin Chinese Russian Spanish
---

b ▶3.41 Listen to Professor Ryan Hunter talking about languages on the radio. Tick (✓) the languages in 1a that he talks about.

c ▶3.41 Match sentences 1–4 with the languages Professor Hunter talks about. Listen and check your answers.

1 He thinks it's a very beautiful language.
2 It's a difficult language for English speakers, but not for Mandarin Chinese speakers.
3 Many people think it's very easy.
4 Over 900 million people speak it.

d ▶3.41 Listen again and answer the questions.

1 What was the first language Professor Hunter learned?
2 How many languages can he speak?
3 Where do people speak Basque?
4 How much of the world's population speak Mandarin Chinese?

e 💬 Choose one thing Professor Hunter said which you think is:
a interesting   b surprising.

2 GRAMMAR Superlative adjectives

a ▶3.42 Complete the sentences with the words in the box. Listen and check your answers.

---
best easiest musical biggest hardest
---

1 Signora Monti was the _____ teacher at my school.
2 Italian is the most _____ language I know.
3 The _____ language to learn is Basque.
4 Spanish is the _____ language to learn.
5 China has the _____ population in the world.

b Read the sentences below and put the languages in order (1 = very easy, 4 = very difficult).

For me, **French** is easier than **Japanese**. But people say that **Spanish** is the easiest language in the world and **Basque** is the most difficult.

c Think about your own language. What number do you think it has (1= very easy, 4 = very difficult)?

d Look at the sentences in 2a. Then complete the rules and the examples.

1 Short adjectives (e.g. *hard*) add _____
   small → _____
2 Write _____ before long adjectives (e.g. *musical*)
   expensive → _____ expensive
3 Some adjectives are irregular (e.g. *good, bad*)
   good → the _____
   bad → the worst

e ▶ Now go to Grammar Focus 10B on p.154

f ▶3.44 **Pronunciation** Listen to these phrases. Notice how the words are stressed.
the <u>big</u>gest   the <u>ea</u>siest   the <u>har</u>dest

g ▶3.45 Listen to these questions. Where's the main stress: on *most* or on the adjective?
What's the most beautiful language in the world?
What's the most useful language to speak?
What's the most difficult language in the world?

h 💬 Ask and answer the questions in 2g with other students.

Professor Hunter

3 READING

a 💬 Ask and answer the questions.

1 Do you read any blogs online? What are they about?
2 Do you use any language websites?
3 What do you think *LinguaBlog* is about?

b Read *LinguaBlog* and check your answer to question 3 in 3a.

c Complete *LinguaBlog* with the superlative forms of the adjectives in the box.

difficult (x2)   fast   heavy   big   long   old   short
expensive   good

d Read *LinguaBlog* again. Who or what are these people talking about?

1 'He could speak to people from many different countries.'
2 'It's a very old language.'
3 'It takes a long time to learn the alphabet.'
4 'I'd love to have this book, but it costs too much.'
5 'She speaks too quickly! I can't understand her.'
6 'I can say the words but I never know how to write them correctly.'

e 💬 Talk about the questions.

1 Which fact do you think is the most interesting? Why?
2 Do you know any other language facts?

4 VOCABULARY High numbers

a Find these numbers in 1c and *LinguaBlog*. What do they refer to?

three thousand	
nine hundred million	
six hundred and three	
six hundred thousand	

b ▶ Now go to Vocabulary Focus 10B on p.162 for more High numbers.

c 💬 Write down a high number for your partner to say.

5 SPEAKING

a Complete the questions with the superlative forms of the adjectives.

What or who is ... ?
1 _____ (nice) word you know in English
2 _____ (beautiful) word in your language
3 _____ (good) language learner you know
4 _____ (ugly) word in your language
5 _____ (long) word you can think of in your language
6 _____ (hard) word to pronounce in English
7 _____ (difficult) word to spell in your language
8 _____ (interesting) book you've got

LINGUABLOG

FACTS OF THE WEEK

One Journalist Harold Williams was one of ¹_____ language learners ever. He spoke 58 different languages.

Two Fran Capo of New York is ²_____ talker in the world. She can say 603 words in 54 seconds.

Three The Tamil language, from Southern India, is probably one of ³_____ languages in the world that people still speak today.

Four With over 600,000 words, the *Oxford English Dictionary* is one of the world's ⁴_____ dictionaries. It costs about £1,000. Is this ⁵_____ dictionary in the world? It's certainly ⁶_____ – it has 20 books and weighs 62 kilogrammes!

Five Rotokas, a language in the Solomon Islands, only has 12 letters, so it has ⁷_____ alphabet in the world. Khmer, the language of Cambodia, has ⁸_____ alphabet. It has 74 letters.

Six Many people say English is ⁹_____ language for spelling. Some of ¹⁰_____ words to spell are: *neighbour*, *foreign* and *awkward*.

b 💬 Ask and answer the questions in 5a with other students.

I think the nicest word in English is *elbow*. I like the sound of it.

Who is the best language learner you know?

10C Everyday English
There's something I don't know how to do

Learn to ask for help
S Checking instructions
P Main stress and tone

1 LISTENING

a 💬 Ask and answer the questions.

1 Are you good at learning how to use new things? Why / Why not?
2 You have a problem with something that you can't fix. What do you do? Why?
   a Read the instructions.
   b Ask someone in your family or a friend for help.
   c Take it to a shop for help.
   d Watch a video about it on the Internet.

b ▶3.47 Annie needs help with her tablet. Watch or listen to Part 1 and answer the questions.

1 Who does Annie want to help her at first?
2 Who can help her in the end?

c ▶3.47 Watch or listen to Part 1 again and answer the questions.

1 Why can't Dan help Annie?
2 What do Annie and Leo decide to do?

2 USEFUL LANGUAGE
Asking for help

a ▶3.48 Look at the different ways to ask for help. Which ones does Annie use? Listen and check your answers.

1 Could you help me?
2 Can you help me?
3 Would you mind showing me?
4 Do you mind showing me?

b ▶3.49 Tick (✓) the correct sentences. Correct the wrong sentences. Listen and check your answers.

1 ☐ Can you explain that?
2 ☐ Would you mind tell me?
3 ☐ Do you mind explaining it to me?
4 ☐ Could you showing me?
5 ☐ Would you mind helping me?

c Match the questions with the correct answers. One answer is correct for both questions.

1 Could you help me?
2 Do you mind helping me?

a No problem.
b Yes, of course.
c No, not at all.

3 PRONUNCIATION
Main stress and tone

a ▶3.48 Listen for the question below and notice the main stress.

Do you mind <u>showing</u> me?

b What kind of word has the main stress when we ask for help?

c ▶3.48 Listen again. Does the tone go up ↗ or down ↘?

d 💬 In pairs, practise saying the sentences in 2b and 3a.

e Think of a small problem you have with studying English. Think of a question to ask your partner for help.

f 💬 Take turns practising asking for help and agreeing to help each other. Use questions from 2a.

I don't understand this word. Would you mind explaining it to me?
No problem.

4 LISTENING

a ▶ 3.50 Annie and Leo have lunch together. Watch or listen to Part 2 and answer the questions.

1 What is Annie having problems with on her tablet?
2 Does Leo help her with the problem?

b ▶ 3.50 Watch or listen to Part 2 again. Leo tells Annie to do these things. Put them in the correct order.

a ☐ Open a new screen.
b ☐ Touch this button.
c ☐ Get into the email.
d ☐ Touch the 'Yes' box.

5 CONVERSATION SKILLS
Checking instructions

a Look at the sentences from the conversation. Who says them: Annie (*A*) or Leo (*L*)?

1 **So first** I touch this button?
2 And it takes me to a new screen. **Like this**?
3 And I touch 'Yes'. **Is that right**?

b Why does Annie ask these questions?

a She wants to be sure she understands the instructions.
b She wants Leo to repeat the instructions.

c Look at the the marked words in 5a. Which expression does Annie use when she's doing something?

d Put the instructions in the correct order.

a ☐ And next go to a new screen.
b ☐ And in the end save the photos here.
c ☐ Touch the word 'Open' here.

e 💬 In pairs, take turns practising giving and checking instructions. Use the instructions in 5d and these phrases. There is no correct answer.

So first   Is that right?   Like this?

> Touch the word 'Open' here.
>
> So first I touch the word 'Open'?

6 SPEAKING

a ▶ **Communication 10C** Student A go to 6b below. Student B go to p.133. Do Conversation 1.

Conversation 1. Read your first card. Think about what you want to say. Then start the conversation with Student B.

① You bought a new phone, but you can't receive text messages on it. Ask Student B for help. Check the instructions he/she gives you.

b **Conversation 2.** Now look at your second card. Think about what you want to say. Then listen to Student B and reply.

② Student B bought a new mouse for his/her computer, but it isn't working. When he/she asks for help, explain how the mouse works. Here are the instructions:
• Turn on the mouse and wait for the green light.
• Double click on the mouse.
• Wait ten seconds and click again. The mouse is working now.

◔ **Unit Progress Test**

CHECK YOUR PROGRESS

You can now do the Unit Progress Test.

1 SPEAKING AND LISTENING

a 💬 Ask and answer the questions.

1 Do you send messages on your phone and on social networking sites?

2 If you do, when do you send them?
- on holiday
- when you're travelling
- at work
- when you go out
Why do you send them?

3 If not, why not? How do you contact people?

b Match messages a–d with pictures 1–4. Where are the people and what are they doing?

c ▶3.51 Listen to three people talking about text messages. Which of texts a–d do you think they sent?

d ▶3.51 Listen again and complete the table.

	Sends texts to	Prefers to	Why?
Speaker 1			
Speaker 2			
Speaker 3			

e 💬 Which speaker's opinion is most similar to yours? In what way?

a
< 160/1 of 6

Take off not till 7:30, so home later than I thought. Maybe around 10. I'll text again when we land. xx

SEND

b < 160/1 of 6

Here's a pic of our first meal in Italy!

SEND

c

Hungry! Anything for dinner? Train gets in 6:35. See you in a bit ;-)

Delivered

d

@bob 16 Aug
Where are you? We're by the fountain. Can't see you.

1 minute

2 READING

a Read the posts on the *Things I hate* discussion board. Tick (✓) who sometimes get annoyed by people who use their phones.

☐ Genji ☐ MadMax ☐ Lars2
☐ Meepe ☐ AdamB ☐ Rainbows

b Read the posts again. Who thinks these things?

¹People who send texts often have nothing to say.

²It can be good fun to send texts to friends.

³People shouldn't send texts when they're eating with other people.

⁴It's rude not to look at someone when they're talking to you.

⁵I don't like people who go online in the middle of a conversation.

c Underline all the adjectives in the posts. Which five are negative?

d Look at the posts again and find:
1 three ways to agree
2 one way to disagree.

Things I hate

Genji
I hate it when people look at their phone when they're talking to you. It's quite clear that if you're talking to somebody, they should look at you, not at their phone. It's the worst thing you can do if you're with someone. I've got a friend who does that.

Meepe
Yes, I agree. I've also got a friend who's like that. You're talking to him and he starts surfing the Internet on his phone! It's so annoying.

MadMax
Yes, you're right, it's really rude. People go online in the middle of a conversation, and some people also send texts while you're talking to them. I hate that.

AdamB
Yes, my sister does that too. We're having dinner and she starts sending texts to all her friends. It's awful.

Lars2
Yes, I feel the same way. And texting is so boring as well. People say the most boring things when they text – they never say anything important. It's like 'I'm on the bus. What are you doing?' or 'I'm at home'.

Rainbows
I don't agree. It can be useful if you want to meet a friend. Also, my friends send really funny texts, so we have a good laugh.

3 WRITING SKILLS
Linking ideas with *also, too,* and *as well*

a Look at the sentences and answer the question.

MADMAX Some people also send texts while you're talking to them.

MEEPE I've also got a friend who's like that.

RAINBOWS It can be useful if you want to meet a friend. Also, my friends send really funny texts.

Where does the word *also* come in each sentence? Underline the correct answer.
1 *before / after* a main verb (*get, send, live* …)
2 *before / after* an auxiliary verb (*be, have, can* …)
3 at the *beginning / end* of a new sentence.

b Look at the sentences below and underline words or phrases that mean the same as *also*. Then answer the question.

1 **ADAMB** Yes, my sister does that too.
2 **LARS2** Yes, I feel the same way. And texting is so boring as well.

Where do they come in the sentence: at the beginning, in the middle or at the end?

c Add *also, too* or *as well* to these sentences.
1 I've got a new PC and I've got a new laptop.
2 We had a satnav in the car and we took a street map.
3 She works for a mobile phone company and she knows a lot about computers.
4 Tablets are very light to carry. They have a large screen so they are easy to read.

4 WRITING AND SPEAKING

a Plan a post about something that annoys you. Use these ideas or your own. Make notes.
- another form of technology (not phones)
- people's bad habits
- an activity you hate doing.

b Write your post. Use the ones on the discussion board to help you. Give your post to another student.

c Agree or disagree with another student's post, and try to add a sentence with *also, too* or *as well*. Then pass your post to the next student.

d Check the linking words in other students' posts. Did they use *also, too* and *as well* correctly?

e 💬 Compare posts. Which do you think is the most interesting? Why?

UNIT 10
Review and extension

1 GRAMMAR

a Complete the conversation with the comparative forms of the adjectives in brackets.

Alba Pro | Plexus Micra

NEIL	Which laptop is ^{1}___*better*___ (good)?
ASSISTANT	Well, the Alba is ^{2}_____ (powerful) than the Plexus, it has 3.5 Gigabytes of RAM. It also has a ^{3}_____ (big) screen. But it's ^{4}_____ (expensive) than the Plexus – it's £1,000 more.
NEIL	Which one is ^{5}_____ (heavy)? The Alba?
ASSISTANT	Yes. The Plexus is ^{6}_____ (light) and ^{7}_____ (thin) than the Alba. So the Plexus is a ^{8}_____ (practical) laptop if you're travelling. And it's a bit ^{9}_____ (fast) than the Alba too.

b Complete the questions with one word from each box. Use the superlative form of the adjectives.

long   big   expensive   hot   good

footballer   country   hotel room   river   place

1 **A** What's ^{a}_____ in the world?
   B Death Valley in California. The highest temperature was 56°C.
2 **A** What's ^{b}_____ in Africa?
   B The Nile. It's 6,695 kilometres long.
3 **A** What's ^{c}_____ in the world?
   B One in the President Wilson Hotel in Geneva. It costs $118,000 for two nights.
4 **A** Who's ^{d}_____ footballer ever?
   B Many people say it's Pelé from Brazil. He scored over 1,000 goals and won the World Cup three times.
5 **A** What's ^{e}_____ in the world?
   B That's easy – Russia. It's 17 million km^2.

2 VOCABULARY

a Underline the correct words.
1 Don't forget to *click on* / *save* the document when you close it. You don't want to lose it.
2 He *visits* / *surfs* the Web for hours every evening. He just goes from one *document* / *website* to the next.
3 How can I *log into* / *click on* your computer? I want to *visit* / *check* my emails.
4 *Click on* / *Visit* this link to download the *file* / *computer*.

b Write the numbers as words.
1 50,000,000   3 256   5 200,000
2 2003   4 1,500   6 2,655

3 WORDPOWER *most*

a Read the text and answer the questions.
1 Which four languages does the family speak?
2 Which language does the writer prefer speaking? Which does her mother prefer speaking? Why?

One family – four languages

My mother is Mexican, my father is from Germany, we spent ten years in England and now we live in Italy. So we speak four languages in our family!

^{1}**Most** of the people we know here are Italian, so when people come to our house we speak Italian ^{2}**most** of the time, but ^{3}**most** of them understand English too so we sometimes speak English and Italian together. I like speaking English ^{4}**most** of all because I was at school in London and also because it's an international language and ^{5}**most** people speak it. But with my parents I usually speak Spanish or German. My mother always prefers to speak Spanish with us – she says it's ^{6}**the most** beautiful language in the world.

b Look at the phrases with *most* in the text in 3a. Which of phrases 1–6 mean … ?
a more than all the others
b nearly all (or about 70–80%)

c Look at the phrases *most of the people* and *most people* in the text. Which is about … ?
a people in general
b a particular group of people

d Complete the sentences with the words in the box.

people   of the way
of the evening   of my friends

1 I spent most _____ at a friend's flat, then I went home.
2 Most _____ in the USA speak English, but there also 35 million Spanish speakers.
3 It's a lovely walk. You go along a river most _____.
4 I'm nearly 70 and most _____ don't work now.

e Write two sentences about your life. Choose two phrases.

most of the time   most of all
most of my friends   most days

f 💬 Tell a partner your sentences and ask and answer questions. How similar are you?

♻ REVIEW YOUR PROGRESS

How well did you do in this unit? Write 3, 2, or 1 for each objective.
3 = very well   2 = well   1 = not so well

I CAN …

compare and talk about things I have	☐
talk about languages	☐
ask for help	☐
write a post expressing an opinion.	☐

CAN DO OBJECTIVES

- Ask and answer about entertainment experiences
- Talk about events you've been to
- Ask for and express opinions about things you've seen
- Write a review

UNIT 11
Entertainment

GETTING STARTED

a 💬 Look at the picture and answer the questions.

1 What do you think these children are watching? Here are some ideas:
- a play
- a cartoon
- someone playing music
- a magic show

2 Look at each child. How you do think he or she feels? Here are more ideas:
- afraid
- excited
- upset
- angry
- surprised
- worrried

b 💬 Talk about what you enjoyed when you were a child. Say why.

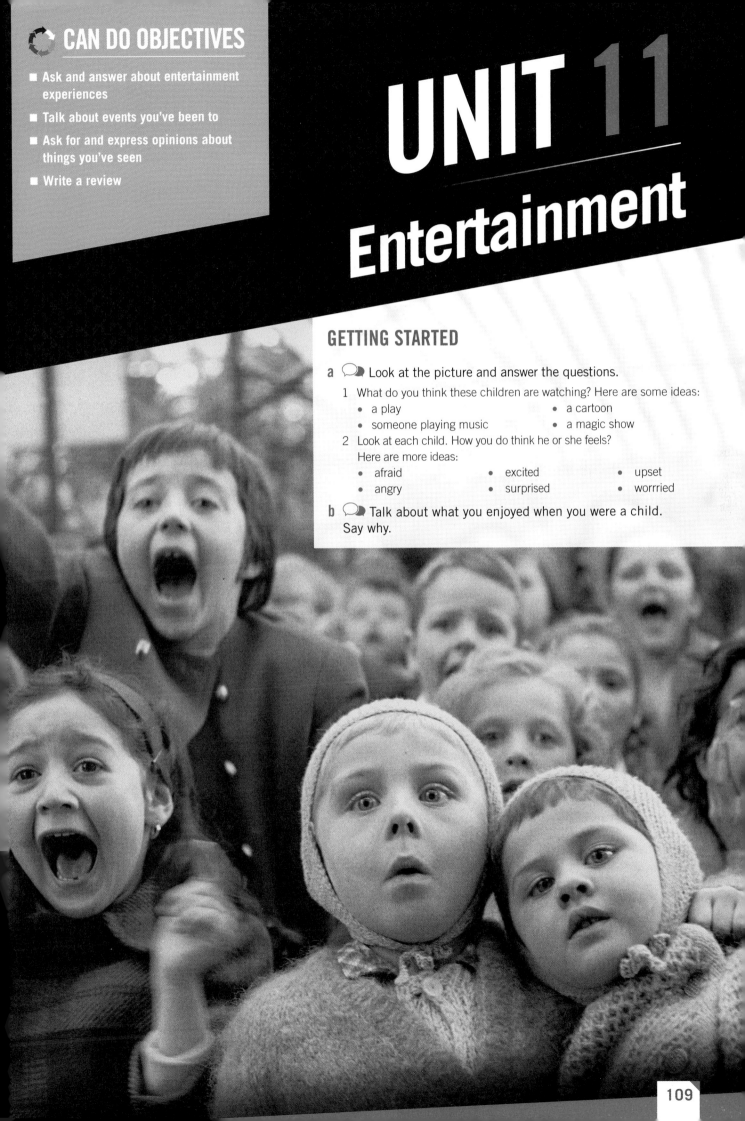

11 A I've heard she's really funny

1 READING

a 💬 Look at the pictures of the three actresses. What do you think they have in common?
- a They went to the same school.
- b They all lived in Australia.
- c They were models before they became actresses.
- d They are married to film directors.

b Read the fact files. Find the answer to 1a.

c 💬 Read the quiz questions about the actresses. Guess the answers.

FACT FILE: *Isla Fisher*
BORN: 1976 MUSCAT, OMAN
CHILDHOOD: AUSTRALIA & SCOTLAND
LIVES: LOS ANGELES

FACT FILE: *Rose Byrne*
BORN: 1979 SYDNEY, AUSTRALIA
CHILDHOOD: AUSTRALIA
LIVES: NEW YORK

FACT FILE: *Mia Wasikowska*
BORN: 1989 CANBERRA, AUSTRALIA
CHILDHOOD: AUSTRALIA & POLAND
LIVES: SYDNEY

THE QUIZ

Is *Hollywood* all they have *in common?*

ISLA, ROSE AND MIA HAVE DONE MANY DIFFERENT THINGS THAT YOU MAYBE DON'T KNOW ABOUT. TRY OUR QUIZ. CAN YOU GUESS WHICH ACTRESS HAS DONE THESE THINGS?

Which actress: ... ?
1 has been in a make-up advertisement
2 can dance well
3 likes to use her camera a lot
4 trained in France
5 enjoys helping people
6 is also a writer

d Read the *Film international* article and find out the answers to the quiz.

e 💬 Talk about the questions.
1 Who do you think is the most interesting actress? Why?
2 Do you know any other famous Australian actors and actresses?

FILM INTERNATIONAL

Isla Fisher, Rose Byrne and Mia Wasikowska are three famous actresses who work in Hollywood, and they have many things in common.

All three come from Australia and before going to Hollywood their very first acting jobs were in Australian TV dramas and soap operas. They've acted in some very popular films. Isla was in *Wedding Crashers* and *The Great Gatsby*, Rose was in *Bridesmaids* and *X-Men: First Class* and Mia was in *Alice in Wonderland* and *Jane Eyre*. They've all won awards in the USA and Australia for their acting.

However, outside of acting, they've done some interesting and unusual things. Isla isn't only interested in films. She studied theatre in France when she was younger and she's written two novels. Rose has worked for UNICEF in Australia. She's also a model and has done TV work for the famous make-up company, Max Factor. Mia, the youngest of the three, trained as a dancer at school, but now she really loves taking photos and has won a national prize in Australia for one of her photos.

Isla, Rose and Mia aren't just three amazing actresses, they're three amazing women.

2 GRAMMAR Present perfect: positive

a Complete the sentences. Check your answers in the text.

1 They _____ _____ in some very popular films.
2 She _____ _____ two novels.
3 Mia _____ _____ a national prize for one of her photos.

b Do we know when in the past the actresses did these things?

c Complete the rule with the correct verb.

> *I / you / we / they* + _____ (*'ve*)
> *he / she / it* + _____ (*'s*)   + past participle (e.g. *worked*)

3 LISTENING

a ▶3.52 Maggie and Stephen answer the magazine quiz about the actresses. Listen and answer the questions.

1 Did they both guess all the correct answers?
2 Tick (✓) the films they talk about:

a ☐ *Wedding Crashers*   d ☐ *X-Men: First Class*
b ☐ *The Great Gatsby*   e ☐ *Alice in Wonderland*
c ☐ *Bridesmaids*   f ☐ *Jane Eyre*

b ▶3.52 Listen again. Tick (✓) if they've seen this actress. Then write the letter (a–f) of the film in 3a they've seen her in.

	Isla Fisher	Rose Byrne	Mia Wasikowska
Maggie			
Stephen	✓ b		

c What did Maggie and Stephen think about the actresses in the films they've seen?

4 VOCABULARY Irregular past participles

a ▶3.53 Complete the sentences from the conversation with the words in the box. Listen and check your answers.

> read   heard   written   seen

1 How did you know Isla Fisher has _____ novels? Have you _____ them?
2 I've never _____ a film with Mia Wasikowska.
3 I've _____ she's really funny in *Bridesmaids*.

Do the verbs end in *-ed*?

b ▶ Go to Vocabulary Focus 11A on p.163

5 GRAMMAR
Present perfect: negative and questions

a ▶3.56 Complete the sentences from the conversation with the words in the box. Listen and check your answers.

> ever   never   seen

1 I haven't _____ any of her films.
2 I've _____ seen a film with Mia Wasikowska.
3 Have you _____ seen any of her films?

b Complete the rules with the words *before* or *after*.

1 When we use *not*, *ever* and *never*, they come _____ *have* in the present perfect.
2 When we make a question in the present perfect, *have* comes _____ the subject.

c ▶3.56 **Pronunciation** Listen again to the sentences in 5a. Do we stress *have* or the past participle?

d ▶ Now go to Grammar Focus 11A on p.156

e ▶3.58 Complete the conversation with the correct form of the verbs in brackets. Listen and check your answers.

A ¹_____ (see) *The Hobbit* films?
B Yes, I have. What about you?
A I ²_____ (see) the first film, but I ³_____ (not see) the others. ⁴_____ (read) the book?
B No, I ⁵_____ (read) *The Hobbit*, but I ⁶_____ (read) *The Lord of the Rings*.

6 SPEAKING

a Think of some popular films, TV programmes and books. Write six questions about these things. Look at the questions in 5e to help you.

b 💬 Ask other students your questions from 6a.

> Have you watched *NCIS* on TV?
> No, I haven't. Is it a good programme?
> Yes, I like it.

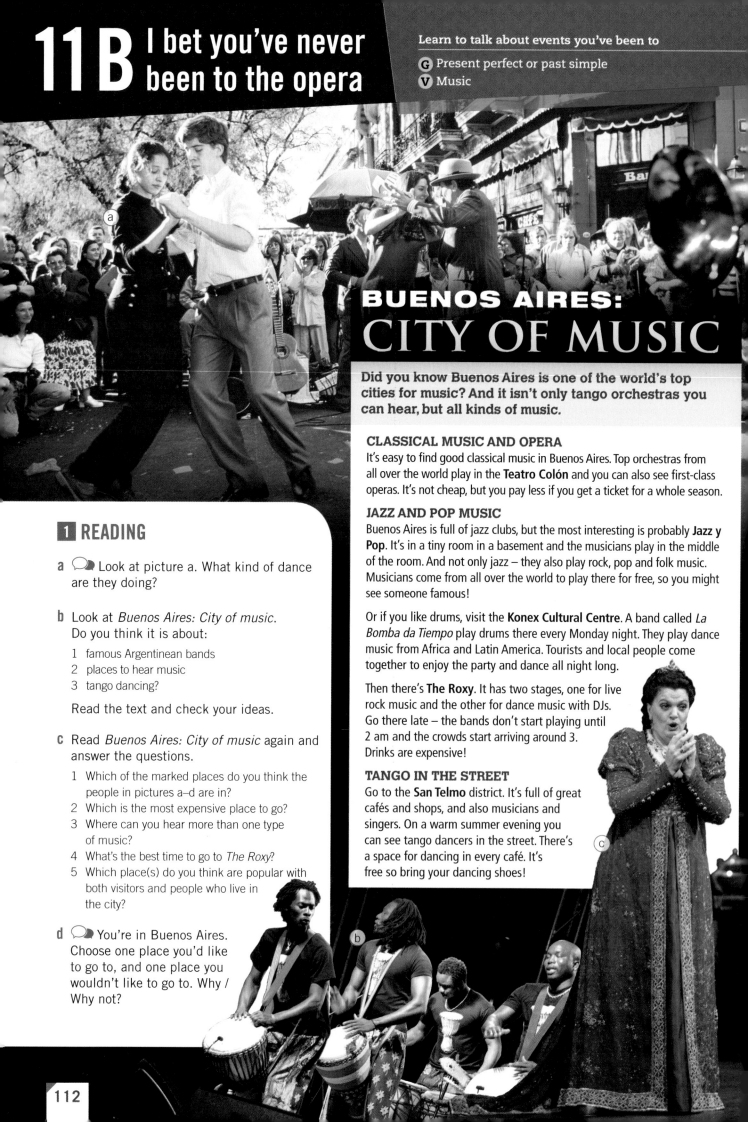

BUENOS AIRES:
CITY OF MUSIC

Did you know Buenos Aires is one of the world's top cities for music? And it isn't only tango orchestras you can hear, but all kinds of music.

CLASSICAL MUSIC AND OPERA

It's easy to find good classical music in Buenos Aires. Top orchestras from all over the world play in the **Teatro Colón** and you can also see first-class operas. It's not cheap, but you pay less if you get a ticket for a whole season.

JAZZ AND POP MUSIC

Buenos Aires is full of jazz clubs, but the most interesting is probably **Jazz y Pop**. It's in a tiny room in a basement and the musicians play in the middle of the room. And not only jazz – they also play rock, pop and folk music. Musicians come from all over the world to play there for free, so you might see someone famous!

Or if you like drums, visit the **Konex Cultural Centre**. A band called *La Bomba da Tiempo* play drums there every Monday night. They play dance music from Africa and Latin America. Tourists and local people come together to enjoy the party and dance all night long.

Then there's **The Roxy**. It has two stages, one for live rock music and the other for dance music with DJs. Go there late – the bands don't start playing until 2 am and the crowds start arriving around 3. Drinks are expensive!

TANGO IN THE STREET

Go to the **San Telmo** district. It's full of great cafés and shops, and also musicians and singers. On a warm summer evening you can see tango dancers in the street. There's a space for dancing in every café. It's free so bring your dancing shoes!

1 READING

a 💬 Look at picture a. What kind of dance are they doing?

b Look at *Buenos Aires: City of music*. Do you think it is about:
1 famous Argentinean bands
2 places to hear music
3 tango dancing?

Read the text and check your ideas.

c Read *Buenos Aires: City of music* again and answer the questions.
1 Which of the marked places do you think the people in pictures a–d are in?
2 Which is the most expensive place to go?
3 Where can you hear more than one type of music?
4 What's the best time to go to *The Roxy*?
5 Which place(s) do you think are popular with both visitors and people who live in the city?

d 💬 You're in Buenos Aires. Choose one place you'd like to go to, and one place you wouldn't like to go to. Why / Why not?

d

2 VOCABULARY Music

a ▶3.59 Underline words in the text for:

1 kinds of music: *tango, …*
2 people who play music, sing or dance:
an orchestra, …

Listen and check your answers.

b ▶3.60 **Pronunciation** Listen to these words again. Circle the number of syllables. Underline the stressed syllable in each word.

dancer	1	②	3	orchestra	1 2 3
musician	1	2	3	opera	1 2 3
classical	1	2	3		

c ▶3.61 Listen to five pieces of music. What kind of music are they?

d 💬 Which kinds of music do you often listen to? Which kinds do you never listen to?

3 LISTENING

a ▶3.62 Kurt and Bea are students in Buenos Aires. Listen to their conversation about *Buenos Aires: City of music*. Tick (✓) the places they talk about.

☐ Teatro Colón   ☐ The Roxy
☐ Jazz y Pop   ☐ San Telmo
☐ Konex Cultural Centre

Which places have they each been to?

b ▶3.62 Complete the table about Bea. Listen and check your answers.

Where?	When?	Did she like it?
1 Jazz y Pop		
2		
3		

4 GRAMMAR
Present perfect or past simple

a ▶3.63 Match the questions with the answers. Listen and check your answers.

1 Have you ever been to *Jazz y Pop*?
   a Yes, I have actually. I went there last year.

2 Where's *The Roxy*? Have you been there?
   b Yes, of course I have. We all went there for Antonia's birthday.

3 I bet you've never been to the *Teatro Colón*.
   c Yes, I went there two weeks ago. They had really good music.

b Answer the questions about 4a.

1 Which two tenses do the speakers use?
   a present simple   c present continuous
   b past simple   d present perfect
2 Which tense do we use … ?
   a if we don't say when something happened
   b if we say when something happened
3 Which tense do we use with … ?
   a *ever* and *never*
   b time expressions (*last weekend, a month ago*)

c ▶ Now go to Grammar Focus 11B on p.156

d ▶3.65 Put the conversation in the correct order. Listen and check your answers.

A ☐ Who did you go with?
A ☐ Did you enjoy it?
A ☐1 Have you ever been to a music festival?
A ☐ Where was it?
B ☐ It was in Novi Sad, in Serbia – the EXIT festival.
B ☐ I went with a group of friends from university.
B ☐ Yes, we all had a great time.
B ☐ Yes, I have. I went to one last summer.

e 💬 Practise the conversation in 4d.

5 SPEAKING

a Think of two things you've seen or places you've been to in your town or city. Here are some ideas:

- a concert or music event
- a film or play
- a cinema, theatre or club

Make notes.

Theatre Royal – Macbeth
football stadium – Jay-Z concert

b Think of two things you haven't seen or places you haven't been to, but would like to. Make notes.

c 💬 Ask other students about the things and places in 5a and 5b. Ask for more information.

Have you been to Mombo's?

When did you go there?

Was it good?

Who did you go with?

1 LISTENING

a 💬 Ask and answer the questions.

1 When you go out in the evening, do you ... ?
   • drive • walk • take a bus • take a taxi • other
2 When was the last time you took a taxi? Where did you go?

b 💬 Look at pictures a and b. Write what you think Dan's saying.

c ▶3.66 Watch or listen to Part 1 and check your answers in 1b. Then choose the correct answers below.

1 Dan and Martina are *going out / on their way home*.
2 Their address is *50 Windsor Road / 15 Windsor Road*.

d ▶3.67 Dan and Martina are in the taxi. Watch or listen to Part 2 and answer the questions.

1 Where have they been?
2 Do they have the same opinion about what they saw?

e ▶3.67 Read the sentences and write Martina (*M*), Dan (*D*) or both (*B*). Watch or listen again to check your answers.

Who thinks ... ?

1 the concert was good
2 not all the bands were good
3 the first band was good
4 Atlantis are a good band
5 Atlantis were too loud

2 USEFUL LANGUAGE
Asking for and expressing opinions

a ▶3.68 Listen and put the conversation in the correct order.

a ☐ Did you enjoy it?
b ☐ How about you?
c ☐ I really liked it.
d ☐ So what did you think of it?
e ☐ Yeah, it was a good concert.
f ☐ Yeah, me too.

b 💬 In pairs, practise the mini-conversation in 2a.

c Now look at these ways to express an opinion. Match opinions 1–3 with reasons a–c.

1 I really liked the first band.
2 I didn't like the first band very much.
3 I didn't like the first band at all.

a I thought they were terrible.
b I thought the singer was great.
c I thought they played quite well, but their songs were boring.

ⓒ

3 LISTENING

▶ **3.69** What do you think's happening in picture c? How does Martina feel? Watch or listen to Part 3 to check.

4 CONVERSATION SKILLS
Responding to an opinion

a Read the mini-conversations. Which replies mean … ?

a I agree.   b I don't really agree.

1 **MARTINA** I didn't like all the bands.
  DAN No, me neither.

2 **MARTINA** I really liked it, how about you?
  DAN Yeah, me too.

3 **MARTINA** I thought they were quite good.
  DAN Did you?

4 **DAN** Really great music.
  MARTINA Do you think so?

5 **MARTINA** They were too loud.
  DAN Yeah, maybe.

b Complete the table with *do* or *did*.

Present	Past
A I think they**'re** good.	**A** I thought they **were** good.
B **Do** you?	**B** ¹____ you?
A Their music **is** interesting.	**A** The concert **was** boring.
B ²____ you think so?	**B** **Did** you think so?

c 💬 In pairs, practise the mini-conversations in 4b. Take turns being A and B.

5 PRONUNCIATION
Main stress and tone

a ▶ **3.70** Listen to these replies. Notice that both words are stressed in each one.

1 Do you?   2 Did you?   3 Me neither.   4 Me too.

b ▶ **3.70** Listen again and answer the questions.

1 Does the tone go up ↗ or down ↘ at the end of each reply?
2 In 1 and 2, do you think the speaker sounds … ?
   a angry   b surprised   c happy?

c ▶ **3.70** Listen again and repeat.

d 💬 In pairs, take turns responding to these opinions. You can agree or disagree.

1 I thought the concert was boring.
2 I didn't enjoy the concert.
3 I think the band play very interesting music.
4 I thought the concert was too long.
5 I think she's a fantastic singer.

> Did you? I thought it was really good.

6 LISTENING

a 💬 Look at picture d. Answer the questions with a partner.

1 Where do you think Dan and Martina are now?
2 What do you think Dan says?

ⓓ

b ▶ **3.71** Watch or listen to Part 4 and check your answers in 6a.

7 SPEAKING

a ▶ **Communication 11C** Student A go to p.131. Student B go to p.133.

Communication 11C Student A go to p.131. Student B go to p.133.

○ Unit Progress Test

CHECK YOUR PROGRESS

You can now do the Unit Progress Test.

1 SPEAKING AND LISTENING

a 💬 Ask and answer the questions.

1 Have you seen any of the films on these pages?
2 Have you ever watched a film more than once?

b ▶3.72 Melissa and Robin talk about a film. Listen and answer the questions.

1 What film are they talking about?
2 Did Robin like it? Did Melissa like it?

c ▶3.72 Listen again. Write Robin (*R*) or Melissa (*M*). Who … ?

1 thinks James Bond films are always the same
2 thinks James Bond films are just for fun
3 thinks the special effects were good
4 is going to see the film again

d Choose a film you've seen and a film you haven't seen. Make notes. Think of:

• why you liked or didn't like the film
• why you'd like to see the other film.

e 💬 Talk about the two films from 1d.

1 Have other students seen them?
2 What did they think of them?

2 READING

a Melissa downloaded the film *Inception*. Read her review. Is it positive or negative?

b Read Melissa's review again and answer the questions.

1 How many times has she watched the film?
2 What is the best way to watch it?

c Robin went to see *Inception* at the cinema. Read his review. Is it positive or negative?

d Read Robin's review again and answer the questions.

1 Why did he go to see it?
2 What are the good and bad things he says about the film?
3 Does he think it's a good idea for other people to see or buy the film?

3 WRITING SKILLS Structuring a review

a Read Melissa and Robin's reviews again. Write the numbers of the sentences that answer the questions below.

a [4] Who are the actors and are they good?
b [ ] When did you see the film?
c [ ] Did you like it?
d [ ] Do you recommend it?
e [ ] Who wrote or directed it?

b Look at some more comments about films. Which questions in 3a do they answer?

1 I loved it!
2 I heard it was good so I went to see it at the weekend.
3 I thought the story was quite interesting.
4 Leonardo DiCaprio is brilliant.
5 It's by Spanish director, Pedro Almodóvar.
6 Don't go to see it. It's terrible!
7 I thought it was a very funny film. I laughed a lot.

| HOME | REVIEWS | INTERVIEWS | FEATURES | PODCASTS |

REVIEWS ☆☆☆☆☆

INCEPTION

❝ **I THOUGHT IT WAS AN INTERESTING AND EXCITING FILM, SO TRY TO SEE IT IF YOU CAN!** ❞

[1] I saw *Inception* at the cinema a month ago and I decided to download it so I could see it again. [2] I've watched it three times now and it gets better every time. [3] It's by British director Christopher Nolan and it's a brilliant story. [4] All the actors are excellent, but I liked Leonardo DiCaprio and Tom Hardy the best. They play Cobb and Eames, part of a team trying to put ideas in another man's head. It's a good idea to watch this film on a big screen because it has great special effects. [5] I thought it was an interesting and exciting film, so try to see it if you can!

c Look at the reviews again. How are sentences 1–3 different from the ones in the reviews?

1 I saw *Inception* at the cinema a month ago and I decided to download *Inception* so I could see *Inception* again.
2 I liked Leonardo DiCaprio and Tom Hardy the best. Leonardo DiCaprio and Tom Hardy play Cobb and Eames …
3 I saw *Inception* last week. My friend Charlie told me *Inception* was good.

d 💬 Answer the questions with a partner.

1 How many times did Melissa and Robin write the name of the film in their reviews?
2 What words did they use in place of the film names?

4 WRITING AND SPEAKING

a Plan a review of a film you've seen. Make notes, using the questions in 3a and the comments in 3b to help you.

b Write your review. Use Melissa and Robin's reviews to help you.

c Swap reviews with another student and check. Does your partner's review answer the questions in 3a?

d 💬 Read other students' reviews. Which film would you like to see?

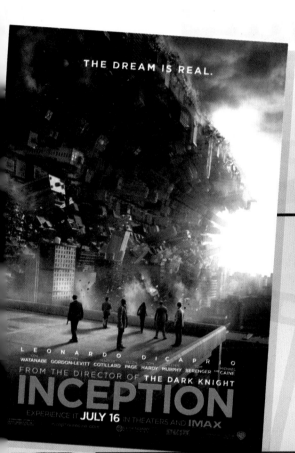

JOSEPH GORDON-LEVITT IS EXCELLENT IN THE ROLE OF ARTHUR

[1] I saw *Inception* last week. [2] My friend Charlie told me it was good. He usually likes the films I like so I went to see it, but I didn't enjoy it very much. [3] Christopher Nolan, who made the *Batman* films, wrote and directed it. [4] There are a lot of well-known actors in the film (Joseph Gordon-Levitt is excellent in the role of Arthur), but I thought the story was quite difficult to understand and also too long. [5] See it if you have a spare two and a half hours …

UNIT 11
Review and extension

1 VOCABULARY

a Underline the correct words.

1 I don't like all *classic / classical* music.
2 He likes old *rock / rocker* music like the Rolling Stones.
3 After years of playing the violin, he finally got a job with an *orchestral / orchestra*.
4 In my opinion, Madonna is the most famous *popular / pop* music singer in the world.
5 Bill only plays his guitar on the street for money. But listen to him – he's a very good *musician / musical*.
6 Would you like to come and see *Così fan tutte*? It's a very famous *opera / operatic* by Mozart.

b Write the past participle of the verbs.

1 be   5 read
2 do   6 see
3 go   7 win
4 hear   8 write

2 GRAMMAR

a Write sentences and questions with the correct form of the present perfect.

1 I / be to South Africa twice.
2 She / meet a lot of famous actors.
3 you / see the latest James Bond film?
4 He / not / work in an office before.
5 We / never / win Lotto.
6 they / read all the Harry Potter books?
7 I / not / hear a lot of jazz music.

b Tick (✓) the correct sentences. Change the verb form in the sentences that are not correct.

1 We've been to Australia only once.
2 He's read a book in English last week.
3 I never saw an *X-Men* film.
4 They've won a pop music competition two years ago.
5 I saw three films at the weekend.
6 She's never been to Argentina.
7 I didn't read a book by Dan Brown.

c Complete the conversation with the correct present perfect or past simple form of the verbs in brackets.

A [1]_____ (you/be) to Australia?
B No, I haven't, but I [2]_____ (be) to New Zealand.
A Have you? I [3]_____ (never/be) there, but I would love to go.
B We [4]_____ (go) about four years ago in the summer.
A How long [5]_____ (you/stay)?
B About three weeks, but it [6]_____ (not be) long enough.
A I [7]_____ (do) a bungee jump when I [8]_____ (be) there. [9]_____ (you/ever/try) anything like that?
B No. I'm too afraid!

3 WORDPOWER Multi-word verbs

a Match 1–6 with a–f to make conversations.

1 Sorry, Mike, I've got a meeting now.
2 Here's my photo ID.
3 Are you from London?
4 Here's a very nice shirt in blue.
5 You're looking a bit tired.
6 I've got nothing to do this evening.

a Yes, I think I need to **lie down** for a while.
b Well, I was born in Manchester, but I **grew up** here.
c That's OK. I can **call** you **back** this afternoon.
d Well, would you like to **come round** for dinner?
e Thank you. Now can you **fill** this form **in**, please?
f Could I **try** it **on**?

b Match the marked multi-word verbs in 3a with meanings 1–6.

1 return a phone call
2 put on clothes and check the size is right
3 complete
4 have a rest on a sofa or bed
5 visit a person's home
6 go from being a child to an adult

c Complete the sentences with the correct form of a multi-word verb from 3a.

1 She never wants to _____ things _____ in the shop and often gets the wrong size.
2 You need this form at the airport. Can you _____ _____ your details here?
3 I've always lived in Sydney. I _____ _____ here.
4 She finally _____ me _____ this morning and told me she was away all last week.
5 Why don't you _____ _____ and read your book?
6 My brother _____ _____ last night and brought a cake for my birthday.

d 💬 Work in pairs. Ask and answer the questions.

1 How often do friends or family come round to your place?
2 Do you sometimes forget to call people back?
3 Where did you grow up?
4 Do you usually try on clothes before you buy them?
5 What was the last form you had to fill in?
6 Do you sometimes lie down in the day?

◯ CAN DO OBJECTIVES

- Talk about holiday plans
- Give advice
- Talk about travel
- Use language for travel and tourism
- Write an email with travel advice

UNIT 12
Travel

GETTING STARTED

a 💬 Look at the picture and answer the questions.

1 Where do you think these people are on holiday? Why?
2 Who are the people in the photo: friends or family?
3 What other things have they planned to do here?

b 💬 In pairs, ask and answer the questions.

1 Do you take photos of friends and family on holidays or other special days?
2 What other things do you photograph?
3 What do you do with your photos after you've taken them?
4 What's your favourite photograph?

12A What are you going to do?

1 VOCABULARY Geography

a Match words 1–10 with pictures a–j.

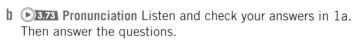

1	island	6	desert
2	mountain	7	lake
3	forest	8	glacier
4	waterfall	9	rainforest
5	beach	10	river

b ▶ **3.73** **Pronunciation** Listen and check your answers in 1a. Then answer the questions.

1 Which two words have only one syllable?
2 Which syllable is stressed in all the other words?

c 💬 Work in pairs. Look at pictures a–j and answer the questions.

1 Which places would you like to live near?
2 Have you been to any of these places?
3 Which place would you like to go on holiday to? Why?

d ▶ Now go to Vocabulary Focus 12A on p.165 for more Geography vocabulary

2 READING

a 💬 What's important for you when you're on holiday? Why?

- nothing – just relax
- meet new people
- do lots of sightseeing
- understand a new culture
- try a new sport
- eat local food

b Read the *WAW* website. Which ideas in 2a can you do on *Work Around the World* holidays?

c Read the website again. What is a good job for someone who likes … ?

- swimming and dancing
- drawing
- outdoor sports

d 💬 Talk about the questions.

1 Would you like to do one of these jobs? Why / Why not?
2 Order the three jobs from hard work (1) to not very hard work (3). Say why.

What are Work Around the World (WAW) holidays?
They're holidays where you work for a few hours every day and you get your accommodation and food free.

Why go on a Work Around the World (WAW) holiday?
Because it's fun, you help other people and you also make a lot of interesting new friends.
Here are some examples of great Work Around the World holidays.

Summer work in a small hotel in the Åland Islands, Finland.
- Jobs include cleaning and taking reservations.
- Great for people who love cycling and kayaking.

3 LISTENING

a ⏵**3.75** Listen to two conversations about holiday plans. Which *Work Around the World* holidays are Emily and Chloe interested in?

b ⏵**3.75** Listen again to the two conversations. Answer the questions.

Conversation 1

1 Why doesn't Emily want to go to university?
2 What does she like about the job she is interested in?
3 Why doesn't Zoe want her to go?

Conversation 2

1 Why does Chloe want to leave her job?
2 What does she like about the job she is interested in?
3 Does Frank think it's a good job for Chloe?

c 💬 Talk about the questions.

1 Do you think it's a good idea for Emily and Chloe to do a *Work Around the World* holiday? Why / Why not?
2 What are the good things and the bad things about going on one of these holidays?

2

A Mexican family is looking for a young person to work in their home in Acapulco on the Pacific Coast.

- Jobs include looking after children and teaching English.
- Great beaches and nightlife – lots of fun.

3

Come and live in an artists' village in the South Island of New Zealand.

- Jobs include helping in the local shop and cleaning.
- Close to amazing scenery: rainforest, mountains and glaciers.

4 GRAMMAR *going to*

a ⏵**3.76** Complete the sentences from the conversations. Listen and check your answers.

1 I'm _____ to email and ask about it.
2 I'm _____ to leave this job.

b Look at the sentences in 4a. Underline the correct words to complete the rule.

We use *be* + *going to* + infinitive when we want to describe *a future plan* / *a present action*.

c ⏵**3.77** Complete the sentences with the correct forms of *going to* and the verbs in brackets. Listen and check your answers.

+ I _____ (find out) more about it.
− I _____ (not go) to university next year.
? What _____ (do)?

d ⏵**3.77** **Pronunciation** Listen to the sentences in 4c again. Which is stressed, *going* or the main verb?

e ⏵ Now go to Grammar Focus 12A on p.158

f ⏵**3.79** Complete the conversation with *going to* and the verbs in brackets. Listen and check your answers.

A I ¹_____ (spend) six months travelling and working next year.
B Great. Where are you ²_____ (go)?
A I ³_____ (travel) around South Africa.
B What jobs ⁴_____ (do)?
A Cleaning, cooking, working in restaurants – things like that. I ⁵_____ (not do) anything too difficult.
B And what about after your trip?
A I ⁶_____ (look) for a job at home.

5 SPEAKING

a ⏵ **Communication 12A** Student A go to p.131. Student B go to p.135.

b 💬 Talk about which of the two working holidays you would like to do.

1 READING

a 💬 Ask and answer the questions.

Would you like to live in a different country? Why / Why not? If yes, which country would you choose?

b Read the texts and match the people with pictures a–d.

c Read the sentences. Who do you think wrote each one: Troy (*T*), Oliver and Kirsten (*OK*) or Cerys (*C*)?

1 Saw some beautiful fish yesterday. Fantastic!
2 We've got a job taking photos for a local newspaper.
3 I think they liked the music I played last night.
4 I'm going to work on Koh Tao Island – the sea is so clear there.
5 We're going to find a local school for our daughter next week.

d 💬 Would you like to go travelling and never stop? Why / Why not?

2 VOCABULARY Travel collocations

a Match pairs of verbs 1–6 with a word or phrase in the box. Use the texts in 1b to help you.

a hotel   a bag   home   abroad   plans   a holiday

1 make / change _____
2 travel / live _____
3 stay at / go back _____
4 plan / have _____
5 book / stay in _____
6 pack / unpack _____

b ▶ **3.80** Six people talk about travelling and holidays. Complete the sentences with verbs in 2a. Listen and check your answers.

1 I always _____ my holidays carefully. I read about the place before I go there.
2 I don't want to _____ abroad. It's better to go on holiday in my own country.
3 I never _____ a hotel. I want to see my room before I decide to stay there.
4 I usually _____ my bags about an hour before I go on holiday. I hate doing it!
5 After a week away I'm always happy to _____ home and see my family again.
6 When I'm on holiday I never _____ plans. I just see what happens when I get there.

c 💬 Which speakers in 2b do you agree with? Why / Why not?

Why not go **travelling** *... and never stop?*

In 2003 Troy sold everything, packed a small bag and left his home in Australia to travel abroad. He was 30. Ten years and 15 countries later, he's still travelling and he says he isn't ever going to go back home. Last year he arrived in Portugal. To earn money, Troy works as an English teacher. He's also a DJ in some local nightclubs.

TROY SAYS: You can use English in most places, but you should try to learn the local language too.

Like many students, Cerys finished university in her home town of Swansea in Wales and decided to have a long holiday. She stayed in cheap hotels and with friends in different countries. Five years later she is still enjoying that holiday. When she was in Australia, she learned how to dive. She loved it and she decided to do a course and learn to teach other people how to dive. Now she works all over the world teaching tourists to dive.

CERYS SAYS: It's a big, wide world out there. I don't want to spend my life in just one place.

Oliver and Kirsten Foster left the UK in 2009. In three years they travelled to Mexico, Peru, the USA, Thailand, China, Dubai and Germany before arriving at their latest home in Egypt. They're both photographers, so they can work anywhere in the world. They now have a three-year-old daughter, Liona, so they have to make plans more carefully. But they don't want to change their lives. Next year they are going to live in Ecuador and then South Africa.

OLIVER SAYS: I love meeting new people, but you shouldn't forget your family back home. I phone my mum every week.

KIRSTEN SAYS: You should live like the local people and try to make friends with people from the country.

3 GRAMMAR *should / shouldn't*

a Look at the sentences. <u>Underline</u> the correct words. Then check in the texts.

1 You *should / shouldn't* try to learn the local language too.
2 You *should / shouldn't* forget your family back home.
3 You *should / shouldn't* live like the local people.

b Choose the correct answer to complete the rules.

You should means:
a you have to do it   b it's a good idea.
After *should* and *shouldn't* we use:
a *to* + infinitive   b infinitive without *to*.

c ▶3.81 **Pronunciation** Listen to sentences 2 and 3 in 3a.

1 Is there a /l/ sound in *should* and *shouldn't*?
2 Is the vowel long or short?

d ▶ Now go to Grammar Focus 12B on p.158

e Read the advice about living abroad. Change the verbs in blue by adding *should* or *shouldn't*.

WOULD YOU LIKE TO LIVE ABROAD?
TAKE OUR ADVICE!

1 **Don't stay** at home all the time.
   Go out and meet people.
   You shouldn't stay at home all the time. You should …
2 **Try** to visit a new place every weekend.
   Don't wait until the last few weeks of your stay.
3 **Read** about the country before you go there.
4 **Don't get** angry when things go wrong.
5 **Remember** that things work differently in other countries.

4 LISTENING AND SPEAKING

a What do you think these people mean?

I'm quite a sporty person.

I'm not really a city person.

I'm a beach person.

💬 What about you and other students? Are you the same?

b 💬 Quickly read the texts again about Troy and Cerys. Which things below do you think Troy likes and which do you think Cerys likes? Why? Write *T* (Troy) or *C* (Cerys).

☐ big cities   ☐ noise   ☐ museums
☐ cafés   ☐ dancing   ☐ the sea
☐ sport   ☐ music   ☐ concerts
☐ shopping   ☐ the countryside ☐ beaches

c ▶3.83 Listen to Troy and Cerys. Check your answers in 4b.

d 💬 Troy and Cerys are going to visit your country. Talk about where they should and shouldn't go, what they should do and why.

e 💬 Work with a student you don't know very well. Find out what they like and don't like doing on holiday.

f 💬 Give your partner some advice about what to do and what not to do in a city you know.

You should go to the centre. There are lots of good cafés.

You shouldn't go to the National Museum. It's very boring!

12C Everyday English
Is breakfast included?

1 LISTENING

a 💬 Ask and answer the questions.

1 When you go on holiday, where do you usually stay? Choose one or more places.
- hotel
- hostel
- camping in a tent
- apartment / house
- with friends
- another place

2 Why do you like staying in this / these place(s)?

b ▶ 3.84 Watch or listen to Part 1 and answer the questions.

1 Who has won a competition?
2 Can Dan and Martina use the prize?

c ▶ 3.84 Watch or listen to Part 1 again. Complete the email. Put a word or number in each gap.

> Dear [1]_____
> Congratulations! You have won a weekend for [2]_____ people in the city of [3]_____. All your travel and hotel expenses are included in the prize.
> You can only use your prize on the weekend of [4]_____ [5]_____ July. Enjoy!

2 CONVERSATION SKILLS Showing surprise

a Look at the conversation. Underline the two ways that Dan shows surprise.

MARTINA I've won a competition.
DAN Have you? Fantastic. What's the prize?
MARTINA A weekend for two in Bath …
DAN Really? That's great.

b Which question in 2a can you use to reply to any news?

c ▶ 3.85 Match 1–4 with a–d. Listen and check your answers.

1 I'm getting married.
2 I really like grammar.
3 I went to New York for the weekend.
4 I've eaten an insect.

a Do you?
b Have you?
c Are you?
d Did you?

d ▶ 3.85 Pronunciation Listen again. Does the tone in a–d in 2c go up ↗ a little or a lot?

e Think of two surprising things. They don't have to be true! Make notes.

f 💬 In pairs, take turns telling each other your surprising things and showing surprise. Use expressions from 2a and 2c.

3 LISTENING

a ▶ 3.86 Who do you think Dan and Martina gave the prize to? Watch or listen to Part 2 and check.

b ▶ 3.86 Watch or listen to Part 2 again. Complete the guest information card.

> ### IMPERIAL HOTEL
> *Welcome to the* IMPERIAL HOTEL.
>
> Your room number is [1]_____.
>
> Please join us for breakfast in the dining room from [2]_____ to [3]_____.
>
> Your check out time is [4]_____.

4 USEFUL LANGUAGE
Checking in at a hotel

a Below are useful expressions for hotel guests. Which two expressions did Annie use?

1 I've got a reservation for a double room for two nights.
2 Is there a car park?
3 Is breakfast included?
4 Is there wi-fi in the room?
5 What time is check out?
6 Is there a safe in the room?

b Which four questions in 4a do we use to ask about things hotels can offer?

c ▶3.87 Complete the conversation between a guest and a hotel receptionist with sentences from 4a. Listen and check your answers.

RECEPTIONIST	Hello, how can I help you?
GUEST	Hello. I ¹_____.
RECEPTIONIST	A double room? Your name, please?
GUEST	Morton.
RECEPTIONIST	Thank you. So, that's two nights?
GUEST	Yes. Is ²_____?
RECEPTIONIST	Yes, it's from 6:30 am until 9:30 am in the dining room.
GUEST	Is ³_____?
RECEPTIONIST	Yes, there is.
GUEST	And what ⁴_____?
RECEPTIONIST	It's 11 o'clock on the day you leave.

5 PRONUNCIATION
Consonant groups

a ▶3.88 Listen to these sentences. Notice how the marked consonant groups with /t/ are pronounced.

1 I've got a reservation for a double room for two ni**ghts**.
2 So, tha**t's** two ni**ghts**?
3 Is breakfa**st** included?
4 I**t's** from 6:30 am until 9:30 am.

b ▶3.89 Listen to these sentences below. Underline consonant groups with /t/.

1 We're away next weekend.
2 I'd like some tourist information.
3 The bathroom is on your left.
4 Can I buy two tickets, please?

c 💬 In pairs, practise conversations like the one in 4c. Use your own name and change some of the questions about things in the hotel. Take turns being the receptionist and guest.

6 LISTENING

a ▶3.90 Watch or listen to Part 3. Complete the information on city bus tours.

Bath City BUS TOURS

Leaves from ¹_____
Price ²_____
Buy tickets at ³_____
Pay by cash or ⁴_____

b 💬 After the bus tour Annie goes to a museum. What do you think happens next?

c ▶3.91 Watch or listen to Part 4 and check your answer to 6b. Then answer the questions.

1 Did Dan and Martina tell Annie their plan?
2 Why do you think they did / didn't?

7 USEFUL LANGUAGE
Asking for tourist information

a ▶3.92 Match 1–5 with a–e to complete the questions. Listen and check your answers.

1 Can you   a for a ticket?
2 Is there a city bus tour b a ticket, please.
3 How much is it   c help me?
4 Can I buy   d I can go on?
5 I'll have   e tickets here?

b You are on holiday and go to a Tourist Information Office to ask about an interesting museum to visit. Answer the questions.

1 Can you use all the questions in 7a?
2 Which one(s) do you have to change?
3 Write a new question for the example(s) you need to change.

c 💬 Work in pairs. Use your answers in 7b to make a conversation at the Tourist Information Office about visiting a museum. Take turns being the tourist and an assistant who works in the office.

8 SPEAKING

a ▶ **Communication 12C** Student A go to p.131. Student B go to p.135.

🔄 **Unit Progress Test**

CHECK YOUR PROGRESS

You can now do the Unit Progress Test.

1 SPEAKING AND LISTENING

a 💬 How much do you plan your holidays before you leave? Choose an answer and say why.

1 I like to plan everything as much as possible so I know what I'm going to do.
2 I plan my travel and accommodation, but nothing else.
3 I only buy tickets. I organise everything else when I arrive.

b 💬 Look at the pictures of places in Sweden and answer the questions.

1 What do you know about Sweden?
2 What can you see in the pictures?

c ▶3.93 Elliot tells Louise about a holiday he's planned. Listen and underline the correct answers.

1 Elliot booked his holiday *online* / *at a travel agency*.
2 He's going to Stockholm for a *weekend* / *week*.
3 He's going to stay in a *3-star* / *4-star* hotel.
4 Elliot's going to go in *March* / *May*.
5 *Louise* / *Elliot* has a friend called Karin in Stockholm.

d 💬 You want to visit Stockholm. What questions could you ask Karin?

2 READING

What should I see in Stockholm?

a Elliot sent an email to Karin. Read Karin's reply. What doesn't she talk about?

a places to visit   b the hotel   c the weather

b Read Karin's email again and complete the table.

Place to visit	Reason to visit
Gamla Stan	historic, [1]_____, excellent [2]_____
Royal Palace	the home of the [3]_____, rooms with [4]_____ things
Skansen	outdoor museum and [5]_____, close to a [6]_____

Re: Stockholm

Hi Elliot

[1]Thanks for your email. [2]I'm very happy to help you plan your holiday in Stockholm. [3]I'm pleased you're going to spend some time in my home town! [4]You asked me about the three top tourist things to do in Stockholm, so here are some ideas. [5]First, you should visit Gamla Stan (which means 'the old town'). [6]You can see a lot of history in this part of Stockholm and it's very beautiful. [7]There are also some great cafés in Gamla Stan. [8]Secondly, you should go to the Royal Palace. [9]This is where our king and queen live, but you can visit some of the rooms and see some amazing things. [10]Finally, the third place that you should go to is Skansen. [11]It's an outdoor museum and the zoo is there. [12]There's also a lovely park nearby. [13]You said you are going to come at the end of May. [14]That's good because the weather is better then. [15]There are a lot of outdoor things to do in Stockholm so there's more to do when the weather is warm. [16]I hope my ideas help you. [17]Perhaps we can meet when you come to visit.

Best wishes

Karin

3 WRITING SKILLS Paragraph writing

a Read Karin's email on page 126 again. Make four paragraphs.

Paragraph 1 talks about Elliot's email: sentences 1 to ___
Paragraph 2 talks about things to do: sentences ___ to 12
Paragraph 3 talks about the weather: sentences 13 to ___
Paragraph 4 finishes the message: sentences ___ to ___

b Look at Paragraph 2. Underline three linking words that order the information.

c Read the email from Alice to you and answer the questions.

1 What is she going to do?
2 What does she want to know?

Hi!

Hi there

[1]My name is Alice and I'm going to visit your home town soon. [2]A friend told me that you can give me useful information, so I have some questions if that's OK. [3]I would like to do some sightseeing. [4]What are some interesting things to see? [5]I'd also like to do some kind of sports activity. [6]What are some interesting things to do? [7]I hope you can help me!

Kind regards

Alice

---

d Make three paragraphs in Alice's email in 3c.

4 WRITING

a Plan an email to Alice.

* answer both her questions
* use paragraphs for different parts of your message
* use linking words to order your ideas.

b Write your email. Use Karin's email on page 126 to help you.

c Swap emails with another student and check.

☐ Are the paragraphs clear?
☐ Are there good ideas of things to see and do?
☐ Are there linking words to order ideas?

Alice

UNIT 12
Review and extension

1 GRAMMAR

a Complete the sentences with the correct form of *going to* and a verb from the box.

travel   move   wear   have

1 He's 30 next week. He _____ a big party.
2 When we're older, we _____ to a cottage in the country.
3 I _____ my new suit and a tie for my interview.
4 She's got two month's holiday before she starts university, so she _____ around Europe with a friend.

b Write the conversation using the prompts with the correct form of *going to*.

PETRA ¹What / you / do after university?
What are you going to do after university?
NADIA ²I / go to New York.
PETRA New York? Sounds great. ³What / you / do there?
NADIA Well, my brother lives there.
PETRA Oh right, ⁴you / stay / with / him?
NADIA Yes. He says ⁵he / find / me / a job.
PETRA Oh, yes? ⁶How long / you / stay?
NADIA Just a month. But ⁷I not / book my flight back. Who knows? If I find a good job, I may stay longer!

c Read the travel advice to people going to Kenya in East Africa. Complete the text with *you should* or *you shouldn't*.

It's very hot in Kenya, so ¹_____ stay in the sun for too long and ²_____ drink lots of water. ³_____ buy bottled water and ⁴_____ drink water from lakes or rivers.

Most people speak English, but ⁵_____ try to learn a few words of Swahili, the local language.

2 VOCABULARY

a Underline the correct words.

1 We went to a Greek *island / mountain*. We just sat on the *forest / beach* and swam in the sea. It was very relaxing.
2 I went across the Gobi *Desert / Lake* on a camel.
3 I watched birds in the Brazilian *desert / rainforest*.
4 The Iguazu Falls are big *waterfalls / mountains* between Argentina and Brazil.
5 I climbed *rivers / mountains* in Norway and we crossed a *glacier / beach*. It was very cold on the ice.

b Put the words in the correct order to make questions.

1 you / abroad / lived / ever / have?
2 you / planned / your next holiday / have?
3 in a hotel / last / stay / you / did / when?
4 always / you / your own bags / pack / do / for a holiday?
5 this weekend / you / at home / are / staying?

c 💬 Ask and answer the questions in 2b.

3 WORDPOWER *take*

a Match sentences 1–6 with pictures a–f. What do you think the people are talking about?

1 You can take the number 23.
2 Please take care!
3 It will only take five minutes.
4 Then you take the first left.
5 Let me take your suitcase for you.
6 Take one three times a day before meals.

b Match the sentences in 3a with the uses of *take* a–f.

a to give street directions
b to talk about time
c to tell someone to be careful
d to talk about using transport
e to talk about medicine
f to talk about carrying something

▶ 3.94 Listen to the conversations and check.

c Complete the sentences with *take* and a word or phrase in the box.

a taxi   the first left   hours
my medicine   my laptop   care

1 I've got two essays to write. It will _____ to finish my homework.
2 There aren't any buses. Why don't we _____?
3 Have a lovely walking holiday and _____.
4 Go along till you come to a supermarket, then _____.
5 I'll carry the bags, but could you _____?
6 Oh, it's 6 o'clock. Time to _____.

d Choose two of the uses of *take* in 3b. Write a short conversation using examples of both uses.

e 💬 Practise your conversations in 3d.

REVIEW YOUR PROGRESS

How well did you do in this unit? Write 3, 2, or 1 for each objective.
3 = very well   2 = well   1 = not so well

I CAN ...

talk about holiday plans	☐
give advice	☐
talk about travel	☐
use language for travel and tourism	☐
write an email with travel advice.	☐

Communication Plus

1A Student A

a Read this web profile. Answer Student B's questions about Roberto.

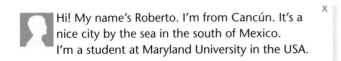

Hi! My name's Roberto. I'm from Cancún. It's a nice city by the sea in the south of Mexico. I'm a student at Maryland University in the USA.

b Ask Student B your questions. Write their answers.

1 What's her name? _____Lora_____
2 What's her nationality? _____
3 What's her home town? _____
4 Where is she now? _____

c ▶ Now go back to p.11

2A Student A

a Read about the job. Complete the sentences with the correct forms of the verbs.

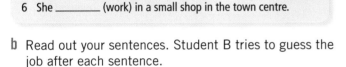

Shop assistant
1 She _____ (start) work at 8:00 am.
2 She _____ (not work) on Sunday.
3 She _____ (like) her job because she _____ (meet) people.
4 She _____ (not wear) a uniform.
5 People _____ (buy) things from her.
6 She _____ (work) in a small shop in the town centre.

b Read out your sentences. Student B tries to guess the job after each sentence.

c Listen to Student B's sentences and guess the job.

d ▶ Now go back to p.21

1C Student A

a **Conversation 1.** Read your first card. Think about what you want to say. Then start the conversation with Student B.

> ① You want to ask about beginner guitar lessons. Talk to the receptionist at the music school.
> • Say what you would like to do.
> • Ask when the first lesson is.
> • Ask where the lesson is.
> • Book a place.

b **Conversation 2.** Now look at your second card. Listen to Student B and reply.

> ② You're a receptionist in a language school. Here's some information about an English course:
> • *Time:* 6:20 pm next Tuesday
> • *Place:* Room 12
> • To book a place, you need the student's name.

4A Student A

a **Conversation 1.** Look at the picture. Answer Student B's questions about what's on your stall. Look at the examples.

> Have you got any apples on your stall?

> I'd like some pears, please.

> Yes, I have.

> I'm sorry, I haven't got any pears.

b **Conversation 2.** You want to buy food to cook dinner. You visit Student B's market stall. Ask about the things in the box. Look at the examples.

lamb	eggs	one lemon	fruit	tomatoes	mushrooms
cheese	pears	vegetables	bread	one onion	apples

> Have you got any eggs on your stall?

> I'd like some mushrooms, please.

2C Student A

a **Conversation 1.** Read your first card. Think about what you want to say. Then start the conversation with Student B.

> ① You're at Student B's home for the weekend. You'd like to do the following things:
> • have something to eat
> • use your friend's computer
> • watch TV

b **Conversation 2.** Now look at your second card. Listen to Student B and reply.

> ② Student B's at your home for the weekend. You're good friends but you don't like it when other people use your things, especially your new phone.

5A Student A

a Look at your picture. Student B has a similar picture. Ask and answer questions to find six differences.

> Is there a park in your picture?

> Yes, there is. / No, there isn't.

b ▶ Now go back to p.51

9A Student A

a Look at your picture for two minutes. What are the people doing? Make notes.

b Student B has a similar picture. Ask and answer questions to find five differences.

> Is Ken drinking coffee in your picture?

> Yes, he is. / No, he isn't. He's …

6C Student A

a **Conversation 1.** Read your first card. Think about what you want to say. Then call Student C.

1
- Think of a reason to phone Student C.
- You call Student C but he/she isn't there. Leave a message with Student B.
- Student C calls you back. Have a conversation.

b **Conversation 2.** Now look at your second card. Listen to Student C and reply.

2
- You return home. Student C has a message for you from Student B.
- Call Student B back. Have a conversation.

c **Conversation 3.** Now look at your third card. Start the conversation with Student C.

3
- Student C calls and you answer the phone.
- He/She wants to speak to Student B, who isn't there. Take a message.
- Student B returns. Give him/her Student C's message.

7A Student A

a You went on a trip from Cape Town in South Africa to Cairo in Egypt. Use the information below to answer Student B's questions about your trip.

countries visited	South Africa, Botswana, Zambia, Tanzania, Kenya, Ethiopia, Sudan, Egypt
transport used	truck, motorcycle, ferry, train
transport not used	plane
opinion	saw fantastic animals, met some amazing people

b Student B went on a journey in South America. Write some questions to ask him/her. Think about:
- countries he/she visited
- transport he/she used
- his/her opinion

Look at the questions in 5e on page 71 to help you.

c Start the conversation with Student B.

d ▶ Now go back to p.71

5C Student A

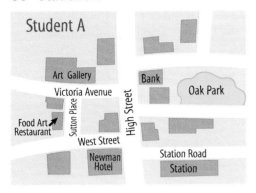

Student A

Art Gallery
Bank
Victoria Avenue
Oak Park
Sutton Place
High Street
Food Art
Restaurant
West Street
Newman
Hotel
Station Road
Station

a Conversation 1. Read your first card. Think about what you want to say. Then start the conversation with Student B.

1. You're at the station with your friend, Student B. The map on your phone isn't clear. You need to go to:
   - the supermarket • Dash Café
   Student B's map is clear. Ask him/her how to get to these places. Someone told you Dash Café is in James Street, but you're not sure.

b Conversation 2. Now look at your second card. Think about what you want to say. Then listen to Student B and reply.

2. You're at the station with your friend, Student B. The map on his/her phone isn't clear. You want to go to:
   - the art gallery • FoodArt Restaurant
   Use your map to tell Student B how you can get there. A lot of people think that FoodArt Restaurant is on the corner of Sutton Place and West Street, but this isn't correct.

12C Student A

a Conversation 1. Read your first card. Think about what you want to say. Then start the conversation with Student B.

1. You're a guest at a hotel. You've got a reservation for a double room for two nights. Check with the receptionist about:
   - the breakfast time • wi-fi in the room
   Ask about this tourist information:
   - interesting local markets near the hotel

b Conversation 2. Now look at your second card. Then listen to Student B and reply.

2. You're a hotel receptionist. Check the guest's name and let him/her know they have a booking. Here is other information you need:
   - check out 10:30 am
   - safe in the room
   - free box of chocolates in the room
   Some important tourist information about Central Park:
   - on the same road as the hotel
   - only half a kilometre away from the hotel
   - large and beautiful park

11C Student A

a Conversation 1. Read your first card. Think about what you want to say. Then listen to Student B and reply about the concert.

1. You went with Student B to a concert last night. You thought the band were really good. You like their music and you thought the singer was good.

b Conversation 2. Now look at your second card. Think about what you want to say. Then start a conversation about your meal with Student B.

2. You went with Student B to La Bodega, an Italian restaurant, last weekend. You didn't like it. You had fish, but it wasn't good and it was expensive. You thought the waiters were unfriendly.

12A Student A

a You're going to go on a working holiday. Look at your plans.

Notes	⊕
	28 Nov 15:46

Where: Australia and Pacific islands
Why: see beautiful beaches, desert in Australia
How long: three months
Possible jobs: hotels and restaurants
Before trip: look on the Internet for jobs
After trip: study at university

b Student B is planning his/her own working holiday. Write questions you can ask him/her about the trip. Use 4f on page 121 to help you.

c Have a conversation with Student B about his/her holiday.

d Listen to Student B's questions about your holiday and reply.

e ▶ Now go back to p.121

10A Student A

a Ask Student B about his/her smartphone. You can use these questions:

How long is your smartphone?
How wide is your smartphone?
How big is the screen?
How much does it weigh?

b Look at the picture of your new smartphone. Compare your phone with Student B's.

57mm
125mm
102mm
114g

My phone is bigger than yours.

c ▶ Now go back to p.101

1A Student B

a Read this web profile. Answer Student A's questions about Lora.

 Hi, my name's Lora. I'm from Berlin, in Germany, but now I'm in England with my family. I'm a teacher in London.   ˣ

b Ask Student A your questions. Write their answers.
1 What's his name? _____ *Roberto* _____
2 What's his nationality? _____
3 What's his home town? _____
4 Where is he now? _____

c ▶ Now go back to p.11

2A Student B

a Read about the job. Complete the sentences with the correct forms of the verbs.

Nurse
1 He sometimes _____ (work) at night.
2 He _____ (not make) a lot of money.
3 He _____ (wear) a uniform at work.
4 He _____ (like) his job because he _____ (help) people.
5 He _____ (give) people medicine.
6 He _____ (work) in a big hospital in the city centre.

b Listen to Student A's sentences and guess the job.

c Read out your sentences. Student A tries to guess the job after each sentence.

d ▶ Now go back to p.21

1C Student B

a **Conversation 1.** Read your first card. Think about what you want to say. Listen to Student A and reply.

1 You're a receptionist in a music school. Here is some information about beginner guitar lessons:
• *Time:* 6:30 pm next Thursday
• *Place:* Room 2
• To book a place, you need the student's full name.

b **Conversation 2.** Now look at your second card. Think about what you want to say. Then start the conversation with Student A.

2 You want to ask about English lessons. Talk to the receptionist at the language school.
• Say what you would like to do
• Ask when the first lesson is
• Ask where the lesson is
• Book a place

4A Student B

a **Conversation 1.** You want to buy food to cook dinner. You visit Student A's market stall. Ask about the things in the box. Look at the examples.

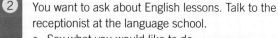
ham   one lemon   beans   fruit   tomatoes   mushrooms
cheese   pears   vegetables   bread   one onion   apples

Have you got any apples on your stall?

I'd like some pears, please.

b **Conversation 2.** Look at the picture. Answer Student A's questions about what's on your stall. Look at the examples.

Have you got any eggs on your stall?

Yes, I have.

I'd like some mushrooms, please.

I'm sorry, I haven't got any mushrooms.

2C Student B

a **Conversation 1.** Read your first card. Think about what you want to say. Listen to Student A and reply.

1 Student A's at your home for the weekend. You're good friends but you don't like it when other people use your things, especially your computer.

b **Conversation 2.** Now look at your second card. Think about what you want to say. Then start the conversation with Student A.

2 You're at Student A's home for the weekend. You'd like to do the following things:
• have a drink
• use your friend's phone
• have a shower

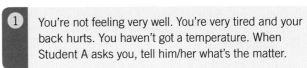

5C Student B

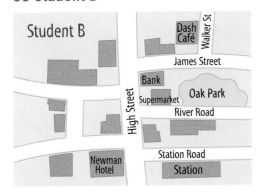

a **Conversation 1.** Read your first card. Think about what you want to say. Then listen to Student A and reply.

> **1** You're at the station with your friend, Student A. The map on his/her phone isn't clear. You need to go to:
> - the supermarket • Dash Café
>
> Use your map to tell Student A how you can get there. A lot of people think that Dash Café is in James Street, but this isn't correct.

b **Conversation 2.** Now look at your second card. Think about what you want to say. Then start the conversation with Student A.

> **2** You're at the station with your friend, Student A. The map on your phone isn't clear. You want to go to:
> - the art gallery • FoodArt Restaurant
>
> Student A's map's clear. Ask him/her how to get to these places. Someone told you that FoodArt Restaurant is on the corner of Sutton Place and West Street, but you're not sure.

3C Student B

a **Conversation 1.** Read your first card. Listen to Student A and reply.

> **1** You aren't free this Saturday because you work at the weekends. You'd like to go out on Friday, to the cinema.

b **Conversation 2.** Now look at your second card. Think about what you want to say. Then start the conversation with Student A.

> **2** You want to meet Student A for a coffee. You think next Friday after work/school is a good time. Decide the following and invite Student A:
> - where to have coffee
> - what time
> - something to do after

c ▶ Now go back to 5c on p.35

8C Student B

a **Conversation 1.** Read your first card. Think about what you want to say. Then listen to Student A and reply.

> **1** You're not feeling very well. You're very tired and your back hurts. You haven't got a temperature. When Student A asks you, tell him/her what's the matter.

b **Conversation 2.** Now look at your second card. Think about what you want to say. Then start the conversation with Student A.

> **2** Student A doesn't look well. Ask him/her what's the matter. When he/she tells you, show sympathy using expressions like *Oh dear!* or *Poor you!*
> Then ask if he/she feels hungry. Tell him/her what to do, e.g. *See a doctor. Have an aspirin/some soup.*

10C Student B

a **Conversation 1.** Read your first card. Think about what you want to say. Then listen to Student A and reply.

> **1** Student A bought a new phone, but he/she can't receive any text messages on it. When he/she asks for help, explain how it works. Here are the instructions:
> - Touch the box that says *Messages*.
> - Wait for a blue screen.
> - Touch the box that says *Receive*. It can receive messages now.

b **Conversation 2.** Now look at your second card. Think about what you want to say. Then start the conversation with Student A.

> **2** You bought a new mouse for your computer, but it isn't working. Ask Student A for help. Check the instructions he/she gives you.

11C Student B

a **Conversation 1.** Read your first card. Think about what you want to say. Start a conversation about the concert with Student A.

> **1** You went with Student A to a concert last night. You didn't like the band very much. You thought they played badly and the music was boring.

b **Conversation 2.** Now look at your second card. Think about what you want to say. Then listen to Student A and reply about your meal.

> **2** You went with Student A to La Bodega, an Italian restaurant, last weekend. You liked it. You had a very good pizza and you thought the food was delicious and not too expensive.

5A Student B

a Look at your picture. Student A has a similar picture. Ask and answer questions to find six differences.

> Is there a bridge in your picture?

> Yes, there is. / No, there isn't.

b ▶ Now go back to p.51

9A Student B

a Look at your picture for two minutes. What are the people doing? Make notes.

b Student A has a similar picture. Ask and answer questions to find five differences.

> Is Ken eating a sandwich in your picture?

> Yes, he is. / No, he isn't. He's ...

7A Student B

a Student A went on a journey in Africa. Write some questions to ask him/her. Think about:

- countries he/she visited
- transport he/she used
- his/her opinion

Look at the questions in 5e on page 71 to help you.

countries visited	Ecuador, Peru, Bolivia, Brazil, Paraguay, Argentina
transport used	plane, ferry, horse, coach
transport not used	train
opinion	met lots of interesting people, saw some beautiful places

6C Student B

a **Conversation 1.** Read your first card. Start the conversation with Student A.

1
- Student A calls and you answer the phone.
- He/She wants to speak to Student C, who isn't there. Take a message.
- Student C returns. Give him/her Student A's message.

b **Conversation 2.** Now look at your second card. Think about what you want to say. Then call Student A.

2
- Think of a reason to phone Student A.
- You call Student A but he/she isn't there. Leave a message with Student C.
- Student A calls you back. Have a conversation.

c **Conversation 3.** Now look at your third card. Listen to Student A and reply.

3
- You return home. Student A has a message for you from Student B.
- Call Student C back. Have a conversation.

b Start the conversation with Student A.

c You went on a trip from Quito in Ecuador to Santiago in Chile. Use the information below to answer Student A's questions about your trip.

d ▶ Now go back to p.71

10A Student B

a Ask Student A about his/her smartphone. You can use these questions:

How long is your smartphone?
How wide is your smartphone?
How big is the screen?
How much does it weigh?

b Look at the picture of your new smartphone. Compare your phone with Student A's.

My screen is wider than yours.

c ▶ Now go back to p.101

10A Listening 3c

Noelle

Thanks to everyone for your advice! I thought about it a lot, but in the end I decided to buy a new tablet. I can use it to do online shopping. Also, I have to do a lot of work when I'm travelling, so it's easier on the tablet.

12A Student B

a You're going to go on a working holiday. Look at your plans.

Notes   ⊕

18 Dec 15:46

Where: South America
Why: see rainforests, old Maya/Inca/Aztec buildings
How long: four months
Possible jobs: looking after children, tour guide
Before trip: send emails to friends
After trip: find a new job

☆ → 🖼 ✉

b Student A is planning his/her own working holiday. Write questions you can ask him/her about the trip. Use 4f on page 121 to help you.

c Listen to Student A's questions about your holiday and reply.

d Have a conversation with Student A about his/her holiday.

e ▶ Now go back to p.121

12C Student B

a **Conversation 1.** Read your first card. Then listen to Student A and reply.

1 You're a hotel receptionist. Check the guest's name and let him/her know they have a booking. Here is other information you need:
- breakfast 7–9:30 am   • free wi-fi in the room
- free dinner at the hotel tomorrow night

Some important tourist information about a local market:
- in a car park opposite the hotel
- biggest market in town
- clothes, paintings, old furniture

b **Conversation 2.** Now look at your second card. Think about what you want to say. Then start the conversation with Student A.

2 You're a guest at a hotel. You've got a reservation for a single room for three nights. Check with the receptionist about:
- check-out time   • safe in the room

Ask about this tourist information:
- nice parks and gardens to visit near the hotel

4B Speaking 5c

Healthy food

Every day you can eat these food quantities:

bread – 4 pieces	rice or pasta – 2 cups
vegetables – 5 pieces	fruit – 2 pieces
cheese – 2 pieces	meat/fish – 1 piece

6C Student C

a **Conversation 1.** Read your first card. Then listen to Student B and reply.

1 • You return home. Student B has a message for you from Student A.
- Call Student A back. Have a conversation.

b **Conversation 2.** Now look at your second card. Start the conversation with Student B.

2 • Student B calls and you answer the phone.
- He/She wants to speak to Student A, who isn't there. Take a message.
- Student A returns. Give him/her Student B's message.

c **Conversation 3.** Now look at your third card. Think about what you want to say. Then call Student B.

3 • Think of a reason to phone Student B.
- You call Student B but he/she isn't there. Leave a message with Student A.
- Student B calls you back. Have a conversation.

Grammar Focus

1A *be*: positive and negative

Positive (+)	
Full form	**Contraction** 1.18
I **am** a student.	I**'m** a student.
You **are** a good cook.	You**'re** a good cook.
He **is** my friend.	He**'s** my friend.
She **is** Spanish.	She**'s** Spanish.
It **is** sunny.	It**'s** sunny.
We **are** sisters.	We**'re** sisters.
They **are** from Japan.	They**'re** from Japan.

Negative (–)	
Full form	**Contraction**
I **am not** a student.	I**'m not** a student.
You **are not** a good cook.	You **aren't** a good cook.
He **is not** my friend.	He **isn't** my friend.
She **is not** Spanish.	She **isn't** Spanish.
It **is not** sunny.	It **isn't** sunny.
We **are not** sisters.	We **aren't** sisters.
They **are not** from Japan.	They **aren't** from Japan.

Remember to use the verb *be* to give information with a noun, adjective, preposition or adverb.
My name**'s Hamid**. NOT ~~My name Hamid.~~
My teacher **is nice**. NOT ~~My teacher nice.~~
I**'m from China**. NOT ~~I from China.~~
We **are here**. NOT ~~We here.~~
Always use a noun or a pronoun before positive and negative *be*:
He's my teacher. NOT ~~Is my teacher.~~
They're Spanish. NOT ~~Are Spanish.~~

> **Tip**
> *you* is the same when we talk to one person or two or more people.
> **You**'re **a good cook**. = one person
> **You**'re **good cooks**. = two or more people

> Hi! No, I'm not at home. We're on holiday in London. It's a beautiful city but ... it isn't very warm.

We use contractions to help us speak quickly. In contractions, the apostrophe (') shows a letter is missing:
You **are not** old. → You **aren't** old.
There are two different contractions for *is not* and *are not*.

is not → **isn't** / **'s not**	He **isn't** = He**'s not**
are not → **aren't** / **'re not**	We **aren't** = We**'re not**

> **Tip**
> We can use *'s* after one name but we don't use *'re* after two names:
> **Tom is** my friend. → **Tom's** my friend.
> **Tom and Jo are** my friends. NOT ~~Tom and Jo're my friends.~~

1B *be*: questions and short answers

In questions with the verb *be*, we change the word order:
They are Russian. → **Are they** Russian?
Our teacher is from Berlin. → **Is our teacher** from Berlin?

 1.25

	Yes/No questions		Short answers	
I	**Am** I	late?	Yes, No,	I **am**. I**'m not**.
you / we / they	**Are** you	ready?	Yes, No,	you **are** you **aren't**.
he / she / it	**Is** it	cold?	Yes, No,	it **is**. it **isn't**.

In *Wh-* questions, we use a question word before *be*.
Where are you from?
What is your name?

> **Tip**
> With positive short answers, we don't use contractions:
> Yes, I **am**. Yes, he **is**. Yes, we **are**.
> (NOT ~~Yes, I'm. Yes, he's. Yes, we're.~~)

> **Tip**
> We can use the contraction of *is* with question words:
> **What is** your name? → **What's** your name?
> **Where is** he from? → **Where's** he from?

1A *be:* positive and negative

a Write the correct form of *be* (*am* / *is* / *are*) in these sentences.

1 We _____are_____ very happy.
2 My father _____ a taxi driver.
3 My parents _____ not old.
4 Carl and Michael _____ brothers.
5 I _____ not a good driver.
6 She _____ at work today.
7 Cambridge _____ not a big city.
8 Our cats _____ hungry.

b Write the sentence again with positive and negative contractions.

1 She is Brazilian.
   ___*She's Brazilian.*___
   ___*She isn't Brazilian.*___
2 It is a beautiful city.
   _____
   _____
3 We are from Berlin.
   _____
   _____
4 They are at a party.
   _____
   _____
5 I am tired.
   _____
   _____
6 You are right.
   _____
   _____

c Complete the sentences with the correct positive (+) or negative (–) form of be. Use contractions if possible.

1 We _____'re_____ (+) at a concert.
2 She _____isn't_____ (–) Japanese.
3 I _____ (+) from Moscow.
4 He _____ (–) at home.
5 It _____ (+) a big hotel.
6 Lena and Thomas _____ (–) friends.
7 My city _____ (+) very beautiful.
8 Hi, my name _____ (+) Michael.
9 My parents _____ (–) at the match.
10 You _____ (+) very nice.

d Write the correct sentences.

1 ~~Russian~~ → French
   She's Russian. ___*She isn't Russian. She's French.*___
2 ~~a doctor~~ → a student
   He's a doctor. _____
3 ~~brothers~~ → friends
   They're my brothers. _____
4 ~~London~~ → Rome
   We're from London. _____
5 ~~good cook~~ → very bad cook
   I'm a good cook. _____

e ▶ Now go back to p.11

1B *be:* questions and short answers

a Put the words in the correct order to make questions.

1 her / what / name / 's ?   ___What's her name?___
2 from / are / you / where ?   _____
3 American / are / you ?   _____
4 she / popular / is ?   _____
5 names / are / what / your ?   _____
6 friends / you / are ?   _____
7 is / cold / it / very ?   _____
8 from / he / is / France ?   _____

b Match questions 1–7 with short answers a–g.

1 [d] Is she Italian?   a No, he isn't.
2 [ ] Are you teachers?   b No, they aren't.
3 [ ] Are Robert and Helen here today?   c No, you aren't.
4 [ ] Is it a beautiful city?   d Yes, she is.
5 [ ] Am I late?   e No, I'm not.
6 [ ] Is he on holiday?   f Yes, we are.
7 [ ] Are you from England?   g Yes, it is.

c Complete the conversations with the correct form of *be.* Use contractions if possible.

1 **A** Hi, I __'m__ Manuel.
   B Hi, Manuel. Where _____ you from?
   A I _____ from Lima, in Peru.

2 **A** See that footballer. What _____ his name?
   B He _____ Philip Lahm.
   A Where _____ he from?
   B He _____ from Germany.

3 **A** Excuse me, where _____ you from?
   B We _____ from Japan. We _____ here for the World Cup.

4 **A** Hi, my name _____ Alice, and this _____ my sister, Marta.
   B Hi, Alice. Hi, Marta. _____ you from England?
   A No, we _____. We _____ American. We _____ from New York.
   B Oh really? My cousins _____ from New York.

d ▶ Now go back to p.13

3A Position of adverbs of frequency

We often use adverbs of frequency with the present simple. Adverbs of frequency tell us how often something happens.

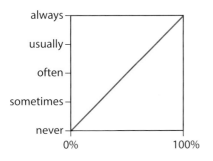

Adverbs of frequency go <u>after</u> the verb *be*.
*I'm **never** late.*
*She **isn't always** happy.*
***Are** they **usually** at home?*

Adverbs of frequency usually go <u>before</u> other main verbs.
*I **always arrive** at 8.45am.*
*Do you **often call** your parents?*
In negatives the adverbs go <u>between</u> *don't / doesn't* and the main verb.
*I **don't usually get** up early.*

We can ask questions with *How often*:
***How often** do you come here?*
***How often** is the bus late?*

▶ **1.59**

Statements with the verb *be*
*I'**m sometimes** late for work.*
*I'**m always** tired.*

Statements with other verbs
*I **often play** tennis in the morning.*
*I **usually go** shopping in the afternoon.*
*I **never do** any sport in the evening.*

Questions
***How often** do you go to the cinema?*
*When do you **usually** see your friends?*

I **often play** tennis in the morning.

I **usually go** shopping in the afternoon.

I never do any sport in the evening. I'm **always** tired.

3B *have got*

have got means *have*.
*I'**ve got** a new phone. = I have a new phone.*
*It **hasn't got** a camera. = It doesn't have a camera.*
We can use *have got* to talk about possessions, appearance and work:
*We **haven't got** a big house.*
*I'**ve got** blue eyes.*
*He'**s got** a lot of homework this week.*

We don't use ***have got*** for actions:
*I **have** a shower before work.*
NOT *I have got a shower before work.*
*I always **have** breakfast with my family.*
NOT *I always **have got** breakfast with my family.*

▶ **1.71**

	+		–	
I / you / we / they have got	*I'**ve***	*got a car.*	*They **haven't***	*got a car.*
he / she / it has got	*She'**s***	*got a car.*	*He **hasn't***	*got a car.*

The full form of *'ve* is *have*.
The full form of *'s* is *has*.

	Yes/No questions		Short answers	
I / you / we / they have got	***Have** you*	*got a car?*	*Yes,* *No,*	*I **have**.* *I **haven't**.*
he / she / it has got	***Has** she*	*got a car?*	*Yes,* *No,*	*she **has**.* *she **hasn't**.*

I'**ve got** a great new phone. It's only 5cm long. It'**s got** a camera. It'**s got** the internet. It'**s** even **got** a satnav so I never get lost.

Have you got it with you?

No, it's at home.

3A Position of adverbs of frequency

a Put the adverbs in brackets in the correct places in each sentence. Use them in the order given.

1 I miss a visit to my parents at the weekend – I go and see them. (~~never~~, always)
never

2 I'm late for work, but my boss gets angry. (sometimes, never)

3 He comes here for a coffee at 10 o'clock – he's late. (usually, never)

4 We have lunch together and talk. It's good to see him. (often, always)

5 They're away on holiday – they're at home. (never, always)

b Write sentences using the information in the table and adverbs of frequency. always = ✓✓✓✓✓, never = ✗✗✗✗✗

	Monday	Tuesday	Wednesday	Thursday	Friday
Paul / have breakfast	✓	✓	✗	✓	✓
My parents / eat in a restaurant	✗	✓	✓	✗	✗
I / play tennis	✓	✗	✓	✗	✓
Natasha / late for work	✗	✗	✗	✗	✗
We / watch TV in the evening	✓	✓	✓	✓	✓

1 _____ *Paul usually has breakfast.* _____
2 _____
3 _____
4 _____
5 _____

c Put the words in the correct order to make questions.

1 often / how / cinema / do / you / to / go / the ?
_____ *How often do you go to the cinema?* _____

2 to work / do / walk / you / usually ?
_____

3 always / are / tired / you / why ?
_____

4 you / where / usually / at weekends / go / do ?
_____

5 football / do / how / they / play / often ?
_____

6 often / is / late / for work / he ?
_____

7 me / you / never / do / write / to / why ?
_____

d ▶ Now go back to p.30

3B *have got*

a Correct one mistake in each sentence.

1 ~~Have~~ she got a laptop?
_____ *Has she got a laptop?* _____

2 Do you have got the Internet on your phone?
_____

3 We not got a car.
_____

4 They got a TV but they haven't got a DVD player.
_____

5 My brother haven't got a digital camera.
_____

6 My parents haven't a printer.
_____

b Use the words to write questions and short answers.

1 you / a fast car
_____ *Have you got a fast car? No, I haven't.* _____

2 your grandparents / a digital camera
_____ Yes, _____

3 your mum / a tablet computer
_____ No, _____

4 your teacher / blue eyes
_____ No, he _____

5 your dad / a satnav
_____ Yes, _____

6 you / a lot of homework
_____ No, _____

c Complete the conversations with the correct form of *have got*. Use the words in brackets to help you.

TOM [1] _____ *Have you got* _____ (you) a laptop?

EMILY No, we [2] _____. But we [3] _____ a tablet computer.

TOM Oh cool! We [4] _____ a tablet computer, but I really want one.

EMILY Yes, it's a great computer. It [5] _____ the Internet, digital camera, everything.

TOM [6] _____ (you) lots of good games on your computer?

EMILY Yes, we [7] _____. But I never play games. My brother plays games all the time. He [8] _____ lots of computer games.

LEO What car [9] _____ (your parents)?

ROB They [10] _____ (not) a car. They don't need a car. My mum [11] _____ a bike – she rides to work every day.

LEO What about your dad? [12] _____ (he) a bike?

ROB No, he [13] _____. He travels by bus.

d ▶ Now go back to p.33

4A Countable and uncountable nouns: a / an, some / any

Countable and uncountable nouns

We <u>can</u> count some things (e.g. *one lemon, eight grapes*). These things (e.g. *lemon, grape*) are **countable** nouns. They can be singular (e.g. *lemon*) or plural (e.g. *lemons*).

We <u>can't</u> count some things (e.g. *cheese* NOT ~~one cheese~~; *pasta* NOT ~~two pastas~~). These things (e.g. *cheese, pasta*) are **uncountable** nouns. They can only be singular (e.g. *cheese*), not plural (~~cheeses~~).

a / an

We use *a / an* with singular nouns. *a / an* means *one*. We can't use them with plurals or uncountable nouns.
We use *a* before a consonant sound:
a lemon, **a p**otato
We use *an* before a vowel sound (*a, e, i, o, u*):
an onion, **an e**gg

some / any

We use *some / any* with plural and uncountable nouns. We use *some / any* when we do not need to say the exact amount.
We use *some* in positive sentences:
*I'd like **some** potatoes.*
We use *any* in negative sentences and questions:
*We haven't got **any** potatoes.*
*Have you got **any** potatoes?*

▶ 2.9

Countable	singular	***a / an*** *I've got **a lemon**.* *I don't need **an onion**.*
	plural	***some / any*** *We'd like **some grapes**.* *We don't want **any potatoes**.*
Uncountable		***some / any*** *They've got **some pasta**.* *Do you want **any cheese**?*

These common nouns are uncountable:

money music hair furniture fruit water cheese *butter bread rice meat chicken* = meat *fish* = meat

---

4B Quantifiers: *much, many, a lot of*

How much? / How many?

We use *How much? / How many?* to ask about quantities.
▶ 2.15
We use *How many?* with countable nouns:
How many eggs *have we got?*
We use *How much?* with uncountable nouns:
How much milk *have we got?*
When we ask about a price, we can just ask *How much?*:
How much *does it cost?*

Large and small quantities

▶ 2.16

	Countable	Uncountable
Large quantity	*a lot of* *I buy **a lot of** grapes.*	*a lot of* *I cook **a lot of** pasta.*
Medium quantity	*quite a lot of* *I eat **quite a lot of** grapes.*	*quite a lot of* *I eat **quite a lot of** pasta.*
Small quantity	*a few* *I eat **a few** grapes every evening.*	*a little* *I've got **a little** pasta.*
	not many *We haven**'t** got **many** grapes.*	*not much* *I haven**'t** got **much** pasta.*
One	*a/an* *Would you like **a grape**?*	–
Zero quantity	*not any* *We haven**'t** got **any** grapes.*	*not any* *I haven**'t** got **any** pasta.*

a lot of / much / many

We use *a lot of / much / many* to talk about large quantities.
We use *a lot of* in positive sentences:
*I need **a lot of** potatoes.*
We often use *much / many* in negative sentences and questions:
*We haven't got **many** potatoes.*
*I don't eat **much** chocolate.*
*Have you got **many** potatoes?*
*Do you eat **much** chocolate?*

> 💡 **Tip**
> Only use *a lot of* before a noun (e.g. *chocolate*) or a pronoun (e.g. *it*). Use *a lot* at the end of a sentence.
> *I eat **a lot of chocolate**.*
> *I eat **a lot of it**.*
> *I eat **a lot**.* (NOT ~~I eat a lot of.~~)

I don't eat **much** chocolate — just **a little** after every meal.

4A Countable and uncountable nouns: a / an, some / any

a Are these things countable (C) or uncountable (U)?

1 bread ___U___
2 carrot _____
3 cheese _____
4 chocolate _____
5 fruit _____

6 furniture _____
7 lemon _____
8 money _____
9 egg _____
10 meat _____

b Complete the conversation between a customer and a shop assistant with *a*, *an*, *some* or *any*.

CUSTOMER Hello, have you got ¹___any___ fruit?
ASSISTANT Yes, of course. This is ²_____ shop and I sell fruit.
CUSTOMER Oh good. I'd like ³_____ grapes, please.
ASSISTANT Ah, sorry, we haven't got ⁴_____ grapes.
CUSTOMER Really? OK, I'd like ⁵_____ orange.
ASSISTANT Just one?
CUSTOMER Yes, please, and ⁶_____ lemon.
ASSISTANT Er … no, sorry, we haven't got ⁷_____ lemons. But we've got ⁸_____ lovely bananas.
CUSTOMER But I don't want ⁹_____ bananas. Well, that's all then, thank you.
ASSISTANT OK, so one orange. That's 15p, please.
CUSTOMER Oh, no! Sorry, I haven't got ¹⁰_____ money.

c Correct one mistake in each sentence.

1 I haven't got some tomatoes.
_____I haven't got any tomatoes._____

2 He hasn't got furnitures.
_____

3 Have you got any moneys?
_____

4 I'd like a onion and a carrot, please.
_____

5 We need a cheese.
_____

6 I don't want some meat.
_____

7 She's got long hairs.
_____

8 Do you want any apple?
_____

d ▶ Now go back to p.41

4B Quantifiers: much, many, a lot of

a Complete the sentences about the pictures.

1 We've got ___a lot of___ apples.

2 We've got a _____ lemons.

3 We've only got a _____ milk.

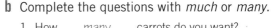

4 We haven't got _____ butter.

5 We've got quite _____ pasta.

6 That's _____ sugar!

b Complete the questions with *much* or *many*.

1 How ___many___ carrots do you want?
2 How _____ money has she got?
3 How _____ does that car cost?
4 How _____ tomatoes do you want?
5 How _____ cheese do we need?
6 How _____ glasses have you got?
7 How _____ do postcards cost?
8 How _____ salt do you eat?

c <u>Underline</u> the correct answers.

1 I don't eat *many* / *much* chocolate.
2 How *many* / *much* butter do we need?
3 How *many* / *much* onions do you want?
4 I just need *a few* / *a little* salt.
5 She hasn't got *many* / *much* money.
6 He eats quite *a lot of* / *a lot* vegetables.
7 Do you drink *many* / *much* coffee?
8 We have *a few* / *a little* good restaurants in my town.

d ▶ Now go back to p.43

5A *there is / there are*

We use *there is / there are* to say that something exists in a place.

We often use *there is / there are* with *a / an*, *some* and *any*.

We use *some* and *any* with uncountable nouns and plural nouns.

We use *some* in positive sentences and *any* in negative sentences and questions.

▶ 2.28

	+		−	
Singular	***There's***	*a river.*	***There isn't***	*a theatre.*
Plural	***There are***	*some restaurants.*	***There aren't***	*any cafés.*

	Yes/No questions		Short answers	
Singular	***Is there***	*a square?*	*Yes,*	***there is****.*
			No,	***there isn't****.*
Plural	***Are there***	*any shops?*	*Yes,*	***there are****.*
			No,	***there aren't****.*

	Wh- questions		
Countable	*How **many***	*people*	***are there****?*
Uncountable	*How **much***	*pasta*	***is there****?*

> 💬 **Tip**
>
> Use *There's* (NOT ~~There are~~) to talk about a list of singular things:
> ***There's a*** *book, a phone and a laptop on the table.*

5B Possessive pronouns and possessive *'s*

Possessive pronouns

Subject	Possessive adjective	Possessive pronoun ▶ 2.34
I	*my* *Those are my shoes.*	*mine* *Those are **mine**.*
you	*your* *These are your pens.*	*yours* *These are **yours**.*
he	*his* *This is his shirt.*	*his* *This is **his**.*
she	*her* *That's her bag.*	*hers* *That's **hers**.*
it	*its* *Those are its wheels.*	—
we	*our* *They're our cats.*	*ours* *They're **ours**.*
they	*their* *They aren't their cats.*	*theirs* *They aren't **theirs**.*

▶ 2.35

We use possessive adjectives (e.g. *my*, *your*) before nouns:
*Is this **your** hat?*

We use possessive pronouns (e.g. *mine*, *yours*) in the place of a possessive adjective and a noun:
*Is this **yours**?*

We can ask about possession with the word *whose*:
Whose *hat is this? / **Whose** is this hat?*

> 💬 **Tip**
>
> - Be careful with *it's* (= *it is / it has*) and *its* (= possessive adjective).
> - Be careful with *who's* (= *who is / who has*) and *whose*.

Possessive *'s* ▶ 2.36

We add an apostrophe (') + *s* to a singular noun or a name to show possession:
*My sister has a car. It's my sister**'s** car.*

If a plural noun already ends in *-s*, we just add an apostrophe after the *-s*:
*My grandparents have a house. It's my grandparents**'** house.*

Other uses of *'s*

- We also use *'s* as a contraction of *is* or *has*:
  *He**'s** (= He is) very lucky. He**'s** (= He has) got four brothers.*

5A *there is / there are*

a Write sentences about a small town using the information in the table.

airport	✗
cafés	six
stadium	✗
shops	a lot

parks	four
schools	not many
river	✓ (one)
bridges	two

1 _____ There isn't an airport. _____
2 _____
3 _____
4 _____
5 _____
6 _____
7 _____
8 _____

b Write questions and short answers about the town, using the information in the table.

1 _____ Is there an airport in the town? No, there isn't. _____
2 _____ How many _____
3 _____
4 _____
5 _____ How many _____
6 _____
7 _____
8 _____ How many _____

c Write sentences about the things in the tables of information about the town in a that are true for your town.

1 _____ There isn't an airport. _____
2 _____ There aren't a lot of cafés. _____
3 _____
4 _____
5 _____
6 _____
7 _____
8 _____

d ▶ Now go back to p.51

5B Possessive pronouns and possessive *'s*

a Complete the sentences with the correct possessive pronouns.

1 It's my pen.

It's ____mine____.

2 They're her shoes.

They're _____.

3 It's their ball.

It's _____.

4 It's his hat.

It's _____.

5 It's our car.

It's _____.

6 He's your dog.

He's _____.

b <u>Underline</u> the correct words.

1 Excuse me. Is this *your* / <u>*yours*</u>?
2 *Its* / *It's* a very interesting book.
3 *Our* / *Ours* apartment is quite small.
4 That's my *parent's* / *parents'* room.
5 Don't touch that lamp – it's *my* / *mine*!
6 *Whose* / *Who's* book is this?
7 *Anita's* / *Anitas* house is in the city centre.
8 What colour are *your* / *yours* curtains?

c Underline the *'s* in the conversation. Write *P* (possessive) or *C* (contraction). Then write the full form of the contractions.

ROSIE Hello. I think I know you. You're in my brother<u>'s</u> [P] class at school.

NADIA What's your brother's name?

ROSIE Paul.

NADIA Paul? Yeah, he's in my class. So, you're Paul's sister.

ROSIE That's right. Well, in fact, Paul's got two sisters.

NADIA Ah, yes, I remember. My name's Nadia. What's your name?

ROSIE I'm Rosie.

NADIA Hi, Rosie. It's nice to meet you.

d ▶ Now go back to p.53

6A Past simple: *be*

We use *was / were* to talk about the past.
was / were are the past forms of *am / is / are*.
We often use past time expressions with *was / were*, e.g. *yesterday*, *last year*, *in 2012*.

▶ 2.49

	+		–	
I / he / she / it	I **was**	at home yesterday.	He **wasn't**	at home yesterday.
you / we / they	They **were**	at home yesterday.	We **weren't**	at home yesterday.

	Yes/No questions		Short answers	
I / he / she / it	**Was** she	at home yesterday?	Yes, No,	she **was**. she **wasn't**.
you / we / they	**Were** you	at home yesterday?	Yes, No,	we **were**. we **weren't**.

	Wh- questions		
I / he / she / it	Where	**was** he	yesterday?
you / we / they	Where	**were** you	yesterday?

We can also use *there was / there were*:
There was a computer on the table.
There were some chairs in the garden.

My grandparents were at school together, but they weren't friends.

6B Past simple: positive

Past simple

We use the past simple to describe completed actions in the past.
We often use past time expressions with the past simple, e.g. *yesterday, last week, when I was a child*.

▶ 2.57

I **arrived** last night.
I **bought** a new car last week.
I often **visited** my grandmother when I was a child.
I sometimes **went** to the theatre when I lived in London.
I **liked** sweets a lot when I was young.
I **had** a lot of friends at school.

Regular and irregular verbs

Past simple verbs are the same for all persons: *I / you / we / they / he / she / it.*
I **worked**. **She** worked. **They** worked.
You went. **He** went. **We** went.
Some verbs are regular. We add *-ed* to make the past simple:
work → work**ed**   help → help**ed**
Some verbs are irregular and you will need to learn their past forms:
meet → **met**   buy → **bought**
There is a list of irregular verbs on p.176.

SPELLING: regular verbs

most verbs → add *-ed*	start → start**ed** watch → watch**ed**
verb ends in *-e* → add *-d*	live → live**d** die → die**d**
verb ends in consonant + *-y* → change *-y* to *-i* then add *-ed*	try → tr**ied** cry → cr**ied**
verb ends in one vowel (*a, e, i, o, u*) and one consonant (*g, n, t*, etc.) → double the consonant and add *-ed*	stop → stop**ped** plan → plan**ned**
never double the consonants *w, x* or *y* → add *-ed* only	show → show**ed** play → play**ed**

My parents bought me a guitar when I was 12. I loved it.

6A Past simple: *be*

a <u>Underline</u> the correct word.

1 I <u>was</u> / *were* on holiday last week.
2 Where *were* / *was* you born?
3 *Wasn't* / *Weren't* there any eggs in the fridge?
4 I *wasn't* / *weren't* at college yesterday; I was ill in bed.
5 There *were* / *was* a lot of people in the queue.
6 Why *was* / *were* your friends late?
7 *Was* / *Were* there a laptop on the desk?
8 When *was* / *were* your children born?

b Rewrite the sentences so that they are about the past.

1 My father's a manager. _____My father was a manager._____
2 They aren't friends. _____
3 **A** Is your grandfather rich? **B** No, he isn't.
    _____
4 We're at school together. _____
5 It's a beautiful day. _____
6 My teacher's name's Miss Smith. _____
7 She isn't at home. _____
8 There are 20 people in my class. _____
9 I'm not tired. _____
10 **A** Are you happy? **B** Yes, I am. _____

c Put the words in the correct order to make questions.

1 born / you / where / were ?
    _____Where were you born?_____
2 good / film / was / the ?
    _____
3 a lot of / there / party / were / people / at / the ?
    _____
4 grandmother's / was / name / your / what ?
    _____
5 school / at / were / yesterday / you ?
    _____
6 was / your hotel / a pool / at / there ?
    _____

d ▶ Now go back to p.61

6B Past simple: positive

a Write *R* (regular) or *I* (irregular) after each verb. Use the list on page 176 to help you.

1	arrive	11	have
2	become	12	like
3	buy	13	plan
4	come	14	play
5	cook	15	spend
6	decide	16	tell
7	enjoy	17	try
8	find	18	win
9	finish	19	work
10	go	20	write

b Write the past simple forms of the regular verbs in **a**. Be careful with spelling!

1 _____arrived_____
2 _____
3 _____
4 _____
5 _____
6 _____
7 _____
8 _____
9 _____
10 _____

c Complete the sentences with the past simple forms of the verbs in brackets.

1 When I was a child, we _____had_____ an old computer. (have)
2 They _____ good friends in 1976 and they stayed friends for many years. (become)
3 I lost my phone for about a week, but then I _____ it under my bed! (find)
4 She _____ me an amazing story about Steve Jobs. (tell)
5 It was a very difficult match, but in the end we _____. (win)
6 My uncle was a famous writer. He _____ books for children. (write)
7 I _____ my first computer in 1995. (buy)
8 I _____ for a walk yesterday. (go)
9 When I _____ home, I checked my emails. (get)

d Correct one spelling mistake in each sentence.

1 He <u>plaied</u> volleyball when he was young.
    _____played_____
2 I buyed a new bed yesterday and it cost £450.
    _____
3 I really liket the concert on Saturday.
    _____
4 She eated a piece of cake with her coffee.
    _____
5 They gotten an email about the new course.
    _____
6 We dicide to stay at home last weekend.
    _____

e ▶ Now go back to p.63

7A Past simple: negatives and questions

 2.75

		+		−	
I / he / she / it / you / we / they	I	*enjoyed* the trip.	He **didn't**	*enjoy* the trip.	
	I	**took** the train.	He **didn't**	*take* the train.	

	Yes/No questions		Short answers	
I / he / she / it / you / we / they	**Did** they	*enjoy* the trip?	Yes,	they **did**.
	Did they	**take** the train?	No,	they **didn't**.

	Wh- questions		
I / he / she / it / you / we / they	*Where*	**did** you	*go*?

💬 **Tip**

Remember, don't change the main verb in questions and negatives:
I didn't **enjoy** it. (NOT ~~I didn't enjoyed it.~~)
Did you **enjoy** it? (NOT ~~Did you enjoyed it?~~)

7B love / like / don't mind / hate + verb + -ing

 2.81

😊😊😊	I **love** driving!
😊	I **like** driving.
😐	I **don't mind** driving.
🙁	I **don't like** driving.
🙁🙁🙁	I **hate** driving!

After *like*, *love*, *hate* and *don't mind*, we can use a noun or a verb + *-ing*.
I love **my car**.   I love **driving**.

SPELLING: verb + *-ing*

most verbs → add *-ing*	*watch* → *watching* *go* → *going* *see* → *seeing*
verb ends in consonant (*g*, *n*, *t*, etc.) + *-e* → take away the *-e* then add *-ing*	*drive* → *driving* *use* → *using*
verb ends in one vowel (*a*, *e*, *i*, *o*, *u*) and one consonant (*g*, *n*, *t*, etc.) → double the consonant and add *-ing*	*run* → *running* *sit* → *sitting*
never double the consonants *w*, *x* or *y* → add *-ing* only	*know* → *knowing* *play* → *playing*

I don't mind going by metro. I like being with other people.

7A Past simple: negative and questions

a Complete the sentences with the past simple forms of the verbs in brackets.

1 We _didn't travel_ (not travel) by plane to Denmark – we took trains.
2 I _____ (not take) an umbrella today, so I got wet.
3 Marion and Neil _____ (not want) a big wedding.
4 He _____ (not answer) the telephone, because he was busy.
5 When I was a child, I _____ (not like) chocolate.
6 We _____ (not see) any wild animals when we went to Egypt.
7 She _____ (not get) back home on time, so I was really worried.

b Change the positive past simple verbs to negative verb forms in these sentences.

1 We went by tram.
_____We didn't go by tram._____
2 They travelled along the Silk Road.
_____
3 We had a good time.
_____
4 The tickets cost a lot of money.
_____
5 She visited China.
_____
6 They stayed in hotels.
_____
7 The people spoke English, so I understood them.
_____

c Complete the questions and answers.

1 **A** ___Did___ you ___go___ (go) through Central Asia?
  B Yes, I ___did___.
2 **A** _____ you _____ (start) your journey in Turkey?
  B No, I _____.
3 **A** _____ he _____ (enjoy) his trip?
  B No, he _____.
4 **A** _____ they _____ (travel) by train?
  B Yes, they _____.

d Write the questions to complete the conversation.

A 1_____ _How did you travel?_____
(how)
B We travelled by train.
A 2_____
(how much)
B The journey cost £750.
A 3_____
(how many)
B We visited five countries.
A 4_____
(where)
B We stayed in hotels.
A 5_____
(when)
B We arrived home yesterday.

e ▶ Now go back to p.71

7B love / like / hate + verb + -ing

a Write the -ing form of the verbs.

1 wait ___waiting___
2 drive _____
3 walk _____
4 get _____
5 fly _____
6 relax _____
7 be _____
8 have _____
9 speak _____
10 sit _____
11 stand _____
12 stay _____
13 run _____
14 try _____
15 use _____
16 agree _____

b Write sentences about Jamie and Lisa.

	eat in restaurants	cook	get pizza	try new food
Jamie	☹	☺	☺	☺☺☺
Lisa	☺	☹☹☹	☹	☺☺☺

1 Jamie ___doesn't like eating in restaurants.___
  He _____
  _____
  _____
2 Lisa _____
  She _____
  _____
  _____

c Circle the correct symbols and write sentences that are true for you.

1 wait for buses
  ☺☺☺ / ☺ / ☺ / ☹ / ☹☹☹
  ___I don't mind waiting for buses.___
2 sit in traffic
  ☺☺☺ / ☺ / ☺ / ☹ / ☹☹☹
  _____
3 play computer games
  ☺☺☺ / ☺ / ☺ / ☹ / ☹☹☹
  _____
4 fly in aeroplanes
  ☺☺☺ / ☺ / ☺ / ☹ / ☹☹☹
  _____
5 cook the dinner
  ☺☺☺ / ☺ / ☺ / ☹ / ☹☹☹
  _____

d ▶ Now go back to p.73

8A can / can't, could / couldn't for ability

We use *can* / *can't* to talk about present abilities:
I **can** read English, but I **can't** speak it.
We use *could* / *couldn't* to talk about past abilities:
When I was young, I **could** dance, but I **couldn't** sing.

I / he / she / it / you / we / they		+		–	
	Present	*I* **can**	**run** *fast.*	*They* **can't**	**run** *fast.*
	Past	*He* **could**	**run** *fast.*	*We* **couldn't**	**run** *fast.*

I / he / she / it / you / we / they		**Yes/No questions**		**Short answers**	
	Present	**Can** *you*	**run** *fast?*	*Yes,* *No,*	*I* **can.** *I* **can't.**
	Past	**Could** *you*	**run** *fast?*	*Yes,* *No,*	*I* **could.** *I* **couldn't.**

> **Tip**
> There is no *-s* on *can* for
> *he* / *she* / *it*:
> *He* **can** *swim.*
> (NOT *He* **cans** *swim.*)

> **Tip**
> The full form of *can't* is *cannot.*

8B have to / don't have to

We use *have to* + infinitive to talk about things we need to do:
I **have to drink** a lot of water when I go running.
She **has to get up** at six every day.
We can use *have to* to talk about rules:
We **have to take off** our shoes before we go inside.
We **have to get to** school by nine.
don't have to means we don't need to do something.
I **don't have to pay** for my lunch at work. (My lunch is free.)
Our teacher **doesn't have to wear** a suit. (There is no rule.)

> **Tip**
> Sometimes, *you* means *everybody* or *people* generally.
> **A** Do **you** have to be fit to run a marathon?
> (= Do **people** have to be fit …?)
> **B** Yes, **you** do. (NOT *Yes, I do.*)

I / you / we / they		+		–	
I / you / we / they	*I*	**have to** **work** *hard.*	*I* **don't**	**have to** **work** *hard.*	
he / she / it	*She*	**has to work** *hard.*	*He* **doesn't**	**have to** **work** *hard.*	

I / you / we / they		**Yes/No questions**		**Short answers**	
I / you / we / they	**Do** *you*	**have to** **work** *hard?*	*Yes,* *No,*	*I* **do.** *I* **don't.**
he / she / it	**Does** *he*	**have to** **work** *hard?*	*Yes,* *No,*	*he* **does.** *he* **doesn't.**

If you're tired, you don't **have to** run anymore. You can walk.

8A can / can't, could / couldn't for ability

a Complete the sentences with *can / can't, could / couldn't*.

1 I ____can____ play the guitar. I want to learn the drums next.

2 I _____ drive last year but I passed my test six weeks ago!

3 She _____ cook really well. Her food is always great.

4 He isn't on the football team, because he _____ run very fast.

5 When I was at school, I _____ do maths. But now I'm much better.

6 My husband _____ speak French, Spanish and Portuguese. It's useful when we travel!

7 I _____ climb trees when I was a child but I'm too old now.

b Write sentences about what Rob *could / couldn't* do in the past and what he *can / can't* do now.

when he was a boy	now
swim 1,000 metres ✗	swim 1,000 metres ✓
cook a meal ✗	cook a meal ✓
ride a bike ✓	ride a bike ✗
run 25 km ✗	run 25 km ✓
speak Spanish ✗	speak Spanish ✓

1 _Rob couldn't swim 1,000 metres when he was a boy. He can swim 1,000 metres now._

2 _____

3 _____

4 _____

5 _____

c Find and correct a mistake in each sentence.

1 I don't can play the guitar. _I can't play the guitar._

2 She cans speak four languages. _____

3 How fast you can swim? _____

4 I could ran very fast when I was a child. _____

5 I didn't could understand what he said. _____

6 **A** Does he can cook? **B** Yes, he can. _____

7 **A** Could he walk before his accident? **B** Yes, he did. _____

d ▶ Now go back to p.81

8B have to / don't have to

a Match questions 1–8 with answers a–h.

1 [d] Do we have to take our shoes off?
2 [ ] How much do you have to pay for a ticket?
3 [ ] Do you have to be a member to use the swimming pool?
4 [ ] Does she have to walk home?
5 [ ] Do you have to walk the dog every day?
6 [ ] Do you have to help in the kitchen?
7 [ ] I want to stay at home. Why do I have to go for a walk?
8 [ ] What time do you have to leave for work?

a Because you have to stay fit.
b No, I don't. My parents do everything.
c Yes, I do. Every day.
d No, you don't. You can keep them on.
e At 8 o'clock.
f Nothing. It's free.
g No, you don't. It's open to everybody.
h No, she doesn't. She's got enough money for a taxi.

b Complete the sentences with the correct form of *have to* or a short answer.

1 In a kitchen, _____you have to work_____ (you / work) very carefully.

2 **A** _____ (you / buy) any new clothes for your new job?
   B Yes, _____.

3 _____ (I / not / pay) rent at the moment, because I'm staying with my parents.

4 I usually wear jeans and a T-shirt, but at work _____ (I / wear) a suit.

5 **A** What _____ (we / do) before we start the game?
   B I don't know. Read the instructions.

6 **A** Do _____ (I / take) them a present?
   B No, _____. But it's a nice idea.

7 My son would like to see this film. How old _____ (he / be)?

8 To get fit, I think _____ (you / walk) for at least half an hour a day.

c Put a tick (✓) or a cross (✗) next to each activity and write sentences that are true for you.

1 I / study for three hours every evening ✓
   I have to study for three hours every evening.

2 I / cook dinner every night
   _____

3 I / do a lot of homework
   _____

4 My teacher / help me with grammar
   _____

5 My best friend / sometimes / wait for me
   _____

6 My father / go to work at 8 o'clock
   _____

d ▶ Now go back to p.83

9A Present continuous

We use the present continuous to describe an activity now or at the moment of speaking. The activity started in the past and will finish in the future.

3.24

	+		−	
I	*I'm*	*waiting.*	*I'm not*	*waiting.*
you / we / they	*You're*	*waiting.*	*We aren't*	*waiting.*
he / she / it	*He's*	*waiting.*	*It isn't*	*waiting.*

Full forms: *am waiting, are waiting, is waiting; am not waiting, are not waiting, is not waiting*

	Yes/No questions		Short answers	
I	*Am I*	*waiting?*	*Yes,* *No,*	*I am.* *I'm not.*
you / we / they	*Are you*	*waiting?*	*Yes,* *No,*	*you are.* *you aren't.*
he / she / it	*Is he*	*waiting?*	*Yes,* *No,*	*he is.* *he isn't.*

	Wh- questions		
I	*Why*	*am I*	*waiting?*
you / we / they	*Where*	*are you*	*waiting?*
he / she / it	*Who*	*is he*	*waiting for?*

talk to you

Past Now Future

9B Present simple or present continuous

The present simple is about things that are normally true. We use it to describe habits, routines, facts and feelings:
*I usually **wear** trousers.   He **loves** cars.*

The present continuous is about now. We use it to describe what is happening now / today / this week etc.:
*Today I'**m wearing** a dress.   I'**m studying** hard this week.*

There are some verbs which we don't usually use in the present continuous:

like   love   hate   not mind   want   know
need   understand   remember   forget

*I **want** to go home. (NOT ~~I'm wanting to go home.~~)*

> 💬 **Tip**
>
> We don't use *have* for possession in continuous sentences:
> *I **have** a new car. NOT ~~I'm having a new car.~~*
> *She **has** red hair. NOT ~~She's having red hair.~~*
> We can use *have* for actions in continuous sentences:
> *We'**re having** dinner right now.*
> *I'**m not having** fun.*

9A Present continuous

a Write about the pictures using the Present continuous.

he / drink / coffee
1 *He's drinking coffee.*

I / do / a grammar exercise
4 _____

they / talk
2 _____

she / not / wear / shoes
5 _____

he / not / ride / a horse
3 _____

they / play / tennis
6 _____

b Complete the conversations using the present continuous and the verbs in brackets. Use short answers where possible.

1 **A** Who ____are____ you __waiting__ (wait) for?
  B I ____'m____ ____waiting____ (wait) for you.
2 **A** Why _____ she _____ (smile)?
  B I don't know. Maybe she _____ _____ (feel) happy.
3 **A** _____ you _____ (sleep)?
  B No, I _____ _____.
4 **A** Where _____ they _____ (stand)?
  B They _____ _____ (not stand). They're sitting at a table.
5 **A** _____ your brother _____ (play) football today?
  B No, he _____. He _____ _____ (play) basketball.

c Complete the telephone conversation using the present continuous forms of the words in brackets.

A What [1] __are you doing__ (you / do)?
B [2] _____ (I / shop) in the city centre. Where are you?
A [3] _____ (We / look) for a parking space. [4] _____ (we / drive) past the museum.
B Really? [5] _____ (I / stand) outside the museum right now!
A I can't see you. What [6] _____ (you / wear)?
B [7] _____ (I / wear) a red t-shirt.
A OK I can see you now, but [8] _____ (we / not stop). The traffic is too busy!

d ▶ Now go back to p.91

9B Present simple or present continuous

a Choose the correct words to complete the sentences.

1 She *usually* / *today* wears black clothes.
2 She's wearing bright colours *usually* / *today*.
3 They *never* / *are not* visit museums. They don't like them.
4 My parents aren't at home. They are visiting a museum *sometimes* / *this morning*.
5 Wow! Look! Tom *dances* / *'s dancing*! He doesn't usually dance.
6 I *enjoy* / *'m enjoying* the party. Thanks for inviting me!
7 I always watch the football *at weekends* / *at the moment*.
8 We don't go out *now* / *often*.

b Complete the conversations with the correct form of the verbs in brackets. Use the present simple or the present continuous.

1 **A** What __are you doing__ (you / do)?
  B _____ (we / get) ready to go out. Would you like to come with us?
  A Not really, no. _____ (I / watch) a film. It's really good.
2 **A** What's that noise?
  B Sorry, it's my friend Harry. _____ (he / sing).
  A Wow! He's quite good.
  B Yes, _____ (he / sing) in a band every weekend. _____ (They / often / play) concerts.
3 **A** _____ (you / play) that computer game again?
  B No, _____. _____ (I / try) to sell my guitar on the Internet.
  A Really? Why _____ (you / do) that?

c Choose the options that are true for you and write sentences.

1 wear bright colours usually ✓ ✗ now ✓ ✗
  I usually wear bright colours.
  I'm not wearing bright colours now.
2 feel happy usually ✓ ✗ now ✓ ✗
  _____
  _____
3 listen to music when I study usually ✓ ✗ now ✓ ✗
  _____
  _____
4 wear a watch usually ✓ ✗ now ✓ ✗
  _____
  _____
5 use a computer when I study usually ✓ ✗ now ✓ ✗
  _____
  _____
6 study in my bedroom usually ✓ ✗ now ✓ ✗
  _____
  _____

d ▶ Now go back to p.93

10A Comparative adjectives

 3.38

We use a comparative adjective + *than* to compare two or more things, people, etc.

My new smartphone is **bigger than** *my old one.*   *My phone is* **more expensive than** *my sister's.*
My tablet is **heavier than** *my phone.*   *Your laptop is* **better than** *mine.*

One syllable		End in -y		Two or more syllables	
adjective + *-er*		adjective – *-y* + *-ier*		*more* + adjective	
old	→ old**er**	heav**y**	→ heav**ier**	useful	→ **more** useful
cheap	→ cheap**er**	eas**y**	→ eas**ier**	expensive	→ **more** expensive
light	→ light**er**	pret**ty**	→ prett**ier**	difficult	→ **more** difficult

> 💬 **Tip**
>
> *good* and *bad* are irregular:
> *good* → *better*   *bad* → *worse*

SPELLING: adjective + -er

most adjectives → add -er	short → short**er** clean → clean**er**
adjective ends in *-e* → add *-r*	larg**e** → large**r** nic**e** → nice**r**
adjective ends in consonant + *-y* → change *-y* to *-i* then add *-er*	dry → dr**ier** easy → eas**ier**
adjective ends in one vowel (*a, e, i, o, u*) and one consonant (*g, n, t*, etc.) → double the consonant and add *-er*	hot → hot**ter** thin → thin**ner**

Life is **easier** *with new technology.*

10B Superlative adjectives

We use the superlative form of adjectives to talk about extremes.
We usually use *the* before superlatives.

 3.43

> 💬 **Tip**
>
> We don't use *the* with words like *my, your,* etc.
> She's my best friend (NOT ~~She's my the best friend.~~)

The most useful *language is English.*
The easiest *language is Spanish.*
What's **the hardest** *language in the world?*
The best *language practice is speaking.*

One syllable		End in -y		Two or more syllables	
the + adjective + *-est*		*the* + adjective – *-y* + *-iest*		*the most* + adjective	
old	→ **the** old**est**	heavy	→ **the** heav**iest**	useful	→ **the most** useful
cheap	→ **the** cheap**est**	easy	→ **the** eas**iest**	expensive	→ **the most** expensive
light	→ **the** light**est**	pretty	→ **the** prett**iest**	difficult	→ **the most** difficult

> 💬 **Tip**
>
> *good* and *bad* are irregular:
> *good* → *the best*   *bad* → *the worst*

SPELLING: adjective + -est

most adjectives → add -est	short → short**est** clean → clean**est**
adjective ends in *-e* → add *-st*	larg**e** → large**st** nic**e** → nice**st**
adjective ends in consonant + *-y* → change *-y* to *-i* then add *-est*	dry → dr**iest** easy → eas**iest**
adjective ends in one vowel (*a, e, i, o, u*) and one consonant (*g, n, t*, etc.) → double the consonant and add *-est*	hot → hot**test** thin → thin**nest**

BETTER   BEST   GOOD

10A Comparative adjectives

a Write the comparative form of the adjectives.

1 angry _____angrier_____
2 bad _____
3 clean _____
4 cold _____
5 comfortable _____
6 crowded _____
7 fast _____
8 fat _____
9 good _____
10 interesting _____
11 modern _____
12 noisy _____
13 old _____
14 popular _____
15 sad _____
16 strange _____
17 strong _____
18 thin _____
19 wet _____
20 wide _____

b Write sentences using the present simple of *be* and comparative adjectives.

1 my new phone / cheap / my old phone
_____My new phone is cheaper than my old phone._____
2 the film / interesting / the book
_____
3 her children / noisy / my children
_____
4 she / a good cook / my dad
_____
5 Dubai / modern / Dublin
_____
6 this hotel / comfortable / the last hotel
_____
7 my friends / fit / me
_____

c Correct one mistake in each sentence.

1 She quicker than me. She always finishes first.
_____
2 The book is good than the film. _____
3 My marks are always worser than yours.
_____
4 This dress is prettyer than that one.
_____
5 The English weather is weter than the weather in Spain. _____
6 Their family is more big than mine.
_____
7 My new teacher is most interesting than my old teacher. _____
8 Is your Internet faster mine? _____

d ▶ Now go back to p.101

10B Superlative adjectives

a Write the superlative form of the adjectives.

1 tidy _____the tidiest_____
2 fit _____
3 funny _____
4 dry _____
5 pretty _____
6 bad _____
7 friendly _____
8 good _____
9 big _____
10 nice _____
11 safe _____
12 exciting _____
13 tiring _____
14 hot _____

English. It's not the most beautiful language in the world. Some people say it isn't the easiest. But when you are lost, it's probably the most useful.

b Complete the sentences using the superlative form of the adjectives in brackets.

1 One of _____the longest_____ (long) words in English is *floccinaucinihilipilification*. But I don't know what it means!
2 _____ (short) words in English are *a* and *I*.
3 In spoken English, one of _____ (popular) words is I – because we think we're _____ (interesting) topic in the world!
4 _____ (useful) noun in English is *time*. We use it all the time!
5 _____ (fast) way to learn a language is to go and live in a different country.
6 Some people think _____ (important) thing for language learners is speaking.
7 I think _____ (good) way to improve your English is to learn lots of words – I try to learn ten new words every day.
8 When you're reading in English, _____ (bad) thing you can do is check all the words in a dictionary. It takes too long and it's not much fun!

c ▶ Now go back to p.102

11A Present perfect

see the film

my life

born   Now

We use the present perfect to talk about past actions in a time period which starts in the past and continues now, for example: today, this week, this year, your lifetime.

I've seen that film four times (in my life).
I haven't had a coffee today.
Have you been to the gym this week?

We make the present perfect from the verb *have* + the past participle of the main verb.

For regular verbs, the past participle is the same as the past form:
I walked to work yesterday.
I've walked to work three times this week.

For irregular verbs, the past participle is usually different. You have to learn the different forms. (See page 176 for a list of irregular verbs.)
I drove to work yesterday.
I've driven to work three times this week.

 3.57

	+	
I / you / we / they	*I've*	*seen the film 400 times.*
he / she / it	*He's*	*seen the film 400 times.*

	–	
I / you / we / they	*They **haven't***	*seen the film.*
he / she / it	*She **hasn't***	*seen the film.*

We often use the present perfect to talk about experiences:
I've seen the film once. (in my lifetime)
She's met him three times. (in her lifetime)
When we ask a question about experiences, we often use the word *ever*.
Have you ever read this book? = Have you read this book in your lifetime?
We use never with the present perfect to say there is no experience.
I've never read her book. = I haven't read her book in my lifetime.

> **Tip**
>
> The past participle of *go* is *gone*. But we often use the past participle of *be* (*been*) instead of *gone*.
> *I've been to France. (= I'm not there now.)*
> *Claire's gone to Scotland. (= she's still there now.)*

Yes/No questions			**Short answers**	
I / you / we / they	***Have** you*	*seen the film?*	Yes, No,	*I **have**. I **haven't**.*
he / she / it	***Has** he*	*seen the film?*	Yes, No,	*he **has**. he **hasn't**.*

11B Present perfect or past simple

We use the present perfect to talk about the past experiences in our life, but we don't say when exactly.
I've been to Buenos Aires. (We don't know when.)

We use the Past simple to say when something happened (e.g. *last year, yesterday, in 2012*).
I went to the theatre last week. (NOT ~~I've been to the theatre last week.~~)

We often start a conversation by asking about or describing an event using the present perfect, and then change to the past simple to ask about or describe the details of the event.

 3.64

A *Have you ever been to Argentina?*
B *Yes, I have. I've been there three times.*
} Focus: my / your life
Tense: present perfect

A *I've been there too, I went there last year.*
B *Really? Which cities did you visit?*
} Focus: a visit last year
Tense: past simple

go to Argentina

last year   Now

I've been to Buenos Aires.

11A Present perfect

a Write the irregular past participles. Use the list on page 176 to help you.

1 see _____seen_____   6 do _____
2 write _____   7 drive _____
3 swim _____   8 ride _____
4 have _____   9 run _____
5 bring _____   10 be _____

b Complete the sentences with the present perfect forms of the verbs in brackets.

1 I have _____read_____ (read) this book twice.
2 We _____ (visit) this museum three times this year.
3 He _____ (not borrow) my car today.
4 We _____ (never eat) at that restaurant.
5 I _____ (walk) down this street many times.
6 She _____ (play) for England in three Olympic Games.
7 They _____ (not do) the housework this week.
8 This country _____ (have) five big storms this winter.

c Complete the conversations with present perfect verb forms of the words in brackets.

1
A ____Have you ever seen____ (you / ever / see) Star Wars?
B Yes, _____. _____ (I / see) it many times. It's my favourite film.
A Really? _____ (I / never / see) it.
2
A _____ (you / ever / meet) a famous person?
B Yes, _____ (I / meet) Bill Gates.
A Wow! _____ (he / visit) Cambridge?
B Yes, he _____. _____ (he / be) here many times.

d ▶ Now go back to p.111

I've watched my favourite film 400 times.

11B Present perfect or past simple

a Underline the correct words.

1 *Have you been / Did you go* out last night?
2 *I've never seen / I never saw* an opera.
3 *We went / We've been* to a rock concert on Saturday.
4 *Have you ever danced / Did you ever dance* the tango?
5 She's a fantastic actress but *she never won / she's never won* an Oscar.
6 *We've visited / We visited* the theatre when we were in Buenos Aires last year.
7 I *didn't eat / 've never eaten* sheep's milk cheese in my life.
8 *Did he win / Has he won* the 100m at the 2012 Olympic Games?

b Match questions 1–8 with short answers a–h.

1 [g] Did she go out?
2 [ ] Have you ever been to Chile?
3 [ ] Was it a good concert?
4 [ ] Has she been in any bad films?
5 [ ] Were you tired when you got home?
6 [ ] Did they help you?
7 [ ] Have they ever visited Tokyo?
8 [ ] Did you have a good time?

a Yes, we were.
b Yes, we did.
c No, I haven't.
d No, they didn't.
e Yes, it was.
f No, they haven't.
g No, she didn't.
h Yes, she has.

c Complete the conversation using the correct present perfect or past simple form of the verbs in brackets.

A [1] ___Have you ever been___ (you / ever / go) to a jazz club?
B Yes, I [2] _____.
[3] _____ (I / go) to a few. My favourite is *Jazz Cellar*.
[4] _____ (I / go) there hundreds of times.
A Yes, I think [5] _____ (I / go) there too. [6] _____ (I / go) there last year.
B [7] _____ (you / like) it?
A Yes, I [8] _____.
[9] _____ (it / be) great. There [10] _____ (be) a brilliant singer – her name [11] _____ (be) Erica something.
B Erica Sousa. [12] _____ (I / see) her a few times. She's amazing. In fact, [13] _____ (she / play) a concert there last week.
A [14] _____ (you / go) to that concert?
B No, I [15] _____.
[16] _____ (I / want) to go but I had a meeting at work and [17] _____ (I / finish) late.

d ▶ Now go back to p.113

12A *going to*

We use *going to* when we have a plan for the future:

▶ 3.78

		+			−	
I	*I'm*	***going to travel*** the world next year.	*I'm not*	***going to work*** in an office.
you / we / they	*They're*	***going to travel*** the world next year.	*You aren't*	***going to work*** in an office.
he / she / it	*She's*	***going to travel*** the world next year.	*He isn't*	***going to work*** in an office.

		Yes/No questions		Short answers	
I	***Am*** *I*	***going to travel*** next year?	Yes, No,	*I* ***am***. *I'm* ***not***.
you / we / they	***Are*** *you*	***going to travel*** next year?	Yes, No,	*you* ***are***. *you* ***aren't***.
he / she / it	***Is*** *he*	***going to travel*** next year?	Yes, No,	*he* ***is***. *he* ***isn't***.

		Wh- questions		
I	*Who*	***am*** *I*	***going to travel*** with?
you / we / they	*Where*	***are*** *you*	***going to go***?
he / she / it	*What*	***'s*** *he*	***going to see***?

I'm not going to stay in this job much longer.
I'm going to travel around the world.

travel the world
Now ———————×————————→ Future

12B *should / shouldn't*

We use *should* to give advice.
You **should** *learn the local language.* (= It's a good idea.)

▶ 3.82

	+		−	
I / he / she / it / you / we / they	*I* ***should***	*go*.	*They* ***shouldn't***	*go*.

	Yes/No questions		Short answers	
I / he / she / it / you / we / they	***Should*** *she*	*go*?	Yes, No,	*she* ***should***. *she* ***shouldn't***.

	Wh- questions		
I / he / she / it / you / we / they	*When*	***should*** *we*	*go*?

> 🗨 **Tip**
>
> We use the infinitive without *to* after *should*.
> *You* **should take** *sun cream with you.*
> (NOT ~~You should to take~~ ….)

12A *going to*

a Match questions 1–8 with answers a–h.

1 [e] Where are you going to stay?
2 [ ] Are they going to visit us?
3 [ ] When are you going to clean your room?
4 [ ] Is he going to get a job?
5 [ ] Who are they going to meet?
6 [ ] Are you going to leave your job?
7 [ ] What are you going to take with you?
8 [ ] How long is he going to be away?

a Not much. Just a few clothes.
b No, he isn't. He's going to travel around the world first.
c Some of their friends.
d No, I'm not. I'm just going to take a long holiday.
e In a hotel.
f About six months.
g Tomorrow – I promise.
h No, they aren't. They don't have time.

b Complete the sentences using the correct form of *going to* and the verb in brackets.

1 I _____'m going to travel_____ (travel) to South America.
2 My sister _____ (get) married next year.
3 We _____ (do) lots of sightseeing on holiday this summer.
4 They _____ (not / stay) in hotels this year.
5 My parents _____ (buy) a new house in the countryside.
6 I _____ (go) to the cinema tonight. Do you want to come with me?
7 He _____ (not / go) to university after high school.
8 We _____ (not / visit) big cities when we go to France.
9 We _____ (stay) in small towns.

c ▶ Now go back to p.121

12B *should / shouldn't*

a Complete the sentences with the verb in brackets and *should* or *shouldn't*.

1 **A** He feels tired all the time.
 B He _____should go_____ (go) to the doctor.
2 You _____ (drink) a lot of water when you run.
3 You _____ (bring) a lot of books. We're only going for three days.
4 You _____ (drive) all night. Stop and get some sleep.
5 It's going to be cold so you _____ (take) some warm clothes.
6 The children _____ (come) into the house – it's getting dark.
7 We _____ (pay) for the meal. The food was horrible.
8 I _____ (say) sorry to him. I broke his cup.

b Put the words in the correct order to make questions.

1 money / much / take / should / I / how ?
 _____How much money should I take?_____
2 museum / we / go / a / should / to ?
 _____
3 clothes / should / what / wear / I ?
 _____
4 I / later / come / should / back ?
 _____
5 we / local / the / should / eat / food ?
 _____
6 we / should / time / arrive / what ?
 _____
7 we / where / stay / should ?
 _____
8 for / should / ask / who / we / advice ?
 _____

c Read the conversation and find six mistakes with *should*.

 A I'm going to Thailand next month. Have you ever been there?
 B Yes I have.
 A Where should I staying?
 B You should look for a hotel when you arrive. You don't should book before you go.
 A Really? I should go to Bangkok?
 B You should to go to Bangkok for a few days. But, you shouldn't stay long. You should visit an island.
 A What do I should do on an island?
 B Do you want to relax?
 A Yes.
 B You should go swimming every day. You should eat at restaurants on the beach… And you should leave your mobile phone at home!
 A Should I take anything with me?
 B Just a bit of money. You should not to worry about money on holiday!

d Correct the mistakes with *should* in **c**.

1 _____Where should I stay?_____
2 _____
3 _____
4 _____
5 _____
6 _____
7 _____

e ▶ Now go back to p.123

Vocabulary Focus

1A Countries and nationalities

a (▶) **1.15** Look at the map below. Write the correct number next to each country in the table. Listen and check.

Country	Nationality	Country	Nationality
A (-ian) Argentina /ɑːdʒəntiːnə/ Australia /ɒstreɪliə/ Canada /kænədə/ Colombia /kəlɒmbiə/ Iran /ɪrɑːn/ Italy /ɪtəli/ Nigeria /naɪdʒɪəriə/	Argentin**ian** /ɑːdʒəntɪniən/ Austral**ian** /ɒstreɪliən/ Canad**ian** /kəneɪdiən/ Colomb**ian** /kəlɒmbiən/ Iran**ian** /ɪreɪniən/ Ital**ian** /ɪtæliən/ Niger**ian** /naɪdʒɪəriən/	**C (-ish)** Ireland /aɪələnd/ Poland /pəʊlənd/ Turkey /tɜːki/ (the) UK /juːkeɪ/ Britain /brɪtən/	Ir**ish** /aɪərɪʃ/ Pol**ish** /pəʊlɪʃ/ Turk**ish** /tɜːkɪʃ/ Brit**ish** /brɪtɪʃ/
		D (-ese) China /tʃaɪnə/	Chin**ese** /tʃaɪniːz/
		E (-i) Pakistan /pɑːkɪstɑːn/	Pakistan**i** /pɑːkɪstɑːni/
B (-an) Mexico /meksɪkəʊ/ South Africa /saʊθ æfrɪkə/ (the) USA /juːeseɪ/	Mexic**an** /meksɪkən/ South Afric**an** /saʊθ æfrɪkən/ Americ**an** /əmerɪkən/	**F (other)** New Zealand /njuː ziːlənd/ Saudi Arabia /saʊdi əreɪbiə/	(a) New Zealander /njuː ziːləndə/ Saudi /saʊdi/

b 💬 Talk about five countries you want to visit.

> I'd like to visit China because I want to see the Great Wall of China.

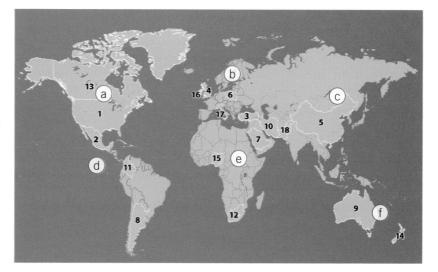

c Match the parts of the world 1–6 with a–f on the map.

1 North America
2 Asia
3 Central and South America
4 Africa
5 Europe
6 Oceania

d 💬 Underline the different country in each group below. Say why.

1 France, Italy, Greece, Poland, China, Germany, Ireland
2 Turkey, Saudi Arabia, Brazil, Iran
3 the USA, Russia, the UK, Australia, Nigeria
4 Argentina, Mexico, Colombia, Spain

e Look at groups A–F in a. Match each nationality from page 10 below to a group.

1 Brazilian
2 Spanish
3 Russian
4 German
5 Japanese
6 French

f (▶) **1.16** Pronunciation Listen to the nationalities in the table. Underline the stressed syllable in each word.

A 2 syllables	Brit|ish, Chi|nese, Tur|kish
B 3 syllables	Mex|i|can, Jap|an|ese,
C 4 syllables	Aus|tra|li|an, Pa|ki|sta|ni, I|tal|i|an

g (▶) **1.16** Look at the nationalities in f again and answer the questions. Listen again and check.

1 In A and in C, which word has a different stress pattern?
2 In B, do the words have the same or a different stress pattern?

h 💬 Student A: choose a new country and a nationality. Tell your partner the part of the world. Then answer his/her questions. Student B: ask questions to guess your partner's new country and nationality. Change roles and repeat.

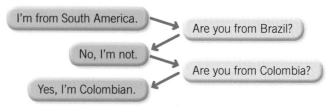

> I'm from South America.
> Are you from Brazil?
> No, I'm not.
> Are you from Colombia?
> Yes, I'm Colombian.

i ▶ Now go back to p.11

1B Adjectives

a ▶ **1.19** Listen to these sentences. Do the marked adjectives mean 'very good' or 'not very good'?

1 This wet and cold weather is **terrible**.
2 I like our new teacher – she's **wonderful**.
3 My new phone does so many new things – it's **amazing**.
4 This colour isn't very nice – it's **horrible**.

b ▶ **1.20** Listen to these sentences. Make pairs of opposites with the marked adjectives.

1 My computer's quite **old** now. I need to buy a new one.
2 I don't think he's got a lot of money – he's quite **poor**.
3 Their new house is finished now and it's very **modern**.
4 He buys anything he wants so I think he's **rich**.

c ▶ **1.21** **Pronunciation** Is the pronunciation of *o* in these words long (/ɔː/) or short (/ɒ/)? Listen and check.

1 m**o**dern   2 p**oo**r   3 h**o**rrible

d ▶ **1.22** Is the pronunciation of *o* in these words long or short? Listen and check. Listen again and repeat.

1 c**o**ffee   4 sh**o**rt
2 **o**ften   5 h**o**liday
3 m**o**re   6 d**oo**r

e Think of things you've got. Make notes. Have you got anything that's … ?

• wonderful   • horrible
• amazing   • old
• terrible   • modern

f 💬 Tell a partner about your things using your notes in e.

g ▶ Now go back to p.13

2A Jobs

a ▶ **1.39** Match the jobs in the box with pictures 1–9. Listen and check. Listen again and repeat.

> businessman /ˈbɪznɪsmən/   businesswoman /ˈbɪznɪswʊmən/   receptionist /rɪˈsepʃənɪst/
> manager /ˈmænɪdʒə/   chef /ʃef/   actor /ˈæktə/   tour guide /ˈtʊə ɡaɪd/
> farmer /ˈfɑːmə/   secretary /ˈsekrətəri/   mechanic /məˈkænɪk/

b Look at the jobs on page 21 and in a. Read the sentences and write the correct job.

a I work in a hospital and look after people.
b I work outside and enjoy showing people my beautiful city.
c I sometimes work in a theatre and I sometimes make films.
d I drive people from one place to another.
e I work in a kitchen and cook amazing food.

f I help people if they have a problem with their teeth.
g I help people if they have a problem with their car.
h I fly people from one country to another.
i I am the first person people meet when they come to our hotel.
j I work outside in the country.

c 💬 Talk about three jobs you would like to do and three jobs you wouldn't like to do. Say why.

d ▶ Now go back to p.21

Numbers

2B Time

a ▶1.45 Match the sentences with the times below. Listen and check.

1 It's (a) quarter past four. *or* It's four fifteen.
2 It's half past four. *or* It's four thirty.
3 It's (a) quarter to five. *or* It's four forty-five.
4 It's twenty past four. *or* It's four twenty.
5 It's ten to five. *or* It's four fifty.
6 It's five past four. *or* It's four oh five.
7 It's twenty-five to five. *or* It's four thirty-five.
8 It's four minutes to five. *or* It's four fifty-six.
9 It's seven minutes past four. *or* It's four oh seven.

b Write down five different times in numbers. Ask your partner to say your times.

c ▶ Now go back to p.23

6A Years and dates

a ▶2.53 Put the months in the correct order. Listen and check. Listen again and repeat.

June /dʒuːn/   September /sepˈtembə/   April /ˈeɪprəl/
November /nəʊˈvembə/   January /ˈdʒænjʊri/
August /ˈɔːgəst/   February /ˈfebruəri/
December /dɪˈsembə/   May /meɪ/   March /mɑːtʃ/
October /ɒkˈtəʊbə/   July /dʒʊlˈaɪ/

b ▶2.54 Complete the sentences with *in* or *on*. Listen and check.

1 We were in Australia _____ 2012.
2 My birthday's _____ the nineteenth of June.
3 Our next holiday's _____ May.

c Correct the dates. Then write them in number form.

1 The next meeting's on ᵗʰᵉ twelfth of April. 12 April
2 Our party's on Saturday the twenty-one of February.
3 We were in Canada in twenty oh seven.
4 Next Saturday's the seventh July.
5 I was at university until one thousand nine hundred and ninety-eight.
6 I'd like to reserve a single room on second of December.

d Think of two people in your family and two friends. Write down their names.

e 💬 Tell a partner the birthdays of the four people. Can they match the birthdays with the names?

f ▶ Now go back to p.61

9A Money and prices

a ▶3.18 Tick (✓) the correct way of saying each price a or b. Listen and check. Listen again and repeat.

1 £25   a twenty-five pounds   b five pounds and twenty
2 £4.50   a four fifty pounds   b four pounds fifty
3 60p   a point six pounds   b sixty p
4 €7.40   a forty cents and seven euros   b seven euros forty
5 €0.25   a twenty-five cents   b quarter euros
6 $28   a eight and twenty dollars   b twenty-eight dollars
7 70c   a seven oh cents   b seventy cents
8 $15.50 a fifteen dollars fifty   b fifteen and half dollars

b 💬 Take turns to say these prices.

1 £2.70   5 $4.75   9 €55.90
2 $120   6 €0.60   10 £9.99
3 €4.30   7 £10.10
4 85p   8 $49.95

c ▶ Now go back to p.90

10B High numbers

a Match phrases 1–10 with numbers a–j.

1 a / one hundred thousand
2 one million three hundred thousand
3 one hundred and twenty
4 a / one million
5 one thousand one hundred
6 one hundred thousand two hundred
7 one hundred and thirty thousand
8 one thousand one hundred and thirty
9 five million six hundred thousand
10 a / one thousand and three

a 120   e 100,200   i 1,130
b 1,003   f 1,000,000   j 130,000
c 1,100   g 1,300,000
d 100,000   h 5,600,000

b ▶3.46 Look at these phrases. Add *and* to four more phrases (sometimes twice). Listen and check. Listen again and repeat.

1 340 = three hundred ᵃⁿᵈ forty
2 2,002 = two thousand two
3 45,800 = forty-five thousand eight hundred
4 381,245 = three hundred eighty-one thousand two hundred forty-five
5 2,000,670 = two million six hundred seventy
6 15,680,430 = fifteen million six hundred eighty thousand four hundred thirty

c Write down a number between:

• 600 and 699
• 3,001 and 3010
• 20,000 and 20,9991
• 1,000,000 and 1,499,999

d Ask a partner to say your numbers.

e ▶ Now go back to p.103

Verbs

3A Common verbs

a ⏵**1.64** Match 1–7 with a–g. Listen and check.

1 How much are the bananas?
2 Do you drink coffee in the morning?
3 Can I **help** you paint the kitchen?
4 Where's your passport?
5 Do you know where I can **buy** an English newspaper?
6 The film starts at 8:15, so let's **meet** outside the cinema at 8:00.
7 Do you want to go for a walk this evening?

a I think they **sell** them in the shop at the station.
b They're very cheap. They only **cost** €2 a kilo.
c No, I just want to **stay** at home and watch TV.
d OK. I'll **try** to be on time but I don't finish work till 7:30.
e Yes, please! But I can't **decide** what colour: blue or green.
f Sometimes, but I **prefer** tea.
g I don't know. I can't **find** it. It isn't in my bag.

b ⏵**1.65** **Pronunciation** Listen to the marked sounds in these words and answer the questions. Listen again and repeat.

b**uy** f**i**nd d**e**c**i**de tr**y** st**ay**

1 Which word has a different sound?
2 Are the two different sounds long or short?

c In pairs ask and answer the questions.

1 What do you prefer to drink in the morning?
2 Think of a small shop near your home. What do they sell? What do you buy there?
3 How much do these things cost in your country?
   a a litre of petrol
   b a cup of coffee
   c a loaf of bread
4 You decide to meet friends in town. Where do you meet?
5 Where do you usually stay on holiday?

d ▶ Now go back to p.31

6B Past simple irregular verbs

a ⏵**2.59** Match the past simple forms in the box with 1–11. Listen and check.

brought	won	lost	found	did	cut
read	thought	sold	became	gave	

1	do	5	bring	9	become
2	read	6	win	10	cut
3	give	7	lose	11	sell
4	think	8	find		

b ⏵**2.60** **Pronunciation** Listen to these sentences. Do the marked letters sound the same or different? Why?

• I r**ea**d a newspaper every day.
• I r**ea**d a wonderful book last month.

c ⏵**2.61** Read the story and <u>underline</u> the correct verbs. Listen and check.

How I ¹*won / lost* the lottery

One day, I went into town and ²*did / made* some shopping. Then, on the way home, I ³*brought / bought* a lottery ticket from a small shop by the bus stop. It had the number of my birthday: 241169. A beautiful woman ⁴*spent / sold* it to me. When she ⁵*gave / took* it to me, she smiled and said, 'Good luck. I hope you win.' I smiled back. A few days later, I opened the newspaper and ⁶*gave / read* the winning number: 2-4-1 ... That was the moment I ⁷*decided / found out*. My life completely changed and I ⁸*became / came* rich. I immediately ⁹*thought / told* of the woman in the shop. I ¹⁰*cost / cut* some fresh flowers from my garden and went back to the shop to give them to her. 'Is the woman who was here on Saturday in today?' I asked. 'I've got some flowers for her.' But she wasn't there and I never saw her again.

d 💬 Cover the text in c and practise telling the story from the pictures. Read it again to check.

e ▶ Now go back to p.63

11A Irregular past participles

a ⏵**3.54** Look at these past participles. What are their infinitive forms? Listen and check.

broken /ˈbrəʊkən/　read /red/　been /biːn/　caught /kɔːt/
written /ˈrɪtən/　seen /siːn/　had /hæd/　eaten /ˈiːtən/
bought /bɔːt/　heard /hɜːd/　flown /fləʊn/
forgotten /fəˈɡɒtən/　fallen /ˈfɔːlən/　grown /ɡrəʊn/

b Complete the questions with past participles from a.

1 Have you ever _____ a fish?
2 Have you ever _____ an email in English?
3 Have you ever _____ octopus?
4 Have you ever _____ in a helicopter?
5 Have you ever _____ to Paris?
6 Have you ever _____ flowers for someone?
7 Have you ever _____ your own phone number?
8 Have you ever _____ an English newspaper?
9 Have you ever _____ an elephant?
10 Have you ever _____ African music?
11 Have you ever _____ your leg?
12 Have you ever _____ breakfast in bed?
13 Have you ever _____ down the stairs?
14 Have you ever _____ vegetables?

c ⏵**3.55** **Pronunciation** Listen to the marked sound in h**ear**d /ɜː/. Which of these words have the same sound as h**ear**d? Listen and check.

g**ir**l　h**ear**　l**ear**n　n**ur**se　G**er**man　w**or**k　y**ear**

d 💬 In pairs ask and answer the questions in b.

e ▶ Now go back to p.111

Food and containers

4A Food

a ▶2.4 Match pictures 1–10 with definitions a–j. Listen and check.

1 garlic /ˈgɑːlɪk/
2 salad /ˈsæləd/
3 burger /ˈbɜːgə/
4 melon /ˈmelən/
5 cereal /ˈsɪərɪəl/
6 yoghurt /ˈjɒgət/
7 jam /dʒæm/

8 cola /ˈkəʊlə/
9 crisps /krɪsps/
10 curry /ˈkʌri/

a People often eat it in India, with rice or naan bread.
b It's a large fruit which grows in hot countries. It's yellow, orange or green.
c It's a quick, cheap meal: meat and salad inside bread, sometimes with cheese.
d It's uncooked vegetables mixed together that you can have with a meal. It's good for you!
e It's like onion and you can use it for cooking.
f It's made from milk. People often have it for breakfast.
g It's sweet and it's made from fruit. You can put it on bread.
h They're made from potatoes and usually come in small bags. They aren't very good for you!
i It's a drink, a bit like lemonade but it's brown.
j Many people eat it for breakfast with milk.

b ▶2.5 **Pronunciation** Listen to the marked sounds in these words. Listen again and repeat.

/k/ **c**ola **c**risps **c**urry
/g/ **g**arlic bur**g**er yo**gh**urt

c ▶2.6 Which words do you hear, a or b?

1 a could   b good   **3** a class   b glass
2 a cold   b gold   **4** a back   b bag

d 💬 Say a word from c for your partner to point to.

e Complete the sentences. Use words from a and page 40.

1 What kind of meat do you want; c_____n, s_____k or l_____b?
2 Let's have a s_____d. We've got tomatoes, o_____ns, c_____ts, green b_____ns and m_____ms.
3 My wife has c_____l and milk for breakfast, but I like y_____t with fruit and then a piece of bread with butter and j_____m.
4 We've got lots of fruit: apples, p_____rs, g_____pes and a m_____n.
5 Of course he's not fit. He always eats c_____ps and drinks c_____a between meals.

f 💬 Look at all the words in a and e. Talk about:

• things you eat or drink nearly every day
• things you eat or drink at least once a week
• things you don't often eat or drink
• things you never eat or drink.

g ▶ Now go back to p.41

4B Containers

a Match phrases 1–6 with pictures a–f.

1 a **jar** /dʒɑː/ of honey
2 a **bag** /bæg/ of potatoes
3 a **can** /kæn/ (or **tin** /tɪn/) of tomatoes
4 a **bottle** /ˈbɒtl/ of water
5 a **bar** /bɑː/ of chocolate
6 a **packet** /ˈpækɪt/ of biscuits

b ▶2.12 **Pronunciation** Listen to the phrases in a. Which words are stressed? Listen again and repeat.

1 the nouns   2 the article 'a'
3 the preposition 'of'

c Change the words in italics using phrases in a. Is more than one answer possible?

> Yesterday I went shopping and I bought ¹*some oil*, ²*some jam*, ³*some spaghetti*, ⁴*some chocolate*, ⁵*some tuna*, and ⁶*some apples*.

1 *a bottle of oil*   4 _____
2 _____   5 _____
3 _____   6 _____

d 💬 Write a shopping list. Use the words in 1 to help you. Tell a partner.

e ▶ Now go back to p.43

Places

5A Places in a city

a ▶️ **2.26** Match the places in the box with pictures 1–6. Listen and check.

post office /ˈpəʊst ˈɒfɪs/ ☐   sports centre /ˈspɔːts ˈsentə/ ☐   theatre /ˈθɪətə/ ☐
police station /pəˈliːs steɪʃən/ ☐   concert hall /ˈkɒnsət ˈhɔːl/ ☐   stadium /ˈsteɪdiəm/ ☐

b Match the definitions with the places in a and on page 50.

a   You go there to watch a sports game.
b   This is a nice place to sit with trees and grass and flowers.
c   When you want to send a postcard, you go to this place.
d   You walk on this from one side of a river to the other side.
e   You can see a play or an opera at this place.
f   If someone steals from you, you go to this place.
g   This is an open area in the centre of a town.
h   You can listen to classical music in this place.
i   When you want to do some exercise, you go to this place.

c ▶️ **2.27** Pronunciation Listen to the words. Are the marked sounds weak or strong? Listen again and repeat.

building   **b**ridge   **p**ark   **p**ost office

d 💬 In pairs ask and answer the questions.
1   Which of the places in b does / doesn't your city have?
2   Which does / doesn't your city need?

e ▶ Now go back to p.51

12A Geography

a Read the emails. Notice the marked words and write them in the pictures.

(a) The _____
(b) _____
(c) _____

📧 Mail

We have a holiday house that we go to at the weekend. It's on the **coast** /kəʊst/, but behind us is a **jungle** /ˈdʒʌŋgl/ with lots of very green trees. Next to the house is a small **hill** /hɪl/. You can walk to the top and the view is wonderful.

(d) The _____
(e) _____
(f) _____

📧 Mail

We live outside the city in the **countryside** /ˈkʌntrɪsaɪd/. There are **fields** /fiːldz/ all around the house and in the distance there is a small **wood** /wʊd/. I like walking there. It's so quiet – I love it.

b ▶️ **3.74** Pronunciation Listen to the words in a. Which words have more than one syllable?

c 💬 Underline the different word in each group below. Say why.
1   lake, river, field, waterfall
2   forest, hill, wood, jungle, rainforest
3   island, mountain, coast, beach

d 💬 Think of the countryside in your country. Talk about what there is and there isn't.

> In my country, there are lots of hills, but there's no desert. We've only got two lakes, but about seven or eight rivers.

e ▶ Now go back to p.120

Collocations

7A Transport collocations

a (▶)**2.70** Read and listen to the text. Match pictures 1–6 with marked phrases a–f.

Erik works in the city centre and he ᵃ**takes the train** to work every morning. He ᵇ**gets on the train** at Kings Park Station, near his home. Then he ᶜ**changes trains** at Central Station in the city centre and he ᵈ**gets off** the train at Riverside Station, near his office.

He usually gets to Kings Park Station at 8:00 so he can ᵉ**catch the train** at 8.05, but sometimes he's a few minutes late and he ᶠ**misses the train**. Then he has to wait for the next train.

b (▶)**2.71** Underline the correct verbs. Listen and check.

1 There were no buses, so I decided to *take / get on* a taxi.
2 It's nearly 10:30. Leave now or you'll *catch / miss* the bus.
3 Excuse me, I want to go to the City Museum. Where do I *take off / get off* the bus?
4 The concert finished at 9:30, so we just *caught / changed* the last tram.
5 The train was expensive, so we *take / took* a night coach.
6 Quick! Let's get *on / off* the bus and find a seat! It leaves in a few minutes!

c (▶)**2.72** Pronunciation Look at these verbs and answer the questions. Listen and check.

bou**gh**t   **g**o**t**   **s**aw   **t**oo**k**

1 Which verbs have the same sound as c**augh**t /ɔː/?
2 Is it a long or short sound?

d 💬 In pairs, ask and answer the questions.

1 When was the last time:
   • you caught a bus or train at the last minute?
   • you missed a bus or train?
   • you changed trains?
2 How do you get from here to your home? What kinds of transport can you take? Where do you get on and off?

e ▶ Now go back to p.71

8A Sport and exercise collocations

a Match the activities in the box with pictures 1–11.

running	golf	judo	sailing
football	snowboarding		volleyball
exercises	fishing	rugby	hockey

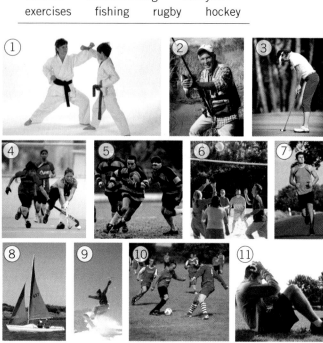

b Write the activities in a in the correct column in the table.

go	play	do
running	golf	judo

c Complete the rules with *go*, *play* or *do*. We use …

1 _____ when we talk about sports, games and music.
2 _____ when we talk about activities that end with *-ing*.
3 _____ when we talk about other activities.

d (▶)**3.5** Pronunciation Listen to the marked sounds in these words. Are they long or short?

f**oo**tball   j**u**do

e (▶)**3.6** Are the marked sounds in these words long or short? Listen and check.

1 f**u**ll   3 p**oo**l   5 f**oo**d
2 g**oo**d   4 p**u**t   6 bl**ue**

f 💬 Which activities in a do people do in your country? Choose a sentence which is true for each activity.

a It's very popular.
b Some people do it but not many.
c It's very unusual.
d You can't do this in my country.

> Some people go snowboarding, but not many.

g ▶ Now go back to p.81

Appearance and clothes

8B Appearance

a Match sentences 1–4 with four of pictures a–h.

1 He's got **short straight dark** hair.
2 She's got **long straight dark** hair.
3 He's got **short curly dark** hair.
4 She's got **long straight fair** hair.

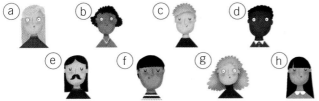

b Notice the order of the adjectives in a. Which adjective always comes first?

c ▶ 3.10 Write sentences about the other four people's hair in a. Listen and check.

d Write a sentence about your hair and one about a partner's hair.

e 💬 Student A: choose a picture in a. Student B: ask questions to guess your partner's picture. Change roles and repeat.

Is it a man or a woman?

A man.

Has he got long hair?

No.

Is it picture f?

Yes.

f Match 1–6 with a–f.

1 People always look at her.
2 You can see he does a lot of sport.
3 Here's a photo of her at the age of five.
4 He always looks great in photos.
5 He should get more exercise.
6 I don't think she eats enough.

a He looks very **fit**.
b He's getting quite **fat**.
c She's looking much too **thin**.
d She was a very **pretty** girl.
e She's a very **attractive** woman.
f He's very **good-looking**.

g ▶ 3.11 **Pronunciation** Listen to these adjectives and underline the stress. Listen again and repeat.

pret|ty   a|ttrac|tive   good-look|ing

h 💬 Talk about famous people who are:

• thin   • attractive   • good-looking   • fit

i ▶ Now go back to p.83

9B Clothes

a ▶ 3.28 Read and listen to the text. Match the marked words 1–8 with pictures a–h. Listen and check.

• She looked lovely. She wore a red ^{1}**skirt** /skɜːt/ and a white shirt and she had a blue and yellow ^{2}**necklace** /'nekləs/.
• It was a hot day, so he decided to wear a ^{3}**T-shirt** /'tiːʃɜːt/, ^{4}**shorts** /ʃɔːts/ and ^{5}**trainers** /'treɪnəz/ without socks.
• I never wear ^{6}**jewellery** /'dʒuːəlri/ – just a ^{7}**watch** /wɒtʃ/, of course, and my ^{8}**ring** /rɪŋ/.

b ▶ 3.29 **Pronunciation** Listen to this word. Which letters don't you hear?

jewellery

c ▶ 3.30 Cross out the letters you don't hear in these words. Listen and check.

1 vegetable   3 chocolate   5 comfortable
2 interesting   4 camera

d 💬 Student A: look at Picture 1 for one minute. Student B: look at Picture 2 for one minute. Try to remember everything the people are wearing. They are all words from a or page 93. Cover the picture and say what you remember.

e ▶ Now go back to p.93

Audioscripts

Welcome!

 1.2

Conversation 1

A Hello. I'm Tony, and this is my wife Joanna.
B Hello. Nice to meet you. I'm Pierre.
C Hello, Pierre. Nice to meet you.

1.3

Conversation 2

A Hi, Nick. How are you?
B I'm fine, thanks. And you?
A I'm OK, thanks.

1.4

Conversation 3

A Hi. Can we pay, please?
B Yeah, sure. That's 13 euros, please.
A 30 euros? For coffee and ice cream?
B No, 13 euros. Six for the coffees and seven for the ice creams
A Ah, OK. … There you are. 15. Keep the change.
B Oh, thank you.

 1.5

Conversation 4

A What's your name and address?
B It's Mike Kato, K-A-T-O.
A Kato, OK …
B 10 Kings Road, Ashley.
A OK, 10 Kings Road …
B Ashley.
A How do you spell that?
B A-S-H-L-E-Y
A Right, OK.

1.6

Conversation 5

A Ah, this is a nice photo. This is my wife and her brother.
B Oh yes. Is that your flat?
A Yes, that's our flat in London.
B Mm, it's very nice.

Unit 1

 1.13

THOMAS Hi, there! My name's Thomas. What's your name?
LENA I'm Lena.
T Hi, Lena! Where are you from? Russia?
L Yeah, you're right! I'm Russian. I'm from St Petersburg.
T Oh, yes! It's a really beautiful city.
L Yes, I think so too. So, where are you from, Thomas?
T Me? I'm from France. I'm French.
L Oh, the French team's really good!
T Of course, we're great!

1.17

LENA So where are you from? From Paris?
THOMAS No, I'm not from Paris. I'm from a town called Rouen.
L Hmm … Where's that?
T Oh, it's a town near Paris. It isn't very big.
L Oh, right.
T So are you here with friends?
L Yes, we're a big group. We're all from St Petersburg.
T But they aren't here.
L No, they're all in the hotel. They say they're tired!
T Oh, right. Well, look, it's only 8:00, the match isn't on yet. So, how about a coffee?
L Hmm, yeah, OK. Good idea!

1.23

1 A This is my good friend Roman. He's really friendly.
B Is he from Poland?
A Yes, he is.
2 A These are my friends Mia and Diego. They're really great.
B Are they married?
A Yes, they are.
B Are they Spanish?
A No, they aren't. They're from Mexico.
3 A This is my friend, Laura. She's really cool.
B Is she Italian?
A No, she isn't. She's from Spain.

1.27 **PART 1**

LEO OK, all finished. Time to go.
DAN I want to finish this. You go. See you tomorrow.
L All this sitting. I need to do some exercise.
D Off to the gym?
L Yeah.
D Say hello to Martina when you see her.
L Sure! … Bye!
D Bye, Leo.

1.28 **PART 2**

SONIA Hi. How can I help?
LEO I'd like to do a fitness class.
S Your card, please?
L Sorry – it's at home.
S OK. No problem. What's your name?
L Leo.
S Sorry, what's your surname?
L Seymour.
S Can you spell that, please?
L S-E-Y-M-O-U-R.
S Seymour – yes, here you are. And what's your address?
L 18 New Street.
S 18 New Street.
L Yes, that's right.
S So, a fitness class?
L Yes, what time's the next one?
S It's at twenty past seven.
L Sorry?
S 7.20.
L And, is it a big group?
S No, only ten people.
L Great. Can I book a place?
S Of course. There you go.
L And where's the class?
S It's in Studio 1.
L So that's 7.20 in Studio 1?
S That's right.
L Thanks for your help.
S You're welcome.

1.31 **PART 3**

MARTINA Leo!
LEO Martina – hi!
M Good to see you here.
L All day at the computer – I need to do something.
M Yes, well, tell my husband that.
L Dan's very busy.
M And a bit lazy! See you later!
L See you later.

1.36

KATE Welcome to the course, very nice to see you all. I'm Kate, as you know, and this is Mike, we're your two teachers on the course and we're both from London. So, first, can we all say our names and where we're from? OK? Carla, you start …
CARLA Yes, of course. Hello, I'm Carla and I'm from Italy. I'm a student in Milan. It's my first time in London, so it's great to be here.
MASATO OK. Well, I'm Masato and I live in Kyoto in Japan. I work in a hotel in Kyoto, so English is really important for me.
CARMEN Yes, I'm Carmen. I'm from Barcelona in Spain. I'm also a student, I study IT. It's not my first time in England, I know London quite well, but it's nice to be here again.
ORHAN I'm Orhan and I'm from Turkey. I live in London now with my family. I work for a bank here.
MARISA I'm Marisa and I'm a student in Recife in Brazil. It's my first time in London, too, but I have a brother here, so I can stay with his family.
K OK, great, thank you. Well, er, to start off then I think I'll just explain what the course is all about …

Unit 2

 1.37

PETER 'Ice Road Truckers' is on this week. It's a really great programme.
KAREN Oh, I don't like 'Ice Road Truckers' at all. I think it's a terrible programme. The truckers only drive their trucks for money. And people watch them because they want to see an accident, it's really bad.
P Oh no, I think it's really good. I really like 'Ice Road Truckers' and I always watch it. You know, a lot of people think it's a man's job to drive a truck, but there's also a really interesting woman in the programme. Her name's Lisa Kelly.
K What! Is she a trucker?
P Yes, she has a big truck and she drives it really well too. I like her – she's always happy. You can see she loves her job.

 1.44

JACK Umm, excuse me. Hi. Look, can I ask you a few questions about your study routine?
TANIA Sorry?
J Your study routine?
T Umm … OK … but I've got to …
J Great! So, first question, do you study full-time or part-time?
T Part-time. I have a job – I'm a nurse and I have a family. I'm really busy.
J OK … and how many hours a week do you study?
T Well, at the university, about five hours.
J And at home?
T I don't know – maybe about ten hours.
J Do you study in the morning or afternoon?
T I usually study early in the morning or late at night.
J When do you start studying each day?
T Usually at half past eight or nine o'clock.
J Do you finish studying very late?
T Well, it changes every day.
J Well, last night, for example.
T Hmm … last night … at quarter past eleven.
J Wow, that's quite late! And where do you study?
T Everywhere! On the bus, at work, at lunch time, in the kitchen, in the bedroom – everywhere!
J And in your free time?
T Free time?
J What do you do in your free time?
T I don't have any free time!

▶ 1.47

JACK Are you the only student at home?
TANIA No, my daughter Ellie is a student too.
J Can I ask about her … ?
T All right, but look, I really have to …
J Thank you so much. So, Ellie is it?
T Yes.
J How many hours a week does she study?
T She's a full-time student so she studies about 40 hours a week.
J What time does she start each day?
T I'm not sure. At about nine o'clock.
J Where does she study?
T Mostly at the university library and sometimes at home.
J Does she study more before an exam?
T Yes, I think so. Look, I really have no idea. I'm in a hurry … I must go. Goodbye!
J Please just one more question. Maybe not.

▶ 1.50 PART 1

DAN What do you want?
LEO Oh, thanks. I'd like a latte.
D Can I have a tea and a latte, please?
SERVER Certainly. Small or large?
D A small tea and …?
L Large for me, please.
S So, a large latte and a small tea?
D Yes. And could I have a croissant as well, please? So, we need to talk about the meeting on Wednesday.
L Oh yes. Is it here or at their office?
D At their office. Could we chat about it now?
L Sorry, I have another meeting in five minutes.
D OK, no problem. We can do it later. How much is that?
S £3.60
D Here you go.
S Thanks.
L So, this meeting on Wednesday …
D Yeah. Oh! Could you pass the milk? Thanks. (*phone rings*) Annie!
A Hi, Dan. Sorry to call you at work.
D That's OK. Don't worry.

▶ 1.51 PART 2

ANNIE Hi, Dan. Sorry to call you at work.
DAN That's OK. Don't worry.
A But you see, I need … well, I'd like some help.
D Sure – no problem.
A It's about this online course I want to do. I'm not sure which one … I mean, I can't decide.
D So you want your big brother to help you … ?
A Yes, I do. Could I come to your place tonight?
D Sorry, we're not at home tonight.
A Oh, that's a pity.
D But, look, come on Friday – for dinner.
A Friday?
D Yes.
A For dinner?
D Yes!
A Lovely!
D OK. See you then. Bye!
A Bye!
D My sister! Always asking me to do things for her. … Eugh! Too much sugar!

▶ 1.56

DANIELA My name is Daniela and I'm a police officer in Mexico City – but just traffic police. I need to speak English because sometimes tourists ask me questions in English, for example, they ask me for directions or some tourist information. I like studying at this college. The timetable works well – we have a two-hour break in the middle of the day. I want to improve my listening. I find listening quite hard and it's difficult to listen to something and make notes at the same time. So I need to do some extra listening practice.

SAID Hi. My name is Said and I'm a dentist in Riyadh in Saudi Arabia. Sometimes English speaking people come to my work, so I need to speak good English. This college is very good – the lessons are very interesting and we do lots of different things in class. I want to stay here for a term – until December. Listening and speaking is OK for me, but I need to work hard at reading and writing. I'd like to read books in English – maybe even some books about my work.

JUSTYNA Hello, my name is Justyna and I'm a photographer for a newspaper in Warsaw in Poland. In the future, I'd like to study at a university in the UK so I need better English to do that. Our teacher, Kate, is great. She is very friendly and she helps us a lot in class. Only one thing worries me a bit: the marks I get in tests. I think my progress is OK and I can speak better, but I'm not very good at tests and exams. But maybe I need to study grammar a bit more too!

▶ 1.57

KATE Hi, everyone. Before we begin the lesson, I just want to tell you about this competition we're having here at school. It's really good because you can win an extra month of English lessons for free. That's right – an extra month for nothing. So all you need is … Well, you need to be a student at this school – and you all are – and you need to complete this entry form by hand – you know, you can't use a computer. But you also need to make sure that what you write on the entry form is correct – no mistakes! So if you want to enter, you can get an entry form from me or you can also get them from reception. It's a really good competition – one more month of study. So are there any questions … ?

Unit 3

▶ 1.60

MARTIN Hey, Kath, I've got an idea.
KATHERINE Oh yeah, what's that?
M I'd like us to have a family dinner together once a week.
K Oh, really? … Why?
M Well, our lives are so busy and we're always in a hurry. You, me and the kids, we never have dinner together these days. Spending some time together – just one night – it feels like a nice idea.
K OK, why not? When do you want to do it?
M When are you free?
K Most nights, but I go to my Spanish lesson once a week. It's usually on Wednesdays, so that's no good.
M OK, so not Wednesday. What about Liz and Pete?
K Well, Liz goes to volleyball training.
M Of course. How often does she go?
K Twice a week – on Monday and Thursday.
M And Pete goes to band practice a lot.
K Yes, three times a week – on Monday, Thursday and Friday.
M OK. So that means … Tuesday! Yes, Tuesday night we can all have dinner together. Everyone's free then.
K No, they're not.
M What do you mean?
K I work late every Tuesday.
M Oh. But you said 'most nights are free'.
K Yeah, *most* nights – not *all* nights. You know I work late on Tuesday. I don't need to tell you that!
M Sorry. Well, this is impossible!

▶ 1.68

Conversation 1

INTERVIEWER So tell me, Don, have you got a smartphone?
D Yes, I've got my daughter's phone. She's got a new phone, so I've got her old one.
I Do you use it a lot?
D No, never. Well, sometimes, but not very often.
I Why not?
D I don't know really. If I'm at home, I use the house phone. Umm … If I go out, I don't want to chat to people or send texts. I just want to be quiet. So, no. In fact, I usually leave my phone at home. I don't want to lose it.

Conversation 2

I So, Bella, have you got a computer?
BELLA Yes of course, in fact I've got two, a PC and a laptop.
I Do you use them both?
B Oh, yes, all the time. I use the PC for studying mainly and also for downloading films. And I use the laptop when I go to university or when I study in the library.

Conversation 3

I Have you got a digital camera?
C Yes, I have. It takes really good photos, but I don't use it very often, just for special photos. I've also got a smartphone, of course, and usually I take photos on that, like holiday photos or photos of friends – the photos are OK but they're not fantastic.

▶ 1.72 PART 1

DAN Here's your coffee, Annie …
ANNIE Thanks, Dan!
D Martina …
MARTINA Thank you.
A My favourite programme's on in five minutes.
M The cooking one?
A Yeah, I love it.
D *Top Cook?*
A That's it – *Top Cook*. Can we watch it?
M Sure! We always watch it too.
A Fantastic! Cooking, food, restaurants. I love all that.
M So do we.

▶ 1.73 PART 2

ANNIE Hey! I know this new restaurant – near my office. Why don't we try it?
MARTINA Yeah! That'd be great. For dinner?
A Yeah.
DAN That's a good idea.
A How about next Wednesday?
M Mmm, maybe. Let me see. I'm sorry I can't. I need to work late next Wednesday.
A Are you free next Friday?
M Mm, possibly. Friday's fine. Dan?
D Friday? Sure, I'd love to.
A Great!
D Mm, can I bring Leo? You know, the guy I work with.
A Leo? Yeah, great idea. Look! My programme!

▶ 1.78

EMRAH I've got a large family and we all live in many different countries. I come from Izmir in Turkey, but I live in England now with my parents. I've got a brother and sister in Germany. My sister Ayda lives in Munich and my brother Mustafa lives in Berlin. Some of our family is still in Turkey, but I've also got an uncle in France – he lives in Lyon with his family – and another uncle in Sweden. And I've also got family in Italy, they live in Milan, but I don't know them very well.

We all stay in contact by Skype and email but we don't often see each other, unfortunately. But we always get together every five years and we spend a long weekend together, and it's always in Turkey because my grandmother is there and she's very old, she's over 80 and she can't travel. We stay with family and we have a big party. It's a great family occasion but we also invite friends, so there are usually about 50 people there. It's a very nice way to keep in contact, and we've always got lots to talk about!

Unit 4

▶ **2.7**

TOM We've got almost nothing to eat for dinner.
MILLY OK. We can order some food then.
T Not again.
M Well, it's the weekend – I don't really want to cook.
T All right, fine. I can cook.
M OK. If you want to.
T But you can come to the shops with me.
M Like I said – it's the weekend. I don't cook and I don't go to the supermarket.
T We can go to the farmers' market then. It's open today.
M OK, fine. What do we need?
T Well, we've got some potatoes, so we can have roast potatoes maybe. But we haven't got any meat.
M Do you want to make that chicken and mushroom dish – you know, the one you like to make?
T Yeah – good idea. Have we got any mushrooms?
M No, I don't think so.
T OK, we can get some. And I need an onion and a chicken, of course.
M So, let's put that on the shopping list – a chicken, some mushrooms and an onion. Is that all?
T Yeah, I think so.
M Oh and Tom … I haven't got any money at the moment, so …
T All right, Milly. I can pay.

▶ **2.13**

OLIVIA I want to try this recipe.
HARRY Which one?
O Ultimate mashed potato.
H Mashed potato? That's a bit boring.
O But it says 'ultimate', you know, the best.
H What's so special about it?
O Well, it says to use 300 grams of butter.
H 300 grams? That's a lot of butter.
O I know, that's why I want to try it. And then you boil the potatoes once, let them get cold and then boil them again.
H Twice?
O Yeah. I don't know why. But I'm going to make it today. Anyway, you look at Heston's book. Which recipe do you want to try?
H Something sweet. Let's see … oh yes, this one, coffee and chocolate sauce. Sounds really good! I can put it on ice cream.
O What's in it?
H Well, some coffee beans, of course.
O How many do you need?
H It says you need 40.
O Woah! That's a lot! And how much chocolate?
H Only a little – 60 grams. But I need dark chocolate, not milk chocolate.
O How many grams of butter?
H None – no butter at all, just water and sugar. It looks really easy to make. I just boil everything together.
O Once or twice?
H Only once with this recipe! Now, no more talking. I'm hungry! Let's get cooking.

▶ **2.18** **PART 1**

DAN Is this it?
ANNIE This is it.
LEO Great.
A It's empty.
MARTINA Maybe it isn't open.
WAITER Good evening, good evening.
A Hello. Are you open?
W Yes, of course. Do you have a reservation?
A No, we don't. Do we need a reservation?
W Erm, not really. It's very early …
A OK, then, we'd like a table for four.
W Certainly.
A Can we have a table by the window?
W Yes. These two over here are both free.
D What do you think? The one on the left?
M Fine.
L Sure.
A What about the one on the right?
D If you prefer …
A Maybe not. The one on the left is fine …
W Of course. This way, please.

▶ **2.20** **PART 2**

WAITER Are you ready to order?
DAN Yes?
MARTINA I'm ready.
LEO Fine.
ANNIE I think so …
W What would you like for your starter?
M I'd like the mushroom soup, please.
W And for your main course?
M I'll have the lamb with roast potatoes.
W And for you, madam? What would you like to eat?
A Oh, dear. It's hard to decide. OK, for a starter I'll have the fish. No wait! I'll have chicken salad and then … yes … I'd like the spaghetti for my main course.
W Very good. And for your starter, sir?
D I'll have chicken salad.
W Chicken salad.
D Then lamb with roast potatoes.
A Oh, lamb – that sounds nice. Can I change my order?
W Of course.
A I'll have the same – lamb for my main.
W Certainly. And finally?
L I'd like the chicken curry.
W Would you like rice with that?
L Yes, please. And for my starter I'd like the fish.
A Fish. My first idea. Sorry, sorry … I'll have the same as Leo.
W So, that's the fish?
A Yes.
L Are you sure about that, Annie?
A What? I think so. Yes.
W And what would you like to drink?
A To drink? Umm …
W Would you like a moment to think about that?

▶ **2.25**

JAKE I'm really bad at cooking. I eat a lot of fast food and ready meals. I'm OK at making pasta – usually spaghetti with sauce. The one sauce I make is tomato and mushroom. It's not very good, but I like it! So I eat a lot of pasta because it's easy to make.
ROSIE My husband's a great cook and he does all the cooking at home. He can look in our fridge and find some vegetables and cheese and then make a dish from it that's wonderful to eat, like vegetable moussaka. I don't know how he does it. But I'm lucky to have a husband like that!
JOHANNA My friends say I'm a good cook. I'm not sure, but I enjoy cooking and if you enjoy something, you're often good at it. I think it's fun to try new dishes and I certainly like eating the things I make! Tonight I want to try a new fish dish. First you grill the fish then you make a lemon sauce. I think it'll go well with a bean salad I often make.

TOBY My mother is a fantastic cook. But isn't everyone's mother a fantastic cook?! I eat everything she makes and I always want more. I really, really like the cakes and cookies she makes. My favourite is her pear cake – I love eating it warm with chocolate sauce.

Unit 5

▶ **2.32**

JIM So, what do you think of this room?
R Mmm … nice and big. I love that armchair.
J Yes, it's quite interesting.
R Is it yours?
J No, it's David's. He's my flatmate.
R I love it. That mirror over there. Is that Mum and Dad's?
J Well, yes, but really it's mine now.
R Well, no it isn't. It comes from my old room. It's really mine.
J Are you sure? I don't remember it in your room. Well, it's Mum and Dad's, not ours.
R But it comes from my old room at their place.
J Yes, well, anyway – let's have a look at another room. … So this is my favourite room, of course.
R Lovely – it's nice and light and clean.
J And it's a good size.
R Whose wardrobe is that? Is it Mum and Dad's?
J Yeah, it's theirs. It's from home. They said I can use it.
R But that's from their bedroom.
J They've got a new one.
R So it's all our parents' furniture in here?
J Well … I guess … some of it. The bed's mine.
R Are you sure?

▶ **2.38** **PART 1**

DAN Come on, Leo. This meeting's really important. We can't be late.
L OK. I don't understand.
D What?
L This says 'Bedford Street', but on my phone it says 'Park Road'.
D Are you sure it's here?
L I think so.
D What street do we want?
L Park Road.
D Are you certain?
L Yes, South Street is off Park Road.
D I don't want to be late for this meeting. Can I have a look at your phone?

▶ **2.40** **PART 2**

DAN This map shows there's a bank on the corner of Park Road and South Street. Excuse me, sorry. Is there a bank near here?
MAN A bank? Yes. There's a bank down there. It's about 50 metres away.
D Thanks very much. Let's go.

▶ **2.41** **PART 3**

LEO Are you sure this is the right bank?
DAN I don't know… this is Henrietta Street, not South Street.
L So, where's South Street?
D Sometimes these maps aren't very clear.
L Excuse me.
WOMAN Yes?
L Can you tell us how to get to South Street?
W South Street. Yes, sure. Go straight on, turn right at the corner.
L Into King Street?
W That's right. Then go along King Street until you come to Park Road.
L Ah! So Park Road is further along?
W That's right, about 100 metres. Turn right into Park Road, go straight on and South Street is on your left.
D So, we turn right and then right again and it's on the left?
W That's it.
D Great, thanks. Let's run!

▶ 2.44

ANTONELLA For me it's very important for a neighbourhood to have lots of cafes and restaurants. I like an exciting neighbourhood. I like going out and meeting my friends a lot. I like a neighbourhood with lots of people in it. My neighbourhood is quite exciting. There's also a museum near my house, so I'm really lucky.

DMITRY I think a good neighbourhood is a quiet one. So, for example, no clubs or restaurants – nothing like that – only houses. My neighbourhood isn't like that – there are lots of shops and restaurants. And there's a cinema close to my house – I really don't like that.

JIA I think a good neighbourhood is a new one – new houses and shops. I also like a neighbourhood that is close to a shopping mall. It's good to have lots of new shops near you – it's interesting. In my neighbourhood, there aren't any shops – there's only a park. It's a little bit boring.

Unit 6

▶ 2.45

FRIEND What's this, Greg?

GREG Oh, it's my family tree. You can download a special programme to make it.

F That's really good. So are these your grandparents?

G That's right. Sally, she's my grandmother and that's my grandfather, Nathan. They're my mother's parents. They've got two children, a son and a daughter. Michael's their son, he's my uncle, and they've got a daughter, Mary, that's my mother.

F And so, Sanjit's your father?

G That's right, yeah. They've got three children – there's me, there's my brother Rick and my sister Ella – that's her there.

F Sanjit's an Indian name, right?

G Yeah, it is, yeah. His parents, Arjun and Priya, are from India, but he was born here in London. And his brother Ravi was born here too – so Ravi's my other uncle.

F Right. So, he's married too.

G Yes, you can see here – he's married to my aunt Alice. And they've got two children, Karl and Kavita. They're my cousins.

F So your grandparents in India have got five grandchildren?

G Yes, they're very happy about it!

▶ 2.47

FRIEND So, your grandparents are all still alive?

GREG Yes, they are. But we don't see my grandparents in India very much.

F Your grandmother, Sally – she looks nice and friendly.

G She's lovely, yes, but she's very old now of course. Look – here's a photo of her with my grandfather. I think this is from about 1963, yeah, you can see that she was a very beautiful woman.

F Oh, yes. She really was. So, when was she born?

G Um, she was born in 1939 I think, I'm not sure. But I know her birthday's the 16th of July. And my grandfather was born two years before her.

F Mmm … interesting.

G Yes, my grandmother's a really interesting woman. She was a doctor at the university hospital in London, for about 40 years I think, until she was 65. So, until 2004.

F Wow, that's a long time. What about your grandfather? Was he a doctor too?

G Yes, he was. And they were at the same school together.

F Really? Were they in the same class?

G No, they weren't. They weren't even friends at school. But then when they were university students, they met again and of course then things were quite different ….

F Ah, right.

G Yes, in fact they were married in 1962. They were still students.

F Oh, so in this photo she was… 24 and just married?

G Yes, that's right.

F Ah, that's so romantic.

▶ 2.58

HANNAH My childhood hobby was sports. I loved it. I played anything and everything: basketball, tennis, swimming, football. But I think my favourite was tennis – I played every summer. Every day of the week I went to some kind of sports activity or game. My parents, poor things, spent all the time driving me to different activities and games and things like that. I never got a train or bus. I think it was really difficult for them! I don't play sports very much now – I don't have the time.

CHARLIE My hobby when I was a child was a bit unusual I think. I really loved sweet things – cakes, biscuits – food like that. So, my hobby was baking. After school and at the weekend I made cakes and biscuits and my friends came to my place and ate them. My parents bought all the things I needed. They told me it cost a lot but they were always happy to eat the things I made. I still bake biscuits and cakes now. My wife loves it because she never needs to bake anything.

▶ 2.63 PART 1

DAN Hello, this is Dan Morton. I can't answer your call at the moment. Please leave a message after the tone.

ANNIE Hi, Dan – it's Annie. Can you call me back? You can call me on my work number or my mobile. Thanks.

A Hi! It's Annie. I'm not here right now. You know what to do after the tone. Have a nice day!

D Hi, Annie. I got your message. I'm here at my desk now. Could you call me back? Bye.

▶ 2.65 PART 2

DAN Would you like a coffee?

LEO Yeah, that'd be great. Thanks, Dan. … Hello, Dan's phone.

ANNIE Oh. Hello. Is Dan there?

L Sorry, he's not here just now. He went to get coffee.

A Oh. It's his sister, Annie. Can he call me back?

L Hi, Annie. It's Leo.

A Leo? Oh … Leo. Hi!

L Can you wait a minute? He'll be back soon.

A Sure … So … Leo. How are you?

L I'm … I'm really well. What about you?

A Oh, great – just great.

L Oh, good. That's, erm … great.

A Yeah.

L He's back. … It's Annie.

D Oh, good. Just a minute.

L He's got coffee for us.

A Lucky you!

D There you are.

L Bye, Annie.

A Bye.

D Thanks. Hi, Annie. It's me.

A Dan – finally!

D You left a message.

A Yes, that's right. I need your help with something.

▶ 2.69

EVA OK, well 1982 was a very important year for me. I was born in that year! I was born in a small town in the north of Colombia. My whole family lived there – my parents, my grandparents, uncles, aunts, cousins, everyone. It's a very nice place, very hot, tropical. I really loved it.

And then 1995 was a very important year. Everything changed. My parents moved to the USA, my father got a job in Minnesota, so we went to live in the USA and I went to school there, I learned English quite quickly.

In 2000, I got my first job. I was a school teacher, I taught small kids, six to ten years old. It was great. Then in 2007, I met Niko – he's my husband. He's German but we met in the USA, and then in 2010 I moved to Germany to be near him, and we got married last year. And then I found a job, I teach English to business people, so here I am today.

Unit 7

▶ 2.73

KLARA My mum said you went on a Silk Road trip.

HANS Yes, it was a wonderful trip – really fantastic.

K How did you travel?

H By train of course. The only way to go.

K Well, not the only way … I went there last year and I travelled by train, and by coach, and by bike!

H By bike? Wow!

K Yes, it was great. So where did you catch the train from – Turkey?

H No, no, from Russia – Moscow.

K Russia?

H Yes, it's the best place to catch the train.

K But did you go through Central Asia?

H Oh yes – all those wonderful cities: Samarkand, Tashkent, Almaty.

K And did you change trains?

H No – the same train all the way.

K Was it comfortable?

H Very. Just like a hotel on wheels – it had everything I needed.

K Great! And how much did it cost?

H I don't remember exactly. Not too much for a trip like that. About $25,000.

K $25,000?

H Well … that was for everything. The train, the food, everything! It was a great trip. And no bikes!

▶ 2.79

ALEX Hi, Svetlana . Sorry I'm late. It was the traffic. So how did you get here?

SVETLANA On the metro, of course.

A Really? Do you use the metro?

S Yes I love going on the metro, it's so quick. It only took half an hour. Don't you use the metro?

A No, I don't like using the metro, it's so crowded. And it isn't always very clean in the trains. And the stations, they're terrible. So many people.

S Oh, I love the stations. I think they're beautiful. So did you come by car?

A Yes, of course, I go everywhere by car. I like driving in Moscow.

S You like it? But it's always so slow. How long did it take you to get here?

A About an hour, maybe. The traffic was bad.

S But it's always bad. I hate sitting in traffic, it's so boring.

A Oh, I don't mind it, it's not too bad. You can listen to the radio, you can chat to people.

S Well you must have a very nice car.

A It is quite a nice car, yes, it's very comfortable and big inside.

S Ah.

ANNOUNCEMENT The train at platform 3 is the 11:50 for Bristol.
ANNIE Oh, no!
PASSENGER Watch out!
A I'm so sorry.
P That's all right.

LEO Excuse me. Excuse me, please. … Excuse me, but I think this is my seat. I booked it online.
ANNIE Oh. I'm very sorry.
L Annie!
A Leo! I'm sorry I took your seat. I just sat down. I didn't check. I'm really sorry.
L No problem!
A Um. Your seat.
L No, no, you have the seat.
A But you booked it.
L It doesn't matter. It's yours now.
A Thank you.
L I can sit here.

ANNIE Are you on your way to Bristol?
LEO No, Reading. I went to university there.
A Really?
L You?
A Bristol. For the weekend.
L To see … a friend?
A A friend? No, no, my mum lives there. I go to see her every month.
L Great!

AHMED So here are the photos and the profiles of the families I can choose from.
FINN Hmm, ok. So two very different kinds of families.
A Yes, it's difficult to decide.
F Well, both families look very friendly.
A Yeah, they do.
F And the Conways look very kind.
A But maybe a bit quiet?
F Mm maybe. Look, the Philips like doing sport – swimming, surfing – that kind of thing.
A Yeah, but I don't like going to the beach much. I prefer playing football.
F You mean, soccer. In Australia we say soccer not football.
A Oh, of course, I forgot.
F And, I have to say, in Australia soccer isn't so popular. Everyone loves rugby.
A But the Conways like watching any sport so maybe I can watch soccer with them. That'd be nice.
F Yeah, that's true. But you like listening to music, don't you?
A Yes, I do.
F And the Philips like listening to music too.
A I'm not sure about children.
F Children are fun.
A Yes, but maybe not so quiet …
F No, not if you want to study.
A And I really want to study a lot.
F You also need to think about transport. It's quite expensive in Sydney.
A So I can save money if I stay at the Conways?
F Yeah, you probably can. You can walk everywhere.
A It really is hard to choose.
F It sure is. But you're the only person who can decide!

Unit 8

INTERVIEWER Welcome to *Focus on Sport*. Today Liv Oldman is with us to talk about how the Olympics can change the host city. Hi, Liv.
LIV Hi, thanks for having me.
I No problem. So, do you think the Olympics can change a city even after the Games finish?
L Oh, yes. It can really change a city and it can also help the people who live there. We see this happen again and again.
I Can you give us some examples?
L Of course. A great example is the Beijing Olympics in 2008. They built a fantastic new swimming centre called the Water Cube, and now families from all over Beijing can use it. And not only for swimming – it's a popular place to spend the day. So it's really made life better in the city. That's just one small example.
I A great example. But many people say the Olympics cost a lot of money, but can it also make money for a city?
L Yes, it can. The Winter Olympics were in Sochi, in the south of Russia, in 2014. Before, tourists always went to Sochi in the summer, because there are some nice beaches there and you can swim in the sea. But after 2014 people knew that you could also ski and do other winter sports there, so now it has tourists all year. And tourists make money for a city. You can ski and skate in the winter and go swimming and cycling in the summer.
I What about children? How can the Olympics change a city for them?
L The Olympics can really help children and young people. After the London Olympics in 2012, a lot of school children in Britain started a new sport. They saw all these sports on TV, sports like badminton and basketball, and they thought yeah, I can do that too. Before the Olympics many of these children preferred to play video games and watch TV. So it's a big change.
I Thank you, Liv. So, next time someone tells you the Olympics cost too much and can't improve the life of a city, tell them to think again. Next up on *Focus on Sport*, we talk to Olympic athlete Martin Fisher …

STELLA Yoga is a great way to be fit, strong and healthy and anyone can do it. My friends and I go to yoga classes every week. My favourite yoga position is quite difficult, but it looks really good. You put your arms on the floor, then you put your legs in the air and try to touch your head with your toes. It's not easy but I love it. But, please, don't try it at home! I needed years of practice to do that!
MARIANA I only started yoga three weeks ago. I'm very lazy, so I wanted to do some exercise that's easy. But, you know, it's not so simple! You need to think about how you move different parts of your body: your stomach, arms and legs … And sometimes you don't move at all – you just stand in one place for two or three minutes. But my favourite part is the end of the class. We all lie on the floor and relax for five minutes. Can I tell you something? Last class I was so tired that I went to sleep on the floor in the middle of the studio!

LEO Right, the running machine next!
MARTINA Hey, are you OK? … Are you all right?
DAN Um, I think so.
M Are you sure? You don't look well.
D Yes, I feel a bit tired. Actually, I feel awful …
M Oh dear. Come and sit down. I'll get you some water.

MARTINA Here's some water.
DAN Thanks.
M You poor thing. What's the matter?
D I'm not sure. I don't feel well.
M Have you got a headache?
D No, I haven't.
M Does your back hurt?
D No, nothing like that.
M Your face looks red, but that's probably from the exercise. … I don't think you've got a temperature.
D No, I'm sure I haven't. I don't feel well, that's all.
LEO Are you OK, Dan?
D Yes, fine.
L Is he OK?
M Yes, I'm sure he's fine. … Did you have lunch?
D No … I didn't have time for lunch. I had too much work to do.
M What about breakfast?
D Just a coffee – I was late for work, remember?
M Oh, yes. So nothing to eat all day?
D I … well … um … no. It was a busy day.
M Poor you. Well, I'm not surprised you don't feel well. You have to work so hard you don't have time to eat!
L That's right. Poor Dan. Are you OK?
D Yes, yes, I'm fine.
L Are you sure you're OK?
D Yes, really!
L Great! There's an aerobics class now. Let's go.
M Come on. I'll take you home.

GINA Did you see the email about writing an article for the company blog?
ANDY Yes, I did.
G I suppose it's true. We don't know each other very well. I mean, I've got no idea if you have a hobby or not. You seem fit so … I don't know … maybe you do some kind of sport?
A Yeah, you're right. About a year ago, a friend of mine asked me to go cycling with him. I laughed and said 'I can't do that – I don't have a bike'. 'No problem,' he said. 'I can lend you one.' Well I went and it was amazing. About two weeks later I bought my own bike.
G That's great!
A Yeah I go cycling all the time – almost every day after work. I love it because it's a way of keeping fit and being outdoors at the same time. I could never go to a gym!
G No, I hate gyms too.
A Cycling can be a bit dangerous in the city, and you always have to be careful in the traffic. A couple of months ago a car sort of hit me.
G Oh dear!
A I wasn't hurt badly – I just hurt my arm and my foot a bit. But I try to get out of the city into the countryside. For example, last weekend I went for a two-day ride in the hills. There was almost no one on the road. It was amazing – I couldn't believe it.
G Well, look, there's something I didn't know about. You could write an article about that.
A Me? Write an article? No, I couldn't do that. I haven't got time.

Unit 9

Conversation 1

SUSIE Hello?
SIMON Hey, Susie. It's Simon. Do you want to go and see a film tonight with Amy and Sandeep?
SU Yeah, great idea, I'd love to.
SI Let's meet at the shopping mall at around seven. OK?
SU Where? The mall's really big!
SI Oh, I don't know. I'll call you when we get there and we can find each other.
SU OK ….

3.20

Conversation 2

SIMON Hello?

SUSIE Simon! Hi! Where are you? Are you having a coffee?

SI No, I'm just buying that new book I told you about. What are you doing?

SU I'm just getting off the bus. So where do you want to meet? It's nearly seven.

SI Let's meet at the entrance in five minutes.

SU All right.

SI And can you call Amy and Sandeep to tell them where to meet?

SU Yeah, sure, no problem. Hurry up!

Conversation 3

SANDEEP Hello?

SUSIE Sandeep, it's Susie. Where are you?

SA Oh! Hi, Susie. I'm just getting some cash. Amy's looking at furniture.

SU Furniture? Are you buying furniture?

SA No, we aren't buying anything. She's just looking.

SU OK, well, can you meet Simon and me at the entrance to the cinema in five minutes?

SA Yeah, sure. See you there!

3.21

Conversation 4

SUSIE Hi, Amy!

AMY Hi!

SU Hi, Sandeep!

SANDEEP Hi!

SUSIE Great to see you!

SA Good to see you too! Where's Simon?

SU I don't know. He told me to meet him here. Let me just call him.

SI Hello?

SU Simon, where are you waiting for us?

SI I'm standing by the entrance – you aren't here!

SU Yes, we are! We're waiting for you. I just bought our tickets.

SI What? ... Oh, no! I'm at the main entrance, not the cinema entrance.

SU What? Quick, run! The film is about to start!

3.26

Conversation 1

LUCAS Hello?

TINA Hi Lucas, it's Tina.

L Oh, Tina – hi!

T I just read your message. Sounds like you're having fun.

L Yeah, it's great here – I love it.

T I can't believe you're wearing red.

L I know, I know.

T You hate red.

L Yes, but it's Chinese New Year – everyone's wearing red – I'm even wearing red socks and a red belt. And someone also gave me a red scarf.

T I hope you're not wearing red shoes.

L No, no – I'm wearing black boots.

Conversation 2

DIANA Hello?

PETE Hi, Diana. It's Pete.

D Oh hi, Pete! Thanks for calling!

P Thanks for the message and the photo.

D No problem. I'm having such a brilliant time here.

P That doesn't look like you in the photo.

D Yeah that's me.

P But you're wearing a dress. You never wear dresses! And gloves too. You look so cool.

D Thanks. I wear dresses sometimes you know.

P Yeah, but I normally see you in jumpers and jeans. And you're wearing jewellery too – those are lovely earrings.

D Well, this is special – it's Carnevale. I'm having so much fun.

3.31 **PART 1**

ANNIE Dan! Hi!

DAN Hi, Annie, how are things?

A Fine.

D Um, look. Are you free at lunchtime?

A Yes.

D Great. Could we meet? I need help to buy some clothes for this evening.

A Yeah, sure. But what about Martina? Can't she help?

D Well I'm meeting her this evening for dinner. She always says I wear the same old clothes, so I want to get something new. I want to surprise her.

A OK, sure. I'm free at 12:30.

3.32 **PART 2**

ANNIE So what are you looking for?

DAN I don't know really. A shirt and trousers. Just something casual.

A OK. What size are you?

D In trousers. 32. ... OK, 34.

A Or 36? And probably a large for the shirt?

D Yeah, I think so.

A What colour would you like?

D Oh, I don't know. Something dark?

A What about this? ... Why don't you try them on?

D OK, excuse me, where are the fitting rooms?

SHOP ASSISTANT The fitting rooms are just over there, sir.

D Thanks.

SA Thank you.

3.33 **PART 3**

DAN What do you think?

ANNIE No ...

D This one?

A Ugh ...

D And this?

A No. Try the next one.

D How about this one?

A No, Dan ... That's it! That looks great.

D These are mine! This is what I came in!

A Well, it looks really good on you ...

SHOP ASSISTANT Can I help you, sir?

D Hi. There's no price on these shoes. How much are they?

SA They're £49.99.

D Great. I'll take them.

A And these trousers and this shirt, please.

SA All together that's £115.97 please.

D Can I pay by card?

SA Yes, of course. Just enter your PIN, please. ... Shall I put the receipt in the bag?

D Yes – thanks.

SA There you go, sir.

D Thank you.

SA Thank you. Take care now.

A Bye.

3.36

AXEL I always give my girlfriend an expensive birthday present. I don't give her flowers or chocolates. I often give her jewellery, maybe a necklace or earrings. Or maybe a beautiful dress. She loves expensive clothes. But clothes are difficult because I don't know what she likes. So, she usually chooses them and then we buy them together.

BOB We don't buy presents. We give the children some cash and then they always buy their own presents. I think that's better because they know what they want. And then we do something nice together, maybe go out for a meal or go to the cinema.

FERNANDA We buy small birthday presents for the children – usually toys or clothes, something small, like a toy car or a T-shirt maybe. Some people buy things like a laptop or a bike, but I don't like giving expensive presents, I prefer to give small presents.

LEILA My husband doesn't think clothes and computers are important. He doesn't need many things, he doesn't like spending money on himself. But he reads lots of books and he likes films – so for his birthday I usually buy him a book or a DVD. He's very easy!

Unit 10

3.39

All the time people ask me "What's the best thing to buy – a phone or a tablet?" There's no easy answer to that question because different people need different things. And they can more or less do the same things – surf the Web, check emails, make calls. However, there are some different ways of helping you decide. And you can be sure these things are not talked about in advertisements and online information. To start with there's: 'pocketability'. 'Pocket-a-what'? I hear you ask. 'Pocketability'. Let me explain. 'Pocket … ability' this means how easy it is to get the phone or tablet into different pockets in your jacket, your jeans – that kind of thing. And another really important thing to think about: 'eatability'. No, it doesn't mean you eat your phone. 'Eatability' is all about how easy it is to use the phone or tablet and eat at the same time. You know, sometimes you want to have lunch and read something. So you see? Two new and very important ways of thinking about phones and tablets: pocketability and eatability. You decide!

3.41

RADIO PRESENTER Good evening and welcome to the programme. Today, we're talking to Professor Ryan Hunter. The Professor is well-known for his love of languages and has a new book in the shops tomorrow. Professor, welcome!

PROFESSOR Thank you. It's great to be here!

RP So let's start with my first question. Professor, in your opinion, what's the most beautiful language in the world?

P That's a very good question. Of course, there is no right or wrong answer here. I'm sure we all have our favourites. But for me the answer is easy: Italian. It was the first language I learned. I still remember my teacher, Signora Monti. Signora Monti was the best teacher at my school and she started my love of languages. Now I can speak more than 20 languages well, but Italian is the most musical language I know. It's the language of opera and love.

RP Ok, next question. What's the most difficult language in the world?

P Hmm. That's an interesting question too. It partly depends on your first language. For example, for a speaker of English, Japanese is very difficult, but for a speaker of Mandarin Chinese it's much easier. However, a few years ago, we did a project at my university and decided that the hardest language to learn is Basque, a language from parts of Spain and France. Last year we did another project on the Internet to find the easiest language to learn. More than 3,000 people answered the question and the most popular answer was Spanish. So perhaps Spanish is the easiest language to learn. That's probably because it's not very different from many other European languages.

RP And one final question, what's the most useful language to speak?

P That's easy – the language of the country where you live. But if you want to learn the most popular language in the world, then take lessons in Mandarin Chinese. More than 900 million people speak it. That's not a surprise as China has the biggest population in the world. So with Mandarin Chinese you can speak to about 14% of all the people in the world. That's pretty useful.

RP That's very useful, indeed! Well, Professor Hunter, thanks for talking with us today. I'm sure our listeners enjoyed hearing your thoughts on language!

▶**3.47** **PART 1**

ANNIE Hi, Leo.
LEO Hi, Annie.
A Where is he?
L Sorry, Annie. I mean, Dan says sorry. He had to go to a meeting.
A What about our lunch?
L He didn't know about the meeting. Someone called him about ten minutes ago.
A I wanted help with this.
L Oh? Right.
A Leo, could you help me?
L Erm …
A There's something I don't know how to do. Do you mind showing me?
L No, not at all – if I can.
A Great, thanks.
L Well, it is lunch time. Would you like to have some lunch and … ?
A … and you could help me with my tablet.
L Yes.
A That would be lovely.

▶**3.50** **PART 2**

LEO So … you wanted some help.
ANNIE Oh yes – I almost forgot. … Everything is fine – it's great. But I don't know how to get into my email. Can you have a look?
L Sure. OK – that's easy. You just need to change one small thing. OK. So what you do is … touch this button here.
A OK.
L And a new screen opens.
A Oh yes.
L And now you just touch here where it says 'Yes'.
A Oh that's easy. OK. So first I touch this button?
L That's right.
A And it takes me to a new screen – like this?
L Correct.
A And I touch 'Yes'. Is that right?
L Yeah. Now you can check your email.
A Great. Thanks, Leo. Thank you so much.
L You're welcome.
A Well, now I have to buy you another coffee.
L Mm, I think I have to get back to work. I've got a meeting with Dan in ten minutes.
A Dan? Oh, don't worry about him. Let's have another coffee!
L Well … OK!

▶**3.51**

1 I sometimes send text messages, usually to my parents to say when I'm coming home, but I usually chat on social networking sites. It's easier if you're online anyway – and it's cheaper! I always have my phone with me so I can see what my friends are doing. It's really good to know what people are doing. I chat to everybody all the time and we send each other pictures.
2 I only really send text messages when I'm travelling. I text my family to tell them when I arrive somewhere new or tell them when I'll be back. It's useful because I'm often away on business trips and of course it's cheaper than phoning. But usually I don't send text messages. I prefer to talk to people on the phone. It's easier and you can say more.
3 I don't really like texting much. I think it's better to talk on the phone. It's friendlier. I sometimes send a text if I'm meeting a friend, but that's about all.

Unit 11

▶**3.52**

STEPHEN How many quiz answers did you get right?
MAGGIE All of them except for numbers one and five.
S I got question two and six wrong. How did you know Isla Fisher has written novels? Have you read them?
M No, I haven't – it was a guess. In fact, I haven't seen any of her films. What about you?
S I've seen *The Great Gatsby*. She's really good in it. I've never seen a film with Mia Wasikowska.
M Really? Try *Jane Eyre* – she's fantastic in that.
S What about Rose Byrne? Have you ever seen any of her films?
M No, I haven't, but I've heard she's really funny in *Bridesmaids*.
S Yes, I've seen that. She's a real laugh.

▶**3.62**

KURT Look, have you seen this article? It says Buenos Aires is one of the world's top cities for music. I didn't know that.
BEA Well, there is a lot of good music.
K I haven't been to any of these places and I've lived here for years. Like Jazz y Pop, it says it's a famous jazz club, but I've never heard of it. Have you been to Jazz y Pop?
B Yes, I went there two weeks ago. They had really good music.
K Oh, right. And what about The Roxy? Where's The Roxy? Have you been there?
B Yes, of course I have. We all went there for Antonia's birthday. We had a fantastic time, we didn't leave till five in the morning. Didn't you come?
K Antonia's birthday…? Oh, I remember. I had exams, I couldn't go. OK, well I bet you've never been to the Teatro Colón.
B Yes, I have actually. I went there last year. It was my dad's 50th birthday, we went to the opera.
K Oh, yeah. What did you see?
B I don't remember, something by Mozart. I didn't like it much.
K You've been everywhere.
B Yeah, well you should go out more, you spend too much time studying. Look, it's a nice evening, why don't we go down to San Telmo and sit in a café, and watch the dancers?
K Mm … Well, I'd love to, actually I've never been there. But I've got this essay to write …

▶**3.66** **PART 1**

DAN Taxi! … Windsor Road – number 15, please.
DRIVER 15 Windsor Road.
MARTINA That's better.
D Tired?
M Yeah, a bit. It's nearly 12. Work tomorrow.

▶**3.67** **PART 2**

DAN So, what did you think of it? Did you enjoy it?
MARTINA Yeah, it was a good concert. I really liked it. How about you?
D Yeah, me too.
M But I didn't like all the bands.
D No, me neither. I didn't like the first band very much.
M Really? Oh, I thought they were quite good.
D Did you? But all their songs were the same. They really only had one song.
M Yeah, but the singer was so good. She's got an amazing voice.
D Yeah maybe. But I just thought they were a bit boring. And I don't really like that kind of pop music.
M Well they aren't really pop, they're sort of folk rock. Anyway, I really liked them.
D But the last band – *Atlantis* – I thought they were really good. Really great music.
M Do you think so? I didn't really like them. They were too loud.
D Yeah maybe.

▶**3.69** **PART 3**

DAN I've got some of their music on my phone. Here, listen. This is one of their tracks. What do you think?
MARTINA No, thanks. I've heard enough of them already.

▶**3.71** **PART 4**

MARTINA Home at last. I'm tired.
DAN How about some music?
M OK, but not *Atlantis*.
D OK, not *Atlantis*. Promise! …

▶**3.72**

MELISSA Have you seen the new James Bond film?
JOHN Yes, have you?
M Yes, I've seen it, yeah. Not very good, is it?
J Oh, I don't agree. I really enjoyed it.
M Well, I thought it was boring. James Bond films are always the same. James Bond is cool, he goes to some beautiful country and he meets a beautiful girl. The bad guys all die at the end. You always know what's going to happen. Of course the special effects were great, but that's about all.
J Well, it's not meant to be too serious, you know. I thought it was fun, I liked it.
M Did you really?
J Yes, I did. I thought it was exciting. It was great to watch, the actors were great and James Bond was fantastic. I'm going to see it again this weekend. Do you want to come?
M What, again? No thanks, once was enough. I'm going to see the new Tarantino film.

Unit 12

▶**3.75**

Conversation 1

ZOE So, about next year – what are you going to do?
EMILY I finally decided yesterday.
Z And?
E Well, I don't really want to continue studying. I'd like to do some travelling. So, I'm not going to go to university next year.
Z Go travelling? Nice idea – but that costs a lot of money.
E I've saved a bit of money. But you don't need a lot. Look. I found this website: *Work Around the World*.
Z OK …
E Well, you can go places and get free food and accommodation – you just have to do a bit of work.
Z I don't know … I heard you work really hard on those things.
E But look at this one. I'm going to email and ask about it. It looks so beautiful there close to the mountains and I love drawing and things so it's perfect.
Z But what about … what about all our friends? I mean, university starts next year.
E I know. Sorry. It starts for everyone, but not for me.

Conversation 2

CHLOE I want to do something different for a while. I'm going to leave this job.
FRANK Get a new one?
C No, I want to go away and have some fun.
F Ah, so a holiday.
C Yes, a very long holiday. Look at this website …
F *Work Around the World* holidays …
C There are some interesting things on it.
F … free accommodation and food … But no pay.
C No, but it doesn't matter. Look at this job I read about. I'm going to find out more about it. It's in such an amazing place. I can go to the beach every day.
F It says you have to spend a lot of time with children. Do you even like children?
C Yeah – I love them.
F And do you know how to teach?
C I'm sure I can learn.

▶ 3.83

TROY I grew up in Melbourne in Australia and I've always lived in big cities. I love cities – I like going to cafés and I love shopping. Every city's different. I've been to London, Paris, Tokyo, Buenos Aires, Lisbon … and I love them all. I'm never very happy in the countryside. There's nothing to do there. I like people and noise.

I'm my free time I listen to music a lot – mainly dance music, but I like rock music too. I don't do much sport, I've never really liked sport … well I like dancing, but that's not really a sport, is it?

CERYS I think I've always been a sporty person, I loved sport at school. And I love water sports of all kinds. I go swimming, surfing, I love being in the water. I spend a lot of time on beaches, it's great to be by the sea.

I'm not really a 'city person', I don't really like big cities and I'm not interested in shopping, I only go shopping if I need to buy something, not for fun. And I never go to museums or concerts. I feel happier in the countryside … or on a beach by the sea somewhere. I live in Swansea now and that's fine because it's got beautiful beaches.

▶ 3.84 PART 1

MARTINA Wow!

DAN What?

M I've won a competition!

D Have you? Fantastic! What's the prize?

M A weekend for two in Bath. Train travel, hotel, museum tickets …

D Really? That's great.

M But we have to use it the weekend after next.

D So, that's Saturday the 20th?

M Yes.

D We have to go to John and Charlotte's wedding – remember?

M Oh, no! I forgot about that. Oh what a pity.

D OK, so, who do we know who could use the prize?

▶ 3.86 PART 2

RECEPTIONIST OK. So here's your keycard. That's room 312 – a single room on the third floor. Turn left as you come out of the lift.

ANNIE Is breakfast included?

R Yes, it's from 7:00 am until 10:00 am in the dining room – just over there.

A Great – thank you. And what time is check out?

R Check out is at 11:00 am.

A Thanks.

▶ 3.90 PART 3

RECEPTIONIST Good morning.

ANNIE Good morning. Can you help me? Is there a city bus tour I can go on?

R Yes, there is. It leaves from just outside the hotel.

A Great. And how much is it for a ticket?

R It's £15.

A Can I buy a ticket here?

R Yes, you can.

A And can I pay by card?

R No problem.

A OK. I'll have a ticket then please.

▶ 3.91 PART 4

LEO Annie?

ANNIE Leo?! I don't believe it!

L What are you doing here?

A Well, Martina won this prize – two nights in a hotel. She gave it to me.

L Oh, really? That's interesting. Dan won a prize – a return train ticket. He gave it to me.

A And she also gave me a ticket to the museum tour at ten o'clock.

L Hmm, Dan also gave me a ticket for the museum tour at ten o'clock.

A Right. So… here we are.

L Yes … here we are. Shall we go in then?

A Why not?

▶ 3.93

ELLIOT Hi, Louise! Here's your coffee.

LOUISE Thanks, Elliot. When's our next meeting?

E In half an hour.

L Good. You look happy today.

E Well, yes, I feel happy.

L Oh – good news?

E Yeah. I've decided to go on holiday!

L Really? Where are you going to go?

E Stockholm. Yeah – a week's holiday in Sweden.

L Very nice.

E Yes, our local travel agent was selling tickets and accommodation to Stockholm at a very good price.

L Lucky you!

E Yes, we're going to stay in a four star hotel with a fitness centre, free wi-fi, indoor swimming pool – it's got everything.

L So, when are you going to go?

E At the end of next month.

L End of May? OK, I think the weather is warmer then.

E Oh, really?

L Yeah. Look, I've got a friend, Karin who lives in Stockholm. You should email her for information so you can plan your holiday. She won't mind helping you. I can give you her email address.

E That'd be great. Thanks, Louise!

L No problem.

Phonemic symbols

Vowel sounds

Short

/ə/	/æ/	/ʊ/	/ɒ/	/ɪ/	/i/	/e/	/ʌ/
breakf**a**st	m**a**n	p**u**t	g**o**t	ch**i**p	happ**y**	m**e**n	sh**u**t

Long

/ɜː/	/ɑː/	/uː/	/ɔː/	/iː/
sh**ir**t	p**ar**t	wh**o**	w**a**lk	ch**ea**p

Diphthongs (two vowel sounds)

/eə/	/ɪə/	/ʊə/	/ɔɪ/	/aɪ/	/eɪ/	/əʊ/	/aʊ/
h**air**	n**ear**	t**our**	b**oy**	n**i**ne	**ei**ght	wind**ow**	n**ow**

Consonants

/p/	/b/	/f/	/v/	/t/	/d/	/k/	/g/
picnic	**b**ook	**f**ace	**v**ery	**t**ime	**d**og	**c**old	**g**o
/θ/	/ð/	/tʃ/	/dʒ/	/s/	/z/	/ʃ/	/ʒ/
think	**th**e	**ch**air	**j**ob	**s**ea	**z**oo	**sh**oe	televi**s**ion
/m/	/n/	/s/	/h/	/l/	/r/	/w/	/y/
me	**n**ow	**s**ing	**h**ot	**l**ate	**r**ed	**w**ent	**y**es

Irregular verbs

Infinitive	Past simple	Past participle
be	was / were	been
become	became	become
begin	began	begun
break	broke	broken
bring	brought	brought
buy	bought	bought
catch	caught	caught
choose	chose	chosen
come	came	come
cost	cost	cost
cut	cut	cut
do	did	done
drink	drank	drunk
drive	drove	driven
eat	ate	eaten
fall	fell	fallen
feel	felt	felt
find	found	found
fly	flew	flown
forget	forgot	forgotten
get	got	got
give	gave	given
go	went	gone
grow	grew	grown
have	had	had
hear	heard	heard
hold	held	held
know	knew	known
learn	learned / learnt	learned / learnt
leave	left	left

Infinitive	Past simple	Past participle
lose	lost	lost
make	made	made
meet	met	met
pay	paid	paid
put	put	put
read	read	read
ride	rode	ridden
ring	rang	rung
run	ran	run
say	said	said
see	saw	seen
sell	sold	sold
send	sent	sent
sing	sang	sung
sit	sat	sat
sleep	slept	slept
speak	spoke	spoken
spell	spelled / spelt	spelled / spelt
spend	spent	spent
stand	stood	stood
swim	swam	swum
take	took	taken
teach	taught	taught
tell	told	told
think	thought	thought
throw	threw	thrown
understand	understood	understood
wear	wore	worn
win	won	won
write	wrote	written